AF506270

# WALTERCIO CALDAS

IN CONVERSATION WITH / EN CONVERSACIÓN CON

## ARIEL JIMÉNEZ

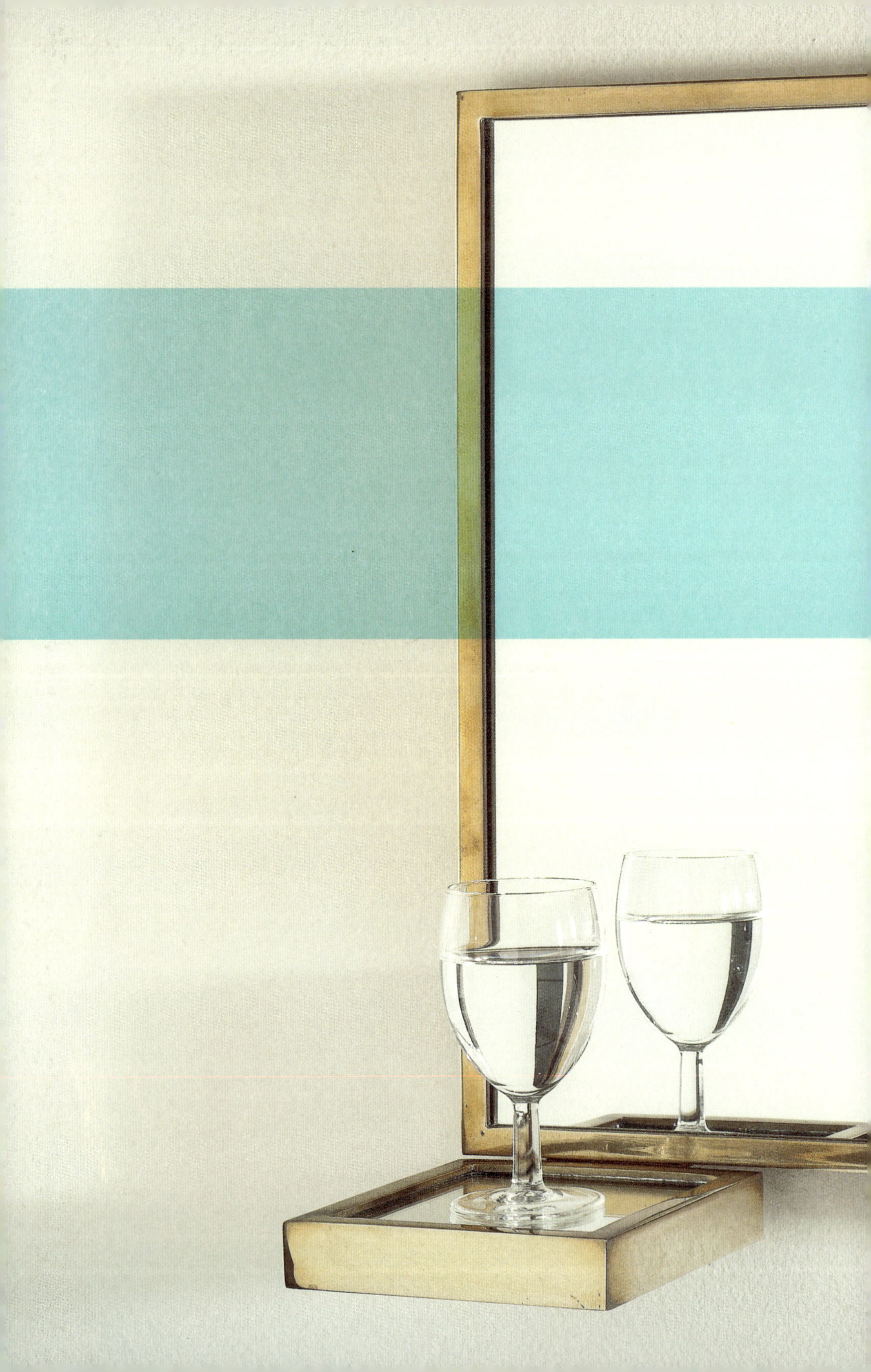

# WALTERCIO CALDAS

IN CONVERSATION WITH / EN CONVERSACIÓN CON

## ARIEL JIMÉNEZ

introductory essay by / ensayo introductorio de
**Guy Brett**

Fundación Cisneros/Colección Patricia Phelps de Cisneros

New York ▪ Caracas

Fundación Cisneros
2 East 78th Street
New York, NY 10075
www.coleccioncisneros.org

Distribution in North America:
ARTBOOK | D.A.P.
155 6th Avenue, 2nd Floor
New York, NY 10013
www.artbook.com

Distribution in Latin America and Spain:
Ediciones El Viso
T 34-915196576, F 34-915196583
www.edicioneselviso.com

Library of Congress Cataloging-in-
Publication Data
Names: Caldas Júnior, Waltércio,
    1946– interviewee. | Jiménez, Ariel,
    interviewer. | Brett, Guy, writer of added
    commentary. | Caldas Júnior, Waltércio,
    1946– Waltércio Caldas in conversation
    with Ariel Jiménez. | Caldas Júnior, Waltér-
    cio, 1946– Waltercio Caldas in conversation
    with Ariel Jiménez. English. Fundación
    Cisneros.
Title: Waltercio Caldas in conversation with
    Ariel Jiménez = Waltercio Caldas en con-
    versación con Ariel Jiménez / Introductory
    essay by Guy Brett = Ensayo introductorio
    de Guy Brett.
Other titles: Waltercio Caldas en conversación
    con Ariel Jiménez
Description: New York : Colección Patricia
    Phelps de Cisneros, 2016. | English and
    Spanish.
Identifiers: LCCN 2016020476 (print) | LCCN
    2016021460 (ebook) | ISBN 9780984017355
    (hardcover : alk. paper) | ISBN
    9780988205598 ()
Subjects: LCSH: Caldas Júnior, Waltércio,
    1946– —Interviews. | Artists—Brazil—
    Interviews.
Classification: LCC N6659.C34 A35 2016
    (print) | LCC N6659.C34 (ebook) |
    DDC 700.92—dc23
LC record available at https://lccn.loc
    .gov/2016020476

Cover: *Escultura para todos os materiais não
transparentes* [*Sculpture for All Nontransparent
Materials/Escultura para todos los materiales no
transparentes*], 1985, detail [detalle].
Title page: *Água/Cálice/Espelhos* [*Water/
Glass/Mirrors / Agua/Vidrio/Espejos*], 1975

Produced by Lucia | Marquand, Seattle
www.luciamarquand.com

Series editor: Gabriel Pérez-Barreiro
Selection of artworks: Waltercio Caldas and
Ariel Jiménez
Editors: Ileen Kohn, Donna Wingate
Copyeditors: Michelle Piranio [English],
María Esther Pino [Spanish]
Translators: Kristina Cordero,
Mariana Barrera Pieck
Proofreader: Elizabeth Chapple
Series design: Zach Hooker
Layout: Ryan Polich
Typesetting: Brynn Warriner
Color management: iocolor, Seattle
Printed and bound in China by C&C Offset
Printing Co., Ltd.

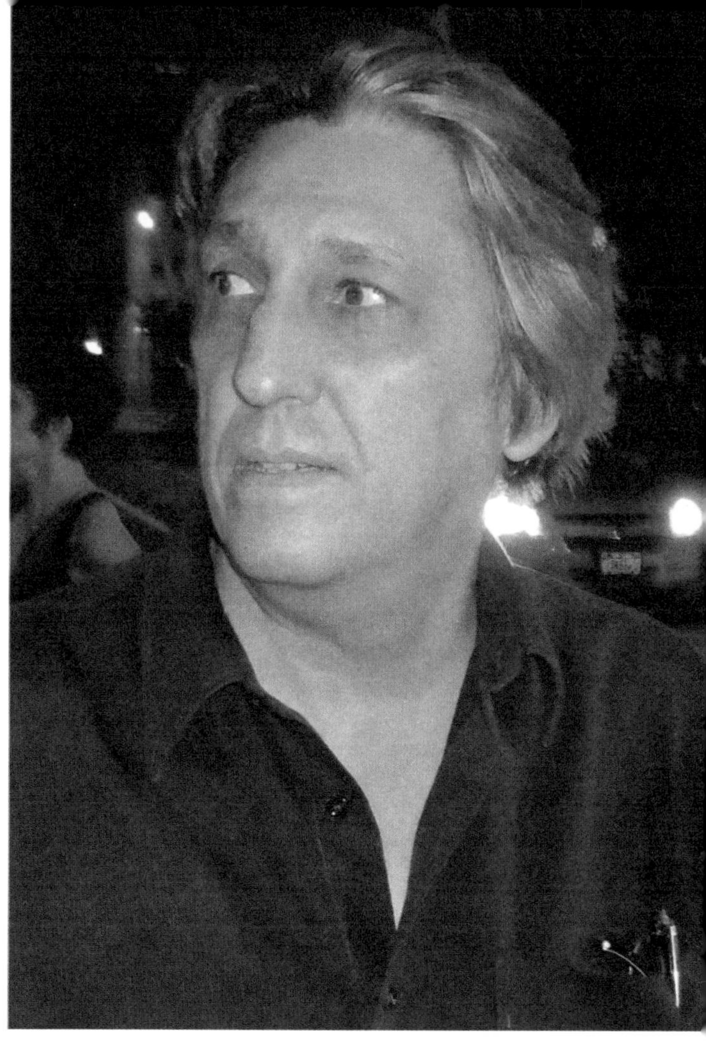

# Contents



# Índice

# INTRODUCTION

Anyone who has had the good fortune of conversing with Waltercio Caldas soon realizes that he has an exceptional gift for expressing himself verbally. Language is certainly one of the central issues in his artistic practice as both a metaphor for communication more generally, and through the incorporation of words into his works more specifically. The titles he gives his artworks are often remarkably poetic and suggestive, and the book form has been a preferred medium for many decades. To make a book of his words about art is therefore a task that is as appropriate as it is daunting. As much as Caldas delights in language, he is also extremely wary of the risks of using words to explain or substitute the visual experience of the objects themselves. He is acutely aware of the dangers inherent in using language that may appear to elucidate a particular work, but in fact can become a poor substitute for the specific magic that only the eye can perceive.

The topics of these conversations between Caldas and Ariel Jiménez range from mirrors and models to music and history. We learn of his passion for Velázquez and jazz, his early encounter with a model of the first airplane at the Rio de Janeiro airport, and of his fascination with an Indian fakir. However broad his interests, we are able to see how each of them emerges and is incorporated into his art during his long and fruitful career.

The former titles in our Conversaciones/Conversations series have tended to follow a chronological model, from each artist's childhood to the present. Caldas, however, resisted this structure from the outset, as his artistic development is perhaps best understood as a spiral rather than a straight line, with various interests and resolutions reappearing over time, creating a dense web of connections. Thus, this volume engages a more thematic approach, exploring the artist's recurring questions over several decades.

Caldas has designed a series of interventions for this book, as a nod to his sustained use of the book format as an artistic medium. The reader will encounter various images and pages that gently disrupt our expectations of how publications deliver information about visual objects. The gestures are subtle, but the point they make—that photographs of objects are not a substitute for the object itself—is one that is explored in multiple ways throughout his career, from the *Manual of Popular Science* to *Velázquez*.

We are deeply indebted to Waltercio Caldas for his commitment and enthusiastic participation in all aspects of this publication and its production. Ariel Jiménez characteristically proved to be a generous and rigorous interviewer, bringing a profound understanding of Caldas's intellectual process, while also challenging many of the assumptions about abstraction and form commonly found in Brazilian art history. We are especially thrilled with Guy Brett's introductory essay for this book, as he was an early and very perceptive champion of Caldas's work, introducing his art to international audiences.

Patricia Vasconcellos provided invaluable support for this project at all stages. On the CPPC team I would like to thank Ileen Kohn and Donna Wingate for their careful editorial oversight, and Lucia | Marquand for their exceptional standards of design and production. Once again, Kristina Cordero has provided expert translation for this volume, as has Mariana Barrera Pieck of Guy Brett's essay, and thanks to Michelle Piranio and María Esther Pino for their skillful copyediting.

*Gabriel Pérez-Barreiro*
*Director and Chief Curator, Colección Patricia Phelps de Cisneros*

# TAKING LIBERTIES

"The distinctive qualities of Waltercio Caldas's creative work—intelligence, precision, conciseness, fine irony and impeccable execution—are present in every piece without exception."[1]

Frederico Morais's generous assessment certainly rings true. To this, I would add "refinement"' to the list, and also "humor," which shows in certain ways a kinship with the humor of Marcel Duchamp. The paradox is that these qualities have been arrived at by a process of negation. The negative can be a great creative force, especially in the work of Waltercio Caldas. It is expressed in the text, *NOT*, written by Paulo Venancio Filho, one of the most beautiful examples of the integration of an artist's forms and the written word, that I know of. They mesh perfectly. The text's first seven lines run:

### "NOT"

*The work insists persistently upon being a border. It further insists upon reducing the border it is. It wants to erase its outlines, its very constitution. Erase itself and, again, erase itself, that is the device itself. In this way, it can continue to disregard everything that proposes to define it. Its definition is more and more expressed by the negative. It is neither this nor that. Perhaps it may not want to be because its being is next to not being. Not is the word that stands for the work.[2]*

In these interviews and conversations with Ariel Jiménez, a highly knowledgeable interlocutor, Caldas describes the evolution of his work. His tone is thoughtful and honest, feeling his way forward as a personal experience, working by his own rules. He is never prescriptive or doctrinaire. The process of inventing himself as an artist was not driven by the search for a *style*, "but by encouraging in us the need to understand what was happening in the things we produced."[3] "This is where the paradox resides," as Caldas sees it, "in the audacity of certain artists to conceive of objects that did not exist

---

1. Frederico Morais, *Aberto Fechado: Caixa e Livro na Arte Brasileira* (São Paulo: Pinacoteca do Estado de São Paulo, 2013), 82.

2. Paulo Venancio, "NOT," in *Transcontinental: Nine Latin American Artists*, trans. Florence Eleanor Irvin (London: Verso, 1990), 66.

3. *Waltercio Caldas in Conversation with/en conversación con Ariel Jiménez*, 31. Unless otherwise indicated, all statements by Caldas are from the interviews with Ariel Jiménez for this book.

previously, but that are now there, here, right in front of us, like an invented reality."[4]

The first sight I had of one such object was in 1986 at Waltercio Caldas's apartment in the then-new "development" of high towers disfiguring the countryside and beach south of Rio de Janeiro. Caldas's ironic adoption of the aspirational and consumerist lifestyle kept alive his attachment to the negative as an instrument of freedom. As I noted in the diary I kept for that trip, the apartment was "a kind of suspended nowhere" and the works created there were "thing and not thing, object or shadow, no form, self-erasure. . . ." The object Caldas showed me was a single block of granite 30 × 24 × 10 cm with rounded corners at the top and at the bottom where they functioned as legs, as in a box or a piece of furniture. The block was placed casually on the floor, and I remember that part of it covered a Persian carpet that Waltercio had in his rooms. The block was both eloquent and dumb at the same time. This is perhaps the reason why I always remember it as an enigma. You would see it in an instant, then it would disappear. You would be constantly re-seeing it. This is a kind of object that is not good to look at for a long time, it will always remain at the exact instant from which it was seen for the first time.

Caldas gently mocks the expectations of the viewer. As with Duchamp, he generates "a new thought for the object." Both draw on commonplace objects as the vehicle for their thoughts. Nevertheless their sensibilities are quite distinct. Caldas reaches toward an extraordinary purity. His objects are always surprising, and sometimes of a devastating simplicity, such as in the early work *Prato comum com elasticos* [*Ordinary Plate with Rubber Bands*; 1978] [Fig. 1]—two rubber bands stretched over a white plate. This object, even the photograph of it, imparts an indescribable feeling of space. Although there is an element of social satire in this and other works of the period, Caldas seems to be reaching for the great expanse of nature, for space in the cosmological sense.

A characteristic and remarkable feature of Caldas's art are his books. They are numerous and strikingly diverse. They do not appear as a subsection of his artistic production but as a continuation of his idea of the object. These are book-objects. Behind the diversity of materials used lies the discernment of Caldas as the passionate collector he is. On one of my visits to the house he had acquired in Rio, it was with pride that he showed me his library, which included his collection of early Brazilian photography, Brazilian satirical magazine prints, and European avant-garde literature.

4. Ibid., 46.

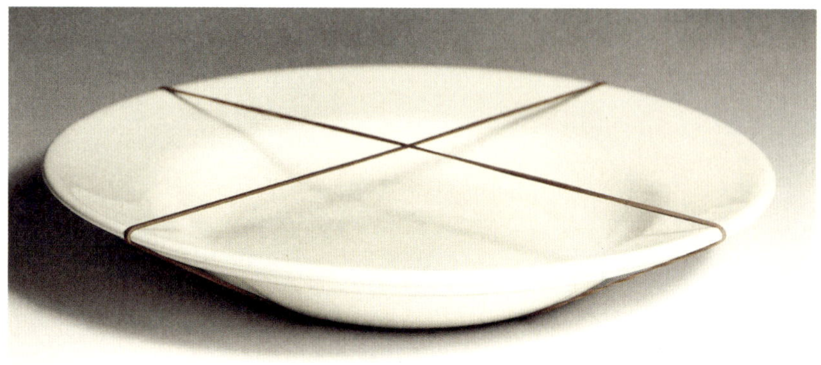

Fig. 1. *Prato comum com elasticos* [*Ordinary Plate with Rubber Bands*], 1978.

The book-form exerted a particular fascination for Brazilian artists in the 1950s to 1970s, producing a climate of questioning that was strongly cross disciplinary in character. It was epitomized by figures such as the physicist Mário Schenberg, who adored Mira Schendel's work and wrote eloquently about it; the art critic and political theorist Mário Pedrosa, whose understanding and support was essential to Lygia Clark, Hélio Oiticica and others; Haroldo de Campos, pioneer of visual poetry and scholar of literature; and Ferreira Gullar, poet and activist, whose intellectual and artistic struggles Gullar so well described in another book in the Conversaciones / Conversations series.[5]

Waltercio Caldas's book-objects can certainly be contextualized within that climate of questioning, whose range was huge, encompassing, for example, Lygia Clark's book version of her participatory work *Livro-Obra* [*Book-Work*; 1964–83], and a work such as Artur Barrio's *Livro de carne* [*Book of Meat*; 1978–79], in which the pages are bloody slices of raw meat. Barrio's work is shown as three photographic prints on paper, and a text. The dichotomy persists between the participatory, hands-on, mode of Clark's book, and that of certain other artists, notably Caldas, whose book-objects cannot be touched. Both in fact produce a shift in the apprehension of what a book may be: to actually touch them would be to disturb their aesthetic balance. This is most delicately conveyed by the book-object, *Matisse, talco* [*Matisse, Talcum*; 1978] [see p. 88], one of Waltercio's best known works, where the talcum powder, spread over the open pages of an art book about Matisse, could be very susceptible to disturbance. We expect to handle books, but Caldas's books are purely visual: books open at a double page as they are commonly shown in museum and library exhibi-

5. Ariel Jiménez, *Ferreira Gullar in conversation with / en conversación con Ariel Jiménez* (New York: Fundación Cisneros, 2012).

tions (an exception is Caldas's book *Velázquez* [1996] [see p. 86], which must be viewed page by page, but even there the book exhibits a constant state, a single perceptual decision).

Coming across *Matisse, Talc*, the viewer experiences the *frisson* of putting together two things which perhaps have never been put together before. This generates a particular kind of humor based on incongruity and the fluidity of meaning. The procedure is familiar from Surrealism: "Beautiful as the chance meeting of an umbrella and a sewing-machine on a dissecting table" (Comte de Lautréamont), and received a boost in the era of conceptualism ("art can be made out of anything," or "a great artist can make art by simply casting a glance" (Robert Smithson).[6]

I take *Matisse, Talc* to be a reflection upon materials in general, and the materials as used in art. The talc is present in every degree, from completely covering the open book to various forms of glimpsing of the printed page. The artist distributes the talc differently for each showing of the work. A link is made to the moment in Western Modernism of the suspension of color in the white monochrome. In the process the powder becomes a graphic instrument of great refinement.

A series of works of the early 1990s carries the intriguing title, *O ar mais próximo* [*The Nearest Air*]. They deploy material with probably the greatest economy of means of any of Caldas's works—large, simple looped cords hung in the air of the gallery. Again, the minimum of physical material reveals the maximum of latent spatial energy, which deeply affects our definition of "the work," as the art critic Paulo Sérgio Duarte describes: "The work is not where we think it is: neither in the ideas that feed it, nor in the form which materializes visually, but in the transparent tension generated between what I am given to see and what I am given to think."[7]

Two developments in Caldas's work have gathered strength over the years and seem to be of a particular significance. These are, firstly, his elaboration of the "exhibition" as a composite whole, made from a selection of individual pieces from various years that each have a meaning as part of the whole. The second is a steady increase in the extent of his outdoor work, its relationships and differences with works conceived for indoors. Works in the outdoor environment developed gradually in Waltercio's practice, after he was able to command sufficient funds to produce his first two outside sculptures, *O formato*

6. Robert Smithson, "A Sedimentation of the Mind: Earth Projects," 1968, in *Robert Smithson: The Collected Writings* ed. Jack Flam (Berkeley and Los Angeles: University of California Press, 1996), 112.

7. Paulo Sergio Duarte, *Waltercio Caldas* (São Paulo: Cosac Naify, 2001), 200.

*cego* [*The Blind Format*; 1978–82] [see p. 107] in Uruguay, and *Jardim Instantâneo* [*Instant Garden*; 1989] commissioned for a park on the outskirts of São Paulo.

There then developed a fascinating dialogue between the indoor and the outdoor in his work, a process full of paradox and reversal. *Jardim Instantâneo* is dais-like in form, overlooking a valley and distant hills. "An invisible place," according to Caldas. It also defined "the relationship of my work with the horizon line, the line that is nowhere."[8] And as we have noted, most of his exterior works are horizontally oriented. (The most notable exception to Caldas's horizontally aligned exterior works is his commission for the streets of Rio de Janeiro, *Escultura para o Río* [*Sculpture for Rio*; 1996] [see p. 101]. The gaze is led upwards by a powerful—and playful—vortex that draws into itself all the constituents of the urban pavement, like a solidified whirlwind. The city's energy is humorously turned back into the cosmic energy of nature.) Although the materials and forms of his outdoor works are often similar to those used for his indoor pieces—platforms, walls, steel tubing, natural stones—the scale of these elements is radically but subtly adjusted not to dominate the human or the landscape, but to enhance the emotional response to the place, to the open air.

These are devices of unmistakable artifice, referencing human culture and construction, which have the effect of accentuating the freedom and openness of the outdoor spaces. This spatial freedom is strongly felt even from photographs of the work in situ. A particularly bold insertion is of four of his favorite "carafe" forms of steel tubing on a slightly raised marble platform in a beautiful enclosed valley near Rio de Janeiro. *Espelhos ausentes* [*Absent Mirrors*; 2003] [Fig. 2], which answers perfectly to Waltercio's once-stated desire to make an object "with the maximum presence and the maximum absence."[9] The carafe shape is rendered as an outline of something that has no outline in reality, while the steel is reflective, giving fluidity to the artificial outline by reflected light. The tubes condense the blue of the surrounding landscape and sky, and the continuous movement and sound of the nearby river. The vessel is empty precisely so that it may fill itself with the nature around it.

In 2008 I was fortunate enough to see one of Waltercio Caldas's "walk through" composite exhibitions at the Fundação Calouste Gulbenkian in Lisbon. Its title is *Horizontes*, a succession of rooms that, in very different ways, evoke the deep space of the universe, a mixture of the homely and the cosmic. Afterward I wrote to Waltercio in ecstatic tones: "Your exhibition is truly beautiful! It is one of the most beautiful exhibitions I've seen in my forty years in

8. Guy Brett, *Transcontinental: Nine Latin American Artists* (London: Verso, 1990), 71.
9. Ibid., 70.

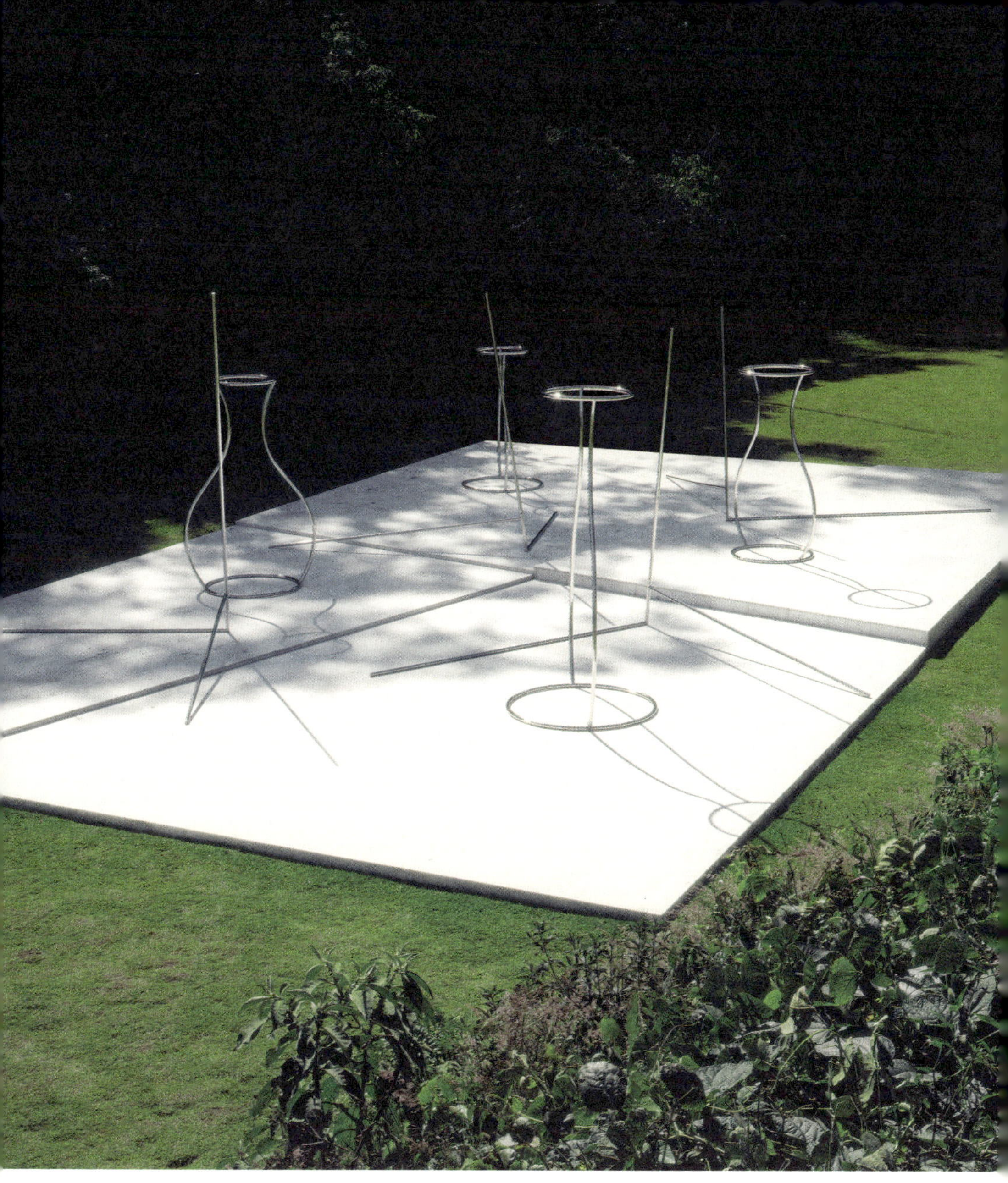

Fig. 2. *Espelhos ausentes* [*Absent Mirrors*], 2003.

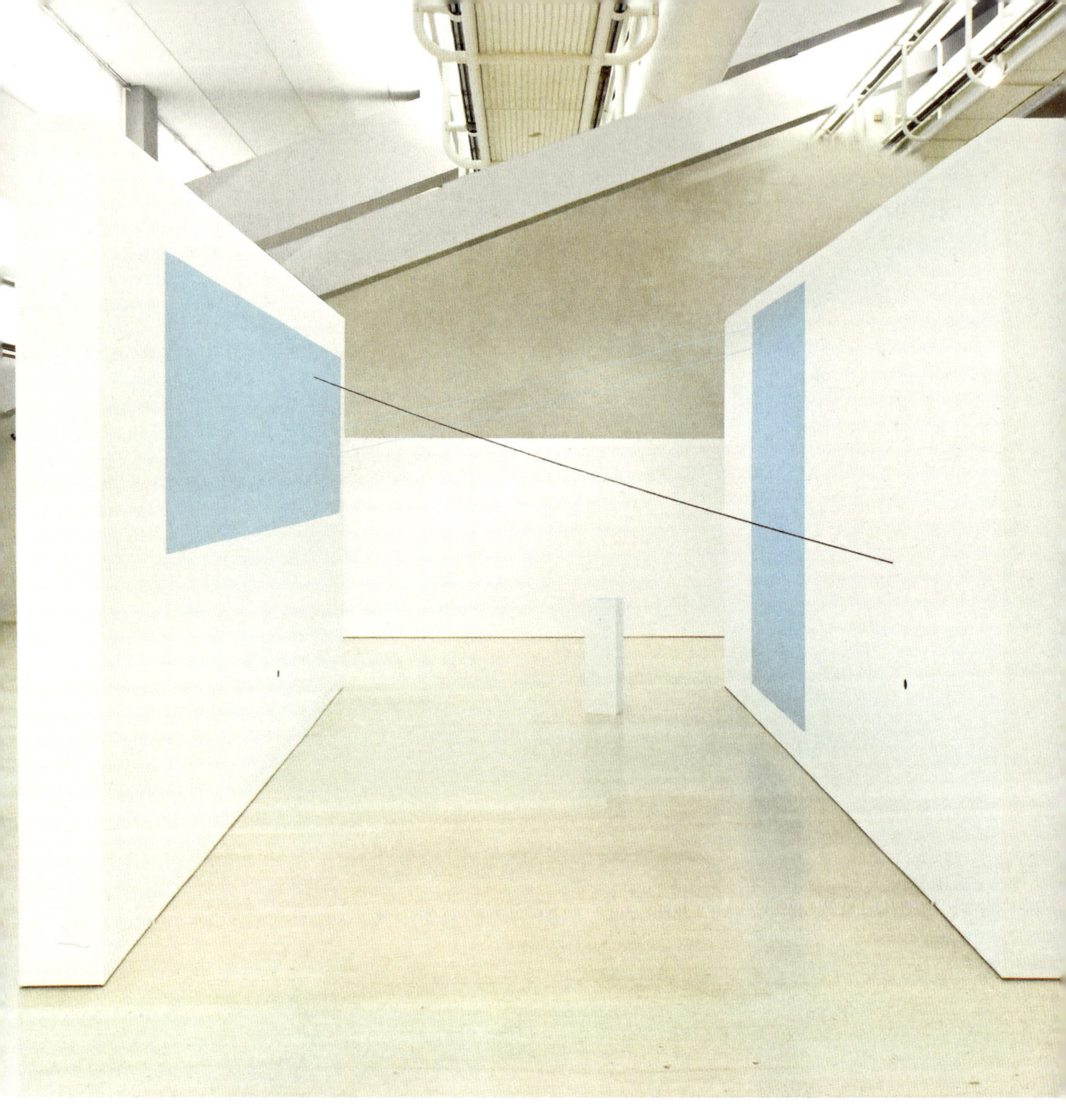

Fig. 3. *Quarto azul* [*Blue Room*], 2007.

the art world. You'll laugh when you read this but it's true. My whole soul was uplifted in the act of entering your space. Such refinement! On the other hand, such intensity of material presence, whether it is wood, steel, or paper. I see that in some ways you are working in sculpture, drawing, and painting simultaneously, so that they go beyond themselves into some sort of rarified world, or atmosphere, or region. . . . And space: the blue-topped empty pedestal of *Quarto azul* [*Blue Room*] [Fig. 3], placed where you placed it, is a stroke of genius. Your show gave me a huge pleasure. Many, many thanks."

Anyone who has been following Caldas's work since the 1970s will have noticed it moving ever closer to abstraction. What kind of abstraction is this? It is one that incorporates a large quantum of empty space, or "silence" as Caldas calls it, and makes much play with transparency [Fig. 4]. In spirit it re-evokes the Zen-influenced position of Mira Schendel ("I would say," Mira wrote in a letter to me in the mid 1960s, "the line, often, just stimulates the void. I doubt whether the word stimulate is right. Something like that. At any rate what matters in my work is the void, actively the void.")[10] Schendel's sensitivity to and modesty before the vastness and ferocity of the universe is echoed in Hélio Oiticica's attitude before nature, expressed in the following beautiful lines: "The work is born from merely a touch upon matter. I wish the matter from which my work is made to remain as it is; what transforms it into expression is nothing more than a breath: interior breath, of cosmic plenitude. Beyond this there is no work. A touch suffices, nothing more."[11]

Nothing more than a breath. . . . The wheel has come full circle and connects us up again with the metaphor of erasure which has played so great a part in the evolution of Waltercio Caldas's artistic work, in pursuit of what he himself has called "a new, fresh kind of spatiality."[12]

*Author's note: some passages in this essay have been incorporated from previous writing when I felt I could not improve on the original expression.*

10. Mira Schendel, extract from a letter to Guy Brett, in *Mira Schendel, No Vazio do Mundo*, ed. Sonia Salzstein (São Paulo: Galeria do Arte do SESI, 1996), 57.

11. Hélio Oiticica, Diary Note of September 6, 1960, in *Hélio Oiticica: Painting Beyond the Frame*, trans. Stephen Berg (Rio de Janeiro: Silvia Roesler Edições de Arte, 2008), 84.

12. Jiménez, *Waltercio Caldas*, 111.

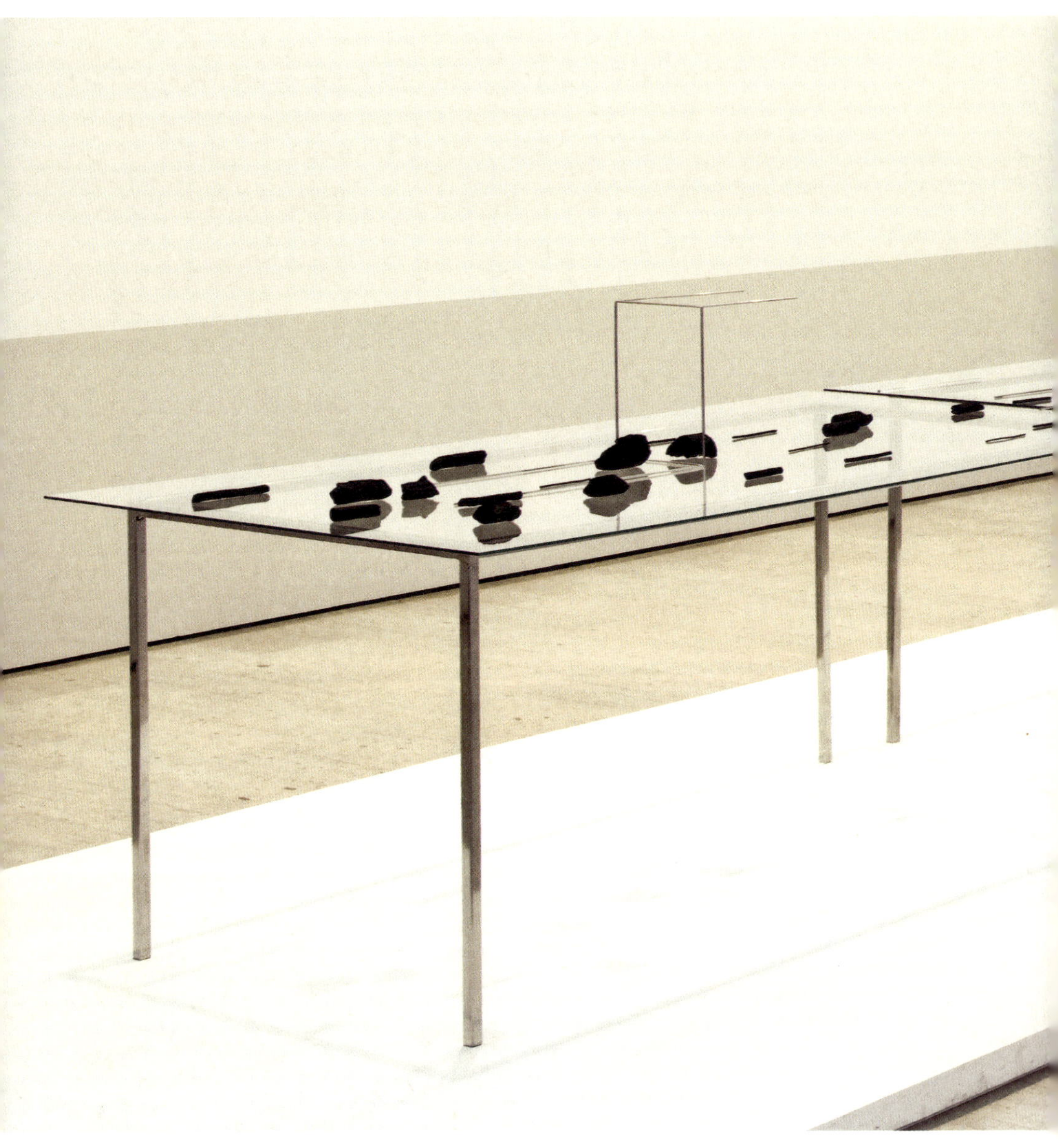

Fig. 4. *Anda uma coisa no ar* [*Something is in the Air*], 2002.

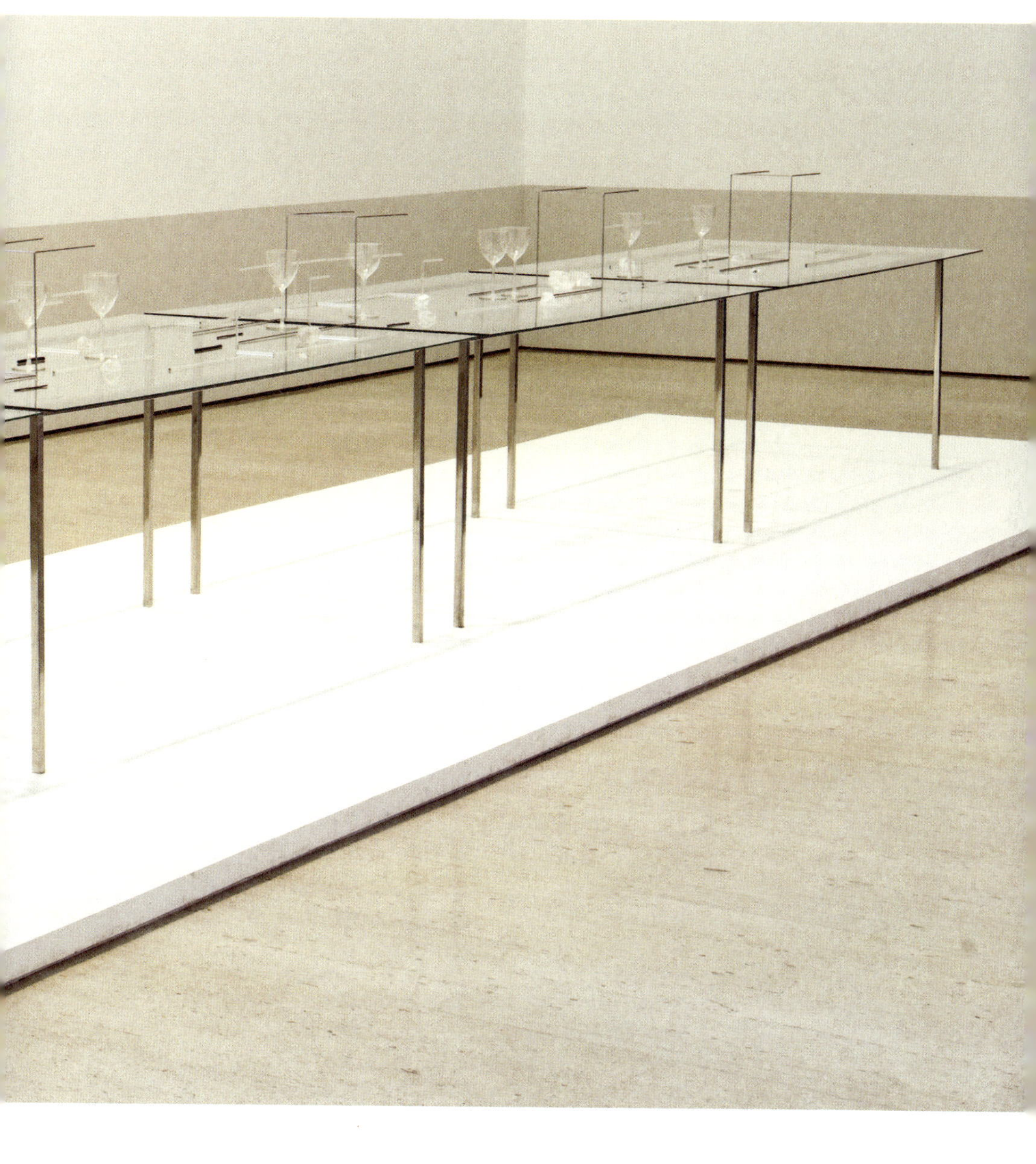

# WALTERCIO CALDAS

IN CONVERSATION WITH

## ARIEL JIMÉNEZ

# DEFINITIVELY UNFINISHED
## Breaking away from the self

*The emergence, during the nineteenth century, of what we now know as modern art can be linked in part to the increasingly significant manifestation of something akin to an inability to complete the work of art. Completion, in this sense, refers to a gesture that would lend the artwork a finished discursive structure, so that it might be interpreted at face value or, as Cézanne said, so that it might be more like "museum art." All modern works have a tendency toward the unfinished and the open. Yet far from being a weakness that we might ascribe to a given artist or generation—as Zola alleged with Cézanne and the Impressionists—this was, in fact, a typical characteristic of a world that was so open to possibilities, a world that, at the time, was still evolving and being built. Moreover, this peculiarity may well be one of the few that remain essential to contemporary art and thought.*

WALTERCIO CALDAS This is true, at least for me, because I confronted that issue from very early on, without knowing, of course, what was happening to me. In the 1960s I made a lot of drawings, and not just one at a time, but thirty all at once, one after the other. I would make a first drawing, and then a second one would come out of the first, and a third out of the second, and so on. And the truth is, that chain reaction was what interested me the most. The shift from one drawing to the next was what stimulated me to keep going [Figs. 1, 1a].

ARIEL JIMÉNEZ That's quite significant, I think—the feeling that something had eluded you in the drawing you just made, something that only another drawing would allow you to define, or capture, in some way.

WC Yes, and maybe I sensed that this thing, whatever it was, would have no end.

AJ That concept of the unfinished is central to modern and contemporary thought, and not just in the visual arts. The awareness that the world we live in is a constantly evolving reality, as Darwin showed us, and the realization that our theories cannot fully explain reality in all its complexity have clear parallels in the evolution of visual art over the past two centuries, through works that are eternally unfinished or, as in the case of your early drawings, possess a structure that entails the awareness of something missing. Balzac had already raised this

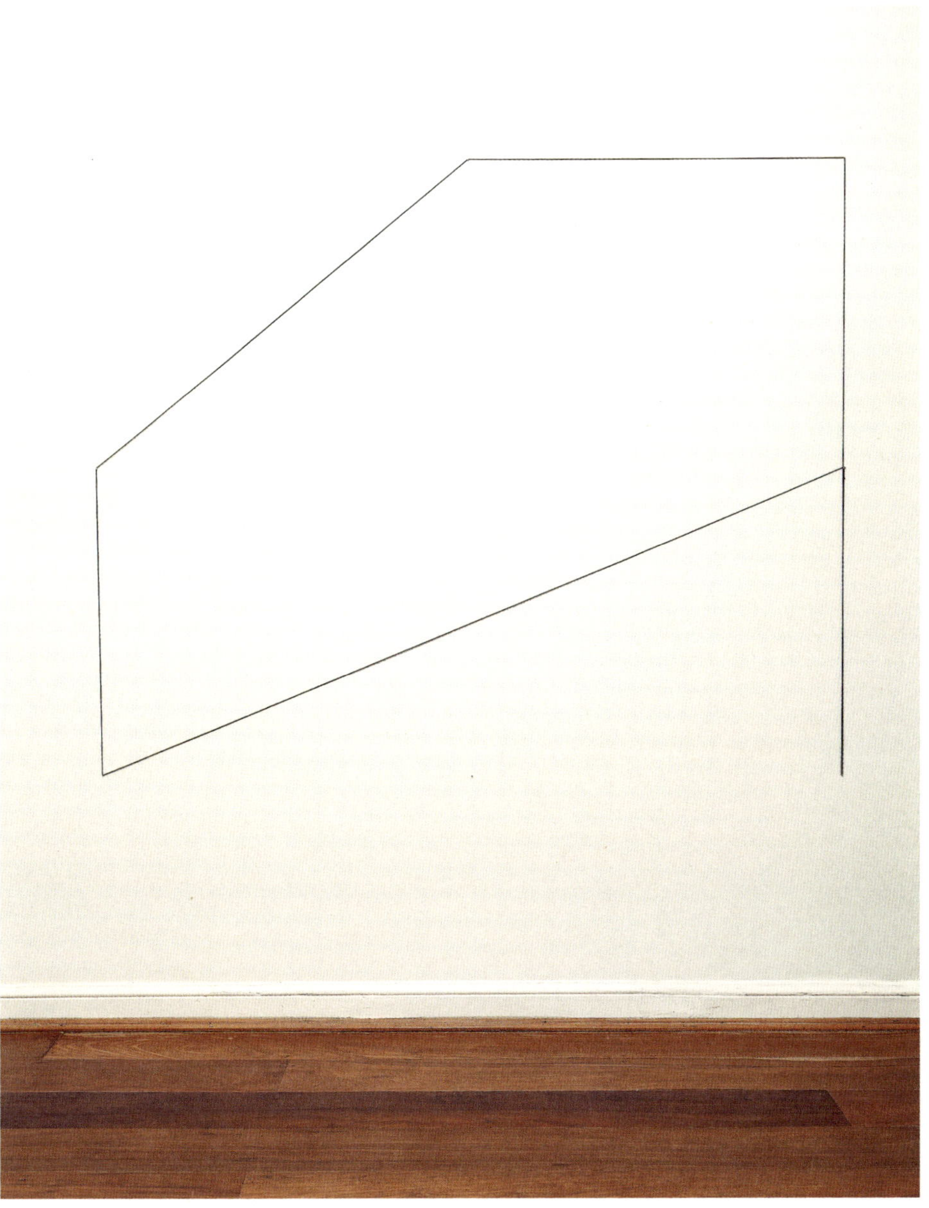

Fig. 1. *Always*, 1967.

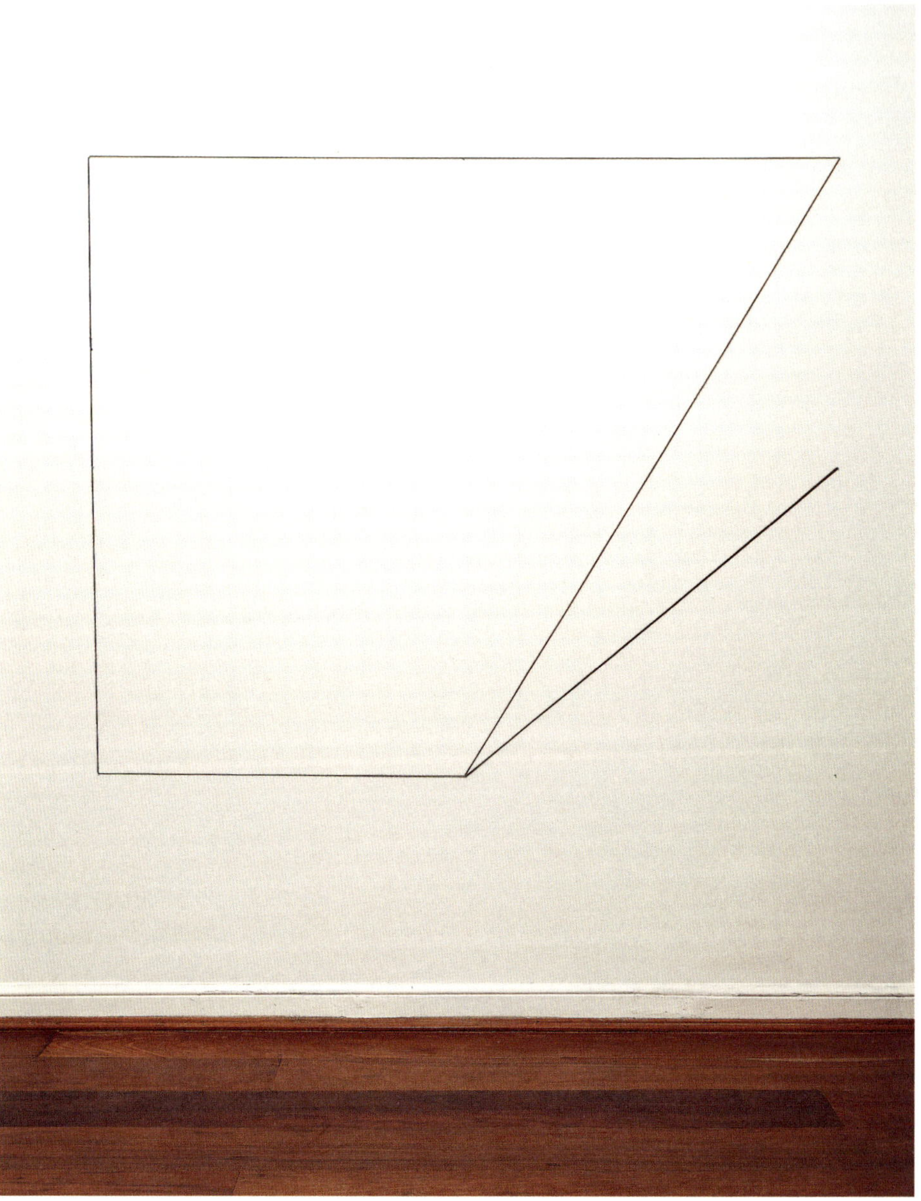

Fig. 1a. *Always*, 1967.

issue in *Le chef-d'oeuvre inconnu* [*The Unknown Masterpiece*], a text published in 1831 and admired by countless artists, including Cézanne and Picasso.

WC Yes, it was something that had no end. And I was deeply drawn to that, to the possibility of creating a finite object—because the operation of making a drawing or producing an object is an action that inevitably ends at a certain moment—that nonetheless unleashed an infinite quality that was specific to it. I suppose this is exactly what I have been doing ever since then. The form is never exhausted, nor is the world as representation.

AJ This experience is clearly related to what Picasso spoke of when he said that the perfect line didn't exist, that the number of possible lines was in fact infinite, and that a drawing materialized only one of those possibilities, the one line that, at that moment, had been possible for him.[1]

WC And they all deserve the same respect, right?

AJ Each one formulates a virtuality of the real, a possibility to explore. I have always been quite moved by those works by Picasso, which he did frequently, that are somewhat like painted drawings, in which the painting prevails upon a background, but it's a background in which you can still see the trace of other lines the artist abandoned in the process of executing the drawing. It's almost as if the drawing retains the memory of the possibilities that presented themselves to the artist as he was working, virtualities that he later abandoned or pushed aside in the quest for a more complete, more accomplished expression, or at least one that best conveyed his thoughts at that moment [Fig. 2].

WC That may be one of the things I find most attractive about Picasso, his total familiarity with error. I think for him there was no such thing as error with respect to his work.

AJ He accepted them as virtualities of the real, as incomplete or unrealized possibilities, as potentialities.

WC It isn't that he accepted the mistake. What I want to point out is something different. It seems to me that he felt certain that if a mistake occurred, it could

1. Hélène Parmelin relates how Picasso described the lines in the drawings he showed her, saying, "they are the only ones that exist, in reality, because they make the only possible line of a thousand . . . possible for me at that moment." Hélène Parmelin, *Picasso dit . . .* (Paris: Gonthier, 1966), 35.

be integrated into the system. It could be a stimulus. In other words, he wasn't worried about the fact of making a mistake, and because he always found that he could integrate the ones he did make, they never bothered him. And that is a very beautiful thing, I think, about Picasso.

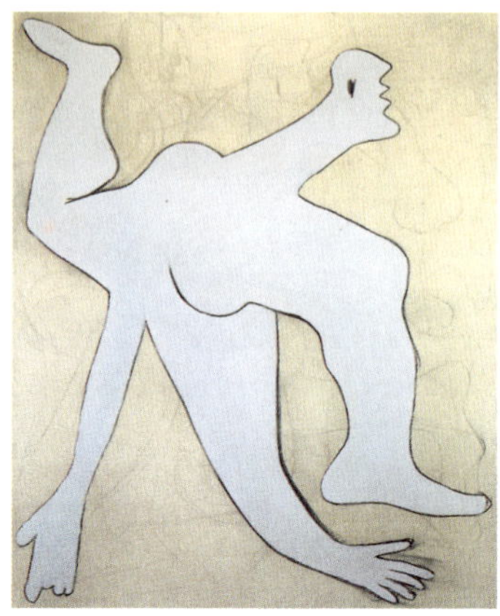

Fig. 2. Pablo Picasso, *The Blue Acrobat*, 1929.

AJ But we could also see the mistake, or that thing we regard as a mistake at a given moment, as an incomplete reality that has yet to achieve its ideal form, as something that simply responds to parameters that are different from the ones that guide us. I'm thinking, for example, about that lack of finish for which the Impressionists were so criticized: the fuzzy edges, the flowing lines, segments of the canvas left unpainted, and so on. For the academics of their age, these were mistakes, or gestures more appropriate for studies than for finished works of art. Well, ultimately, those mistakes were the indications of new concepts in painting, and in viewing the world itself. And those concepts evolved and proved their meaning many times over during the twentieth century.

WC In that case, I think, what we call reality is not enough. There is no such thing as the perfect line. It is something to be done, and the result is an invented reality, because the artist does not just produce an illusion, he generates an illusion that then becomes part of reality. And of course some people, in their resistance, question art's utility or purpose, saying things like "art doesn't change the world." But, you see, art doesn't *have* to do that; it's enough for art to change language, expectations, people. That in itself is a real achievement. In other words, maybe some people who are more conservative express a certain frustration because they expect art to fulfill a purpose that was never the purpose of art in the first place. I am talking about the expectation or hope that the work will be a faithful representation of the world, as if a work of art could be a substitute for reality. Some people will condemn certain kinds of art when it doesn't meet their expectations.

AJ As Paul Valéry said, the only real thing in art is art. In other words, more than imitating what is real, art creates realities.

<sup>WC</sup> Yes, and you can see there how generous Valéry was with his concept of reality, and that is very provocative—a concept of reality that, in some way, art promotes or builds. Reality as something that is made, not accepted. It isn't something that is incorporated into something else; reality is something that exists in a process of constant formation and always will be. And maybe that's why reality is always different from what people hope or expect it will be. The good health and strength of art depend on whether or not it possesses precisely that critical capacity to stand up to what the public generally expects.

<sup>AJ</sup> And that's why the early experiences you described before are so meaningful, the ones in which a first drawing prompted the creation of a second drawing, and so on after that, with no preassigned limit. The interesting thing there, I think, is that it wasn't something you decided to do consciously. It was something that imposed itself on you, as a demand of your artistic practice at that time.

<sup>WC</sup> Each drawing was a step, and they just grew from there, one after the other. I remember one day, when I was twenty-one years old, feeling terrified by the quantity of drawings I had done. I felt oppressed, I think, by the accumulation of operations I had performed in search of something that I couldn't even define very clearly for myself, perhaps even working without any specific goal, just experimenting, looking for a path, which is very different. And so this huge pile of drawings became somewhat authoritarian and obsessive for me. What happens, when you produce something, is that the thing you produce becomes part of your life, and it can become a burden if it isn't used in the right way. I was fortunate to learn relatively early on that not all that material necessarily needed to become a work of art. At that moment I decided that if I wanted to move forward, I would have to free myself from everything I had accumulated, and that it would be enough to keep a selection of things in my memory. I think I threw out around four thousand drawings that I had done between the ages of fourteen and twenty-one. It was one of the most crucial decisions of my life, because it helped me to understand the importance of starting over, again, from the beginning. This act left a lasting impression on me, and it is still present in my mind whenever I need to make a decision. It's as if a piece both raised an issue and then closed the book on it entirely. In that situation, everything was closed, and from there I had to start all over again, with a different material, a different procedure, a different attitude. That idea of starting over is fundamental; it's the determination not to get caught in the trance of a formal style, or by the presence of previous works.

<sup>AJ</sup> Every time I see an artist fighting with him- or herself, fighting what he or she has created, I recall Roland Barthes's very lovely observation that if something new needs to emerge in an artist's oeuvre, it can only come out of the artist's constant struggle with what he described as two blind forces—those two horizons of style and the history of art.

<sup>WC</sup> It's very funny that you should say that, because those are two challenges that, to some degree or another, are always permeating my work. That, in fact, is the reason I use art history as if it were another material to work with. Because one can incorporate that material without being quotational, when talking about an artist, or even talking about everything that came before. You see, the history of art is entirely present for us; it is as if it were a second nature.

<sup>AJ</sup> That is exactly the term that Barthes used to name that blind force of art history. For him it is something that imposes itself on us like a horizon, a second nature.

<sup>WC</sup> For me, this is a critical issue, because artists today are inundated with information as never before, and this has come to be something of a second landscape for us. In this sense, today's artist, as compared to those of past eras, has a more critical need to free him- or herself from that past. Nowadays, if you go to a library, you will find the history of cave paintings alongside German Expressionism, Cubism, Surrealism, Dada, and a thousand other things. All of this has been accumulated in our present moment through the editorial form. It is impossible to deny that current presence of the past, of the history of art.

<sup>AJ</sup> And it is something that intellectuals and artists began to perceive as soon as the publishing industry reached a certain degree of maturity. I am thinking, for example, of an essay written by André Malraux in 1947, "Le musée imaginaire" [later published in English as *The Museum without Walls*]. What he talks about, precisely, is the possibility of having a kind of imaginary museum of all those artworks that we don't have access to in our own museums but that imprint themselves upon us in some way, and he talks about the impact those works had on the world then. I think that impact is still felt today. Those works begin to interact, in books and in our minds. One of the most interesting arguments in that essay addresses the burden represented by the reproduction of artworks, as it imposes a reading that decontextualizes them and brings them closer to the cultural texture of our gaze. The published book can integrate them into our collective awareness in a way that works of art had previously never done.

This is quite a recent phenomenon, since the second half of the twentieth century, no earlier than that. Is this how it operates with you? Do you attempt to domesticate the weight of history by integrating it?

WC No, it's not about integrating it; I just can't avoid taking it into account. It's the fact of that presence of art, that constant flow, which owes as much to Duchamp as to Rembrandt, Braque, Vermeer, or the person who made the first cave drawing. What I mean is that art couldn't be what it is without the contribution of every one of those artists.

AJ It's as if that second nature of art were as immediately present here and now, for us, as the forests and mountains were for the nomads of prehistoric times, wouldn't you say? It's something that is simply too present to avoid, because you live inside it, you are part of it.

WC That's exactly how I see it. And that river has neither source nor outlet, no sea to empty into.

AJ And you would be—we all would be—a new species of nomads in the middle of that other nature. In today's world, culture and its natural environment, the enormity of the contemporary city, stand as our true form of nature. From there we emerge, from time to time, to admire the vestiges of the natural world, what still remains of the animal and vegetable universe of the dawn of time. It seems to me that the maquette, as the intimate projection of a possible, imaginable space, is one of the most logical paths for confronting that artificial—and eminently human—world of the city. That is, in any event, the path you have taken since your first solo exhibition.

WC That's right. My first show was in 1965, at the academic center of a university philosophy department, in Rio de Janeiro. For that exhibition I showed small objects made out of cardboard and other materials, with which I took on a relatively juvenile topic, my first sexual experiences. I had read some Surrealist texts and was very taken with the way they dealt with sexuality. At that moment, at least, I felt that the Surrealists had invented a revolutionary way of dealing with subjectivity.

AJ And how did those maquettes work?

WC I was interested in studying adolescent sexual experiences, and in the violence

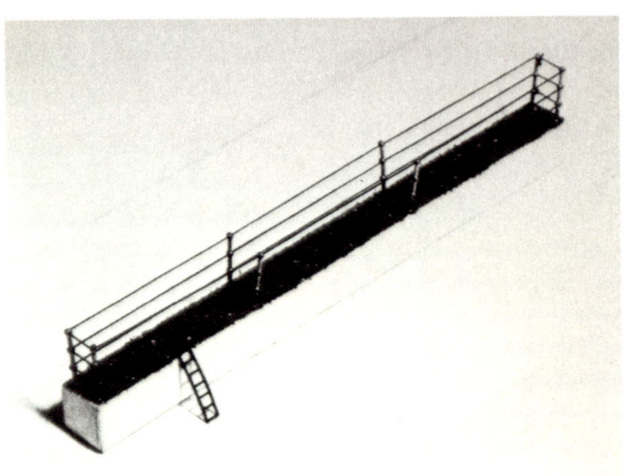

Fig. 3. *Maquette II*, 1967.

of that transition from being a dependent family member to being an autonomous individual. And so in those early maquettes I began to explore the topic of the individual confronting society. Even though today I may feel that they completely lack artistic transcendence, I still know that they were important to my process of learning the possibilities for building a reality outside of myself through small-scale three-dimensional montages. All those constructions were subjective manifestations (how could they have been anything but?), and it was not happenstance that it was a philosophy department that invited me to put them on display. The one thing, maybe, that I disliked about this exhibition is that even though I might have perceived subjective qualities in my work, I didn't want the focus of the show to be my subjectivity. After that exhibition, in about 1966–67, I started working on the maquettes of three-dimensional objects in the world, which are those maquettes of imaginary architectural constructions.

For this work my starting points were themes suggested by Jorge Luis Borges, the writer whom I was most fascinated with at the time. Borges gave me the idea that it was possible to create imaginary constructions. And so I approached those maquettes as if I were a Borgesian architect, as if that kind of architect could actually exist. It was a way of delocalizing my subjectivity and orienting it toward the world [Fig. 3]. I was also strongly influenced by the utopian architecture of Étienne-Louis Boullée,[2] an eighteenth-century French architect who was known especially for his almost metaphysical designs

2. Étienne-Louis Boullée (1728–1799) was a visionary French architect and member of the Royal Academy of Architecture. He was very influential in his day, both for his teaching and for the audacity of his architectural projects, which were often utopian in nature. Inspired by Ancient Rome and Greece, he ascribed a central role to geometric forms such as the sphere, the cube, and the pyramid, from which he conceived a number of striking, grandiose structures.

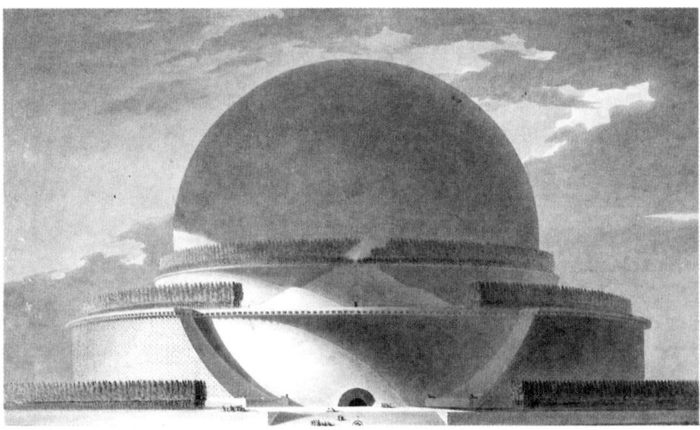

Fig. 4. Étienne-Louis Boullée, *Cénotaphe à Newton* [*Cenotaph for Newton*], 1780–93.

of buildings that couldn't have been erected with the techniques of his age, because they defied the limits of what was possible then [Fig. 4].

<sup>AJ</sup> Your maquettes from 1966–67, then, which were oriented toward the world, came about as a reaction, in a way, to those first objects from 1965?

<sup>WC</sup> Reaction might be too strong a word. I would rather speak of a correction in perspective. In any event, it was at that moment that I understood something important, perhaps intuitively. I seem to have realized that maybe I had been too naive in the beginning, because I allowed myself to get carried away, too blindly, by the influences that came my way. I think it's important to mention that I was raised in a middle-class home, in an environment and in a house where there was no library. My father had books on architecture and engineering, and a bit, but just a very little bit, of literature. What I mean by this is that my upbringing did not instill in me any notion about that second nature of culture. Culture was a real discovery for me, because even though my father supported me very much, always, my education was a personal effort on my part. It was about understanding that culture was something to be discovered, and I felt that culture had actually arrived at my doorstep as a new life possibility.

<sup>AJ</sup> When you organized that first exhibition in 1965, you had already begun studying with Ivan Serpa at the Museu de Arte Moderna [Museum of Modern Art] in Rio, isn't that right?

<sup>WC</sup> Yes, the classes with Serpa had started before that. It was there that I began to understand how the art world functioned. I found my way to him in 1964 in

a rather unusual way. I had known, of course, that the Museum of Modern
Art offered art classes that were, in ways, more interesting than the classes
available to me at the Escola de Belas Artes [School of Fine Arts]. I had been
to two or three painting workshops at the school, live-model workshops, for
example, and it all felt extremely tedious, because the model would just stand
there, motionless, the entire time. It was as if she wasn't a woman at all, or had
been expelled from her sexuality in order to be used in this way. And the artists
painted that body reduced to the condition of model. And I felt that the person
was somehow outside of reality, as were, of course, the representations created
by the students in the class. And the classes themselves also just felt lifeless to
me. I don't know where I got the idea that they were supposed to be stimulating, but there was certainly a difference between that experience and what I
expected and hoped for from art.

AJ  What you were experiencing, in some way, was precisely the modern doubt
about the capability of pictorial representation to approach the truth of the
world. Like when Cézanne wondered if it was true that color and form existed
separately, as he had been taught at the academy, or if they constituted an indi-
visible unit, as he believed he observed in nature.

WC  Maybe I saw something there that made me doubt representation, or its autonomy. In any case, because I was also a person who felt drawn to the possibility
of knowing the world through a willingness to feel wonder, it was inevitable
that at some point I would discover books. It was evident that I would eventually need information that, in those days, was not as easy to access as it is now. I
had to scour books for information that I couldn't find anywhere else. Around
that time, I heard about a professor at the Museum of Modern Art who gave
art classes, and I was intrigued. Not long after that, one day in 1964, I was at
a bookstore that sold secondhand books, and while leafing through some art
publications, I spotted a man who had just bought a book by Jean Cocteau,
*Opium*. So I started talking to him, and he really piqued my interest. Later on,
I learned from the bookstore manager that I had been talking to Ivan Serpa.
That was where the seed was planted for me: two or three months later I signed
up for one of his classes. It was because I had gotten the sense that Serpa was
a very well-informed person—and I confirmed this in his classes—and for that
reason he would be able to introduce me to that second nature of culture, and
specifically culture as it related to art.[3]

3. Caldas's interest in the book and its function extends far beyond the norm and has led him to amass a
considerable collection of first-edition art books that are closely and significantly linked to his artwork.

 What were his classes like?

 They were like a training camp. We would go home and do whatever we thought we ought to do, and then we would come back to class to subject our work to the scrutiny of both our professor and our classmates. This was actually a bit cruel, but I have to say it was the first great lesson I learned from him, because that boundary between what it means to create something for yourself and what it means to create something for other people was completely destroyed, obliterated. That was how it was. On the one hand, you objectively had the chance to do whatever you wanted at home, but on the other, you had to present your work to a group of other people, one of whom—Serpa—was extremely competent and knowledgeable about things.

In his classes I learned a few basic lessons. First, I learned about that confrontation with the world. Second, he gave us detailed information that allowed us to situate what we did in the world of art, which was something none of us knew anything about, because we had no idea how much of what we had done was new. Third, I found his classes extremely interesting because even if he indirectly and ultimately stimulated personal expression, he elicited this not by having us search for a style, but by encouraging in us the need to understand what was happening in the things we produced. It was a much more intelligent way of approaching visual creation. This might have been difficult for an artist seeking his or her own possibilities of self-expression and who might have felt lost when confronting such a vast range and wealth of meanings in Serpa's classes. But for me it was totally the opposite, possibly because I was not obsessed with the quest for personal expression.

Another aspect of Serpa's classes that I recall was the atmosphere: the fact that he conducted the class in the Museum of Modern Art, in the proximity of the other professors and the exhibitions on view at the time. That was when I started to take a look at the exhibitions at the museum, and at other galleries too. This taught me what it means to be an artist, because in those days nobody really knew what that meant. So it was there that I began to get an idea of how I, too, might find a way to express myself through art.

# THE NATURE OF ART
## Inventing your own artist

<sup>WC</sup> In those days I wasn't very sure of what it meant to be an artist, and I think many of us were quite clueless in this sense. The first I ever heard of Lygia Clark was in a fashion magazine, in a spread that showed her making objects, a housewife who had an unusual, unexpected hobby. It was a profession without a very clear job description. Artists were people who made things that were called "art"—meaning, they produced objects that were neither useful nor functional nor recognizable, and so the assumption was that these things could only be art. I would almost say that as a result of this very absence of a definition, all the Brazilian artists of that period invented their own individual ways of being artists. I certainly found myself forced to invent the kind of artist I wanted to be, and I see this in all the Brazilian artists. I see Hélio Oiticica inventing the artist he would have liked to be, I see Lygia inventing her own thing, I see Tunga, José Resende, and Cildo Meireles all inventing a particular way of being an artist.

What I mean to say with all this is that typically in Brazil it is very hard to look at an entire generation of artists and not recognize a general style that allows you to connect their work. For example, this is the case with the Neo-Concrete artists [of the late 1950s and early 1960s]: beyond certain individual differences, it is possible to discern a certain degree of relationship, a kind of formal affinity among them. But this does not happen with my generation, precisely because of that need to invent an "other" artist for an "other" art. No longer was it enough to replace one "ism" with another.

<sup>AJ</sup> And yet, isn't it logical to think that the need for artistic self-invention would have been even stronger among the Neo-Concrete artists, precisely because they created their works in a milieu in which nobody was quite sure what it meant to be an artist?

<sup>WC</sup> That's a very good question, because it's a challenge. I would say, however, that the Neo-Concrete artists did not feel obliged to self-invent because the model of the modern artist was still convenient for them. They didn't do it because the model of the artist is only questioned when it achieves a certain level of complexity in the cultural sphere. For example, when there is a great diversity of isms to choose from, a situation that admits many different ways of being an artist, the artist must confront the difficulty of defining his or her own form of

being an artist. This is what occurred in the case of Lygia Clark, when around mid-career she came to believe that she was outside the realm of art, and was even known to deny her own status as an artist.

<sup>AJ</sup> The artist and poet Ferreira Gullar publically agreed with Clark's stance, because in reality after the *Bichos* [*Animals*], she stopped making art.

<sup>WC</sup> That's another very interesting issue. . . . The way I see it, what happened there was different, because I believe Gullar was using a revolutionary statement, that of an artist aware of the boundaries she needed to push through, to deduce a limitation that is inherent to all contemporary art. From my perspective, Lygia never doubted the efficacy of artistic practice in a general sense; she just perceived it as insufficient, as and how she perceived it, for her new objectives. I don't see a denial of art there, just a very clarifying and precise critique of the programmatic naïvetés of her time.

<sup>AJ</sup> And that was precisely the moment when your generation began working. She must have understood that her objects could no longer be perceived from the perspective of the traditional concepts of art, and must have felt that, to some degree, she was no longer an artist. But your group, having begun to practice as artists at a time when those traditional notions had lost their relevance and force, understood in some way that part of your efforts involved, precisely, defining the characteristics of that new realm of art and what it meant to be an artist within it. That's how I see it, at least: until quite late into the twentieth century, creating a work of art involved producing an image that could maintain a close relationship with the world—an "informed" duplicate of the world, conceived of course from the realm of culture and fulfilling its objectives, wouldn't you say? That would be a Romantic landscape, a Van Gogh still life, or even a Cubist still life. They are images of the world, or of a piece of the world, informed by culture. But with artists like Duchamp, and then individuals like Clark and Oiticica in Brazil, art began to operate in a different way. Possibly because now the artist was situated firmly in the cultural sphere (because we knew there was no "outside" possible for us), and from there generated, produced objects, situations, or even just tensions capable of enriching that cultural environment from which we observe the world and define our interaction with it. And of course, by now, neither the artist's mode of functioning nor his products were equivalent, exactly. And that's why it makes sense that people like Joseph Beuys and Lygia Clark must have felt expelled from the realm of art.

271 × 322 × 894 × 765 × 1485 × 136 × 69801 KM

<sup>WC</sup> Exactly. And that's why I say that denying oneself as an artist, which is what happened with Lygia, is different from what my generation had to deal with, which was the need to build a new possibility for art. What I mean is that at a certain point she was able to create another possibility, perhaps without defining it so clearly. What distinguishes her generation from mine, possibly, is that we found ourselves facing a much more complex set of variables, and that excess made us question all of them. It wasn't just about the difficulty of choosing one from a variety of aesthetic options and programs. That's where the novelty lay. What happened with us was similar to what the Dada artists produced in their day, because they didn't even want to be artists, at least in the traditional sense of the term.

<sup>AJ</sup> They were either unwilling or unable to continue operating as traditional artists, but they produced actions in the realm of language—and did so within the parameters of art—and for that reason it was natural for these parameters to become integrated into the realm of meaning created by art.

<sup>WC</sup> That's right, but it would be naive to think that that integration occurred without the medium exacting a very high price for it. There is something perverse in that insertion, in the sense that once a new object of art becomes part of the culture, it immediately begins to erode and ultimately transform it.

<sup>AJ</sup> It's as naive as believing the old anti-art story. Because you would have to establish a difference between the will to break free from a given way of creating art (that negative work waiting to be done, as Tristan Tzara put it) and the thing that some people call anti-art, which to my mind doesn't exist. An action in the field of art is, by nature, already a form of artistic creation, even if one's quest is to destroy a way of thinking about and creating art.

<sup>WC</sup> Of course. When I talk about anti-art, in reality I am referring to the restricted character of what, at the time, was understood to be art.

<sup>AJ</sup> That's exactly what [Maurice] Merleau-Ponty meant when he said that modern art was less about choosing between drawing and color or figuration and the creation of signs, and more about "multiplying the systems of equivalence."[4] In other words, that "realist" style of pictorial representation was a system of equivalence, one among many such systems, but until the late nineteenth

---

4. Maurice Merleau-Ponty, *L'œil et l'esprit* (Paris: Gallimard, 1964), 71.

century it was believed to be the only one, or at least the only one that maintained an efficient, correspondent relationship with reality.

<sup>WC</sup> It was perfect, and in that sense, all of us who began working as artists in the 1960s did so in a world where the notion of art in its most restricted sense had long since died. But for the Dadaists, things were very different because they were working before the existence even of Surrealism, which allowed artists to explore themes from dreams, for example, and other things not necessarily related to the real world. Thanks to Surrealism, the boundaries of art in those days broadened considerably. And in the same way, each successive generation opened new possibilities that have grown and grown until the present day, to the point where, now, information gives you simultaneous access to multiple versions of things, in addition to all the things that a multitude of artists are exploring all over the world. And as you confront that chaos as an artist, you have to assume some kind of position. No longer is it about being figurative or abstract, Pop or Conceptual, because all those possibilities exist together, they recombine and produce new subinterpretations.

<sup>AJ</sup> Maybe that's why you have said that your group was an alternative in Brazil, because you had no alternative.

<sup>WC</sup> Not exactly. When I said that, I was referring to two catchwords that many people used in the 1970s to describe any situation they didn't understand or something that was being done in an unconventional way. Every time an artist searched for a personal expression for what he or she was doing, it was deemed "experimental." The experimental gallery at the Museum of Modern Art in Rio had been created especially for young artists who, because of the kind of work they were doing, could not find a place in the gallery circuit. And artists like me, who worked in that vein, who confronted that risk, were a little offended, because it felt like a frivolous classification, a comfortable label to cover everything that was not understood and that went beyond the usual boundaries of art. For me, experimentation was so intimately linked to the learning process and the artistic practice that it couldn't be used against art. In the end, art is the process of experimenting, which Mário Pedrosa expressed so well when he said that art was an experimental exercise of freedom. That's why, when I heard Pedrosa speak so radically about the process of experimentation, I felt that he had redeemed the term "experimental." He had identified the perfect formula for it; no longer was the experimental a simple, precarious reaction to existing

art. The world was, in truth, experimental, precisely because of its very urgent need for transformations.

Another oversimplified concept was the notion of "alternative" art, which had the same problem. It was as if the cultural realm wanted to cheapen the value of any activity that eluded the parameters of the system it wanted to uphold. And so for me, these two words took on a reactionary quality, and that was why I said that we preferred the alternative because we had no alternative. It was a way of saying that what was at stake was much more essential and complex than the naïveté of wanting to do something new, against established forms.

<sup>AJ</sup> Something similar took place in Venezuela in the 1970s and 1980s, when the only way these kinds of regenerative experiences could be accepted was by assimilating them into another genre: the experimental genre. It was a comfortable way to deal with things because it broadened the traditional categories of painting, sculpture, and printmaking without posing a risk to the established order. And in addition to that—this was actually very funny—some critics and even some artists would attempt to create new categories for perfectly conventional proposals, in the hope of giving them a bit of avant-garde swing. This is what happened, for example, with so-called experimental drawing. The most clumsily representative drawings would pass for the most radically young, avant-garde artistic expression, and a great many people in the field accepted them as such.

<sup>WC</sup> That was exactly what happened. Plus, in those days painting and printmaking were very rigid categories, and there were groups of printmakers who were very resistant to any genre other than printmaking, who wanted to work only within the boundaries of a specific technique. Much later on [in 1980] I began to experiment with printmaking, and when I did I was shocked, because I discovered that all the rigor they invoked was actually very relative. If there is one artistic practice in which the resulting work can turn out different from what the artist might foresee, it is printmaking. And I remember thinking about that for a long time, because I couldn't understand how it was possible that a process so regulated by norms could tumble so wildly out of the printmaker's control.

<sup>AJ</sup> It's very interesting, because I see you creating a personal vision of art out of the clash you experienced in the encounter with that conservative vision. In a way, your work is almost the product of the bewilderment that emerged from that clash.

<sup>WC</sup> Yes, absolutely. It was almost as if I had sensed, and continue to sense even

now, that one must always be conscious of those boundaries, because they go through a period of renewal with each decade and in some way they surround the creator, especially as the creation becomes freer and freer. I almost think that as systems of representation grow more and more sophisticated, they increasingly need a critical vision, because the possibilities grow narrower and broader at the same time, and artists are gathered up ever more efficiently by the culture of entertainment.


*As we talked about this, and I tried to reconstruct the process of his visual production over time, our conversation and his mode of argumentation kept bringing us back to the present moment, as if with each question I asked, his response reflected all his work, regardless of when it was made—as if today's problems were the same as the problems of his early years, or as if his present methods of dealing with problems, through new experiences, were the only methods that could possibly shed light on his oeuvre.*

AJ I am having a hard time maintaining the chronological thread of this conversation, because with each question I ask, even when I mention a very specific moment in your artistic practice, we end up talking about your most recent work.

WC What happens in these kinds of situations is that when I start talking about one piece in particular, I tend not to define it as an isolated case but as something within the general program of my oeuvre. It's like saying each fragment is the whole, each work is the entire body of work.

AJ That's exactly what Merleau-Ponty said about painting, that all painting—understood as any dense work—always extended out to the very depths of painting, in the sense of touching its deepest essence, no matter when the work being painted was created, in the past or in the present.[5]

WC In the end, in a certain sense, what gets produced is an object that catalyzes all the others, without being any one of them.

AJ In any event, our conversation does bring us back, over and over again, inevitably, to the present.

5. "Well, yes, neither in painting nor any other experiences, even, can we establish a hierarchy in civilizations or speak of progress, not because some fate is holding us back, but because in a certain sense the very first painting extended out to the very depths of the future." Merleau-Ponty, *L'oeil et l'esprit*, 92.

<sup>WC</sup> For me it's a very fruitful process, because every time you go back, you start again in a different way, and you shed a new light on your ideas.

<sup>AJ</sup> Let's go back, then, to the mid-1960s, when you began your studies with Ivan Serpa and your immersion in the world of museums and galleries.

<sup>WC</sup> That was a time in which a very essential process took place for me; it was about the way I responded, in my work, to the exhibitions and the constant exchange with other artists and their work. In some way, my art making began when I was a viewer, in dialogue with other people's work. While looking at a piece of art and trying to understand what the artist meant to say, I seemed to be asking myself, "How would I say that?" or "How would I respond to what this artist is saying?" This forced me—and it was very enjoyable to do this—to be extremely attentive not just to what other artists were trying to say, but to *how* they were trying to say these things. I always paid very close attention to what was on the canvas and the way in which it had been executed and thought out. Because I was interested in discerning the kind of language I was observing. I was confronting those works as an observer who wanted to learn, never as an artist myself.

<sup>AJ</sup> You wanted, simply, to learn how that work had been made, what it had achieved. And, I suppose, you also wanted to discern its limitations . . .

<sup>WC</sup> I am still learning about those limitations. Those observations taught me that each artist had a particular way of facing the challenges that he or she wanted to deal with in the effort to achieve something. I began to focus on identifying the characteristics of this or that painter, this or that sculptor. And that was when I realized that each one, more than creating a repertoire of forms, had invented a destiny. Each one responded, so to speak, to an obsession, and the effort to respond to that obsession was made manifest in the artwork itself. And to me this seemed absolutely critical to constructing one's own expressivity. I am not talking about the will to be an artist, but about the will to propose a voice, an expression for myself. And I found that expression through art. That marked the beginning of a very key process for me, because that was when I began to find in the world an immense variety of art objects and, for reasons I can't quite explain, I began to manufacture objects that I couldn't find anywhere, just to watch them emerge. Those were the objects I showed at my first solo exhibition in 1965.

# Papel-carbono entre espelhos

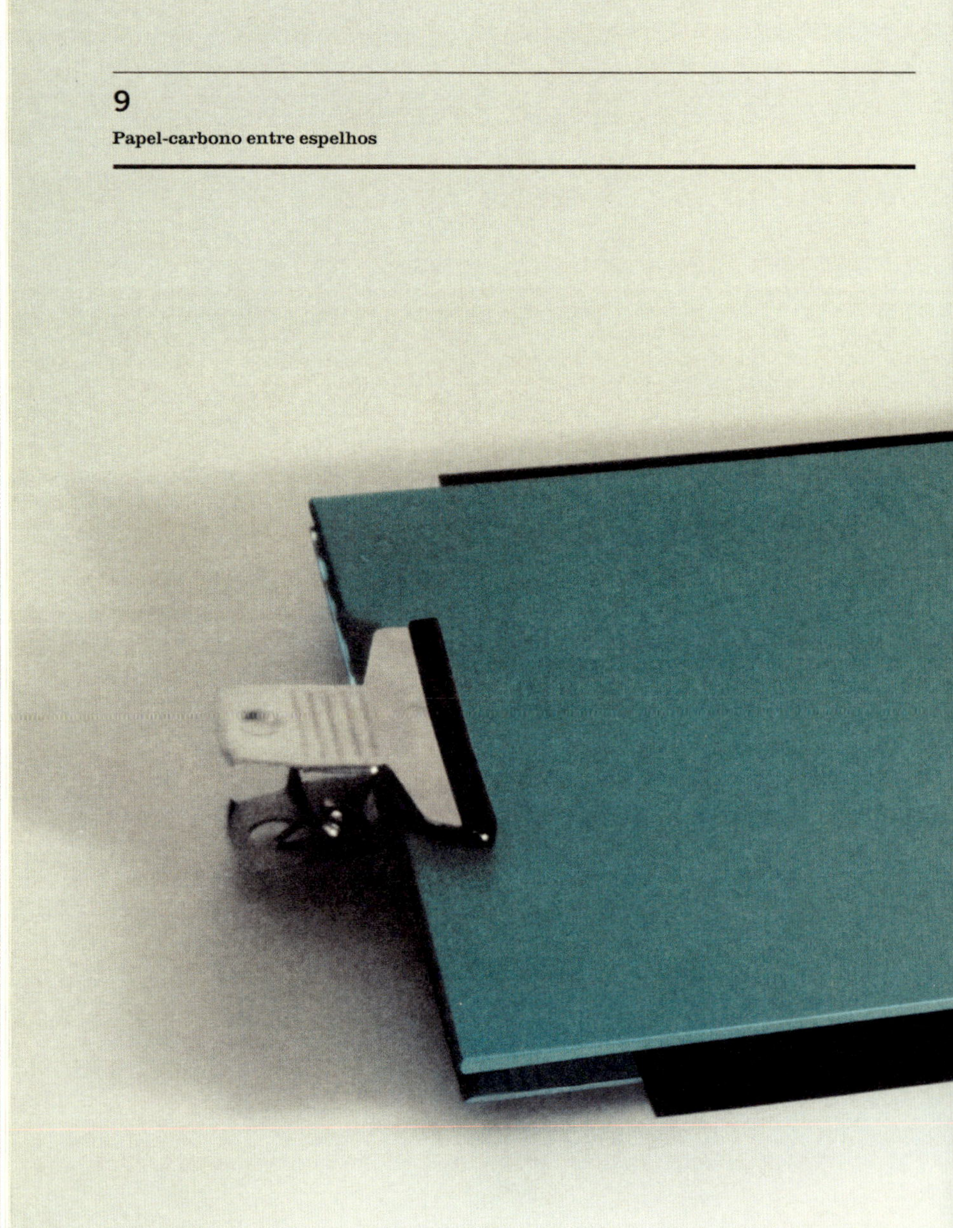

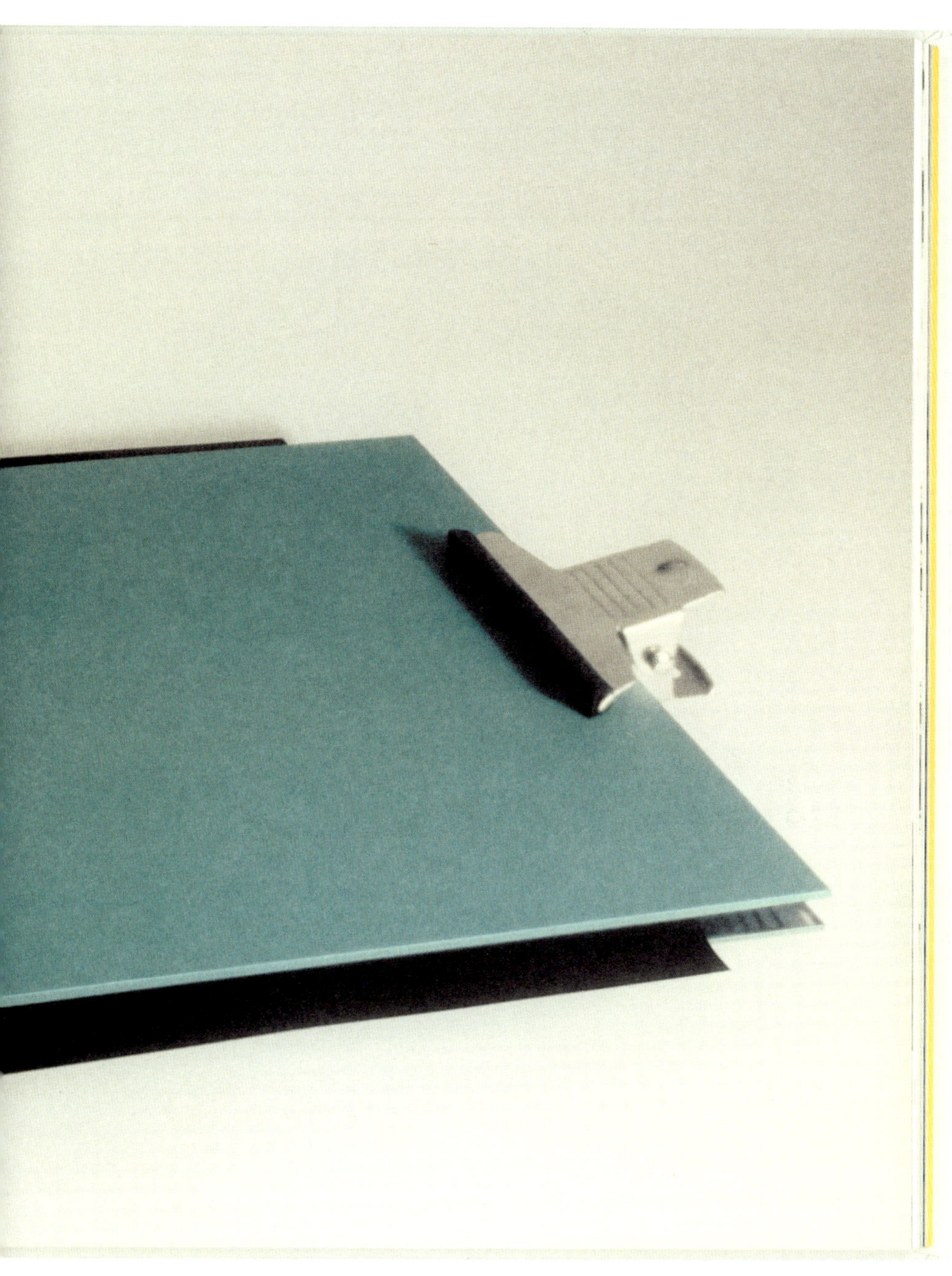

That is, possibly, the moment when I recognized my own need for expression, and in those objects an even greater capacity for asserting their independence from me. This was something that fascinated me back then, and it still does: the capacity of an object to resist becoming the personal expression of one and only one individual, to become something independent of its creator.

*A dense work of art is something that, most certainly, transcends its creator and the ideas that made it possible. It is a kind of organism that, once it has been given to the world, evolves over time and takes on new forms for those who observe it. It becomes a source of unexpected meaning, because life changes and with it, so does our perspective. And so, in this way, a truly powerful work says even more than what its creator believed he or she imbued it with. All it needs is fertile terrain and a complicit gaze. Important works often languish in a state of obsolescence for centuries (Hieronymus Bosch's* Garden of Earthly Delights *is one example) until a fresh perspective, from premises unanticipated by the work's creator, brings it back into the light and makes it relevant. How will future generations regard our works of art? What will they say about us?*

 That is what I learned during that time, specifically with the maquettes I did soon afterward, from 1966 to 1967, when I abandoned personal issues in order to deal with questions of space and architecture. It might be important, now, to bring up the strategic nonauthorship of my work, which belongs to its deep poetic nature, because that deliberate deauthorization taught me a great deal about who I am.

The work of art on its own says something, asserts itself. Its materials and its structure also assert themselves as visual evidence, as does the mood of the artist. There are so many variables that come into play in the creation of a work of art that it's impossible for me to single out one as more important than the others. When an artist says he is only creating what he feels, it's a lie, because an artist never has pragmatic access to his sensibility. An artist's sensibility is not just there, freely available for us. Rather, it is subjected to a series of uncontrollable pressures—at the most, the artist manages to control a few of them and modifies or alters the rest. The best thing about a work of art is that the result of the effort invested in making it, what comes out of it, is essential to the whole of the work. Not to recognize that would mean losing the new perspectives that the work can generate. Today, I depend almost completely on the productive wonder that justifies my work.

<sup>AJ</sup> In 1967 you also built the set designs for a play by Eugène Ionesco, which gave you the chance to work at the borderline between two artistic practices, between visual art and theater.

<sup>WC</sup> What interested me then was the possibility of working with literal rather than metaphorical spaces. That was the great lesson I took from my work in the theater, even if it seems ironic that that work began with the creation of a maquette. That experience reminded me of when I visited the São Paulo Biennial in 1965, where I first saw the maquettes of the great Czech set designer Josef Svoboda [Fig. 5].[6] I was mesmerized by his set designs because they had something in common with my own—not formal similarities, of course, but they evoked something about the way I understood and dealt with space. I always liked small scales that suggested larger ones, as if imaginary spaces could, in fact, be built. They show the world from a distance, the represented space coming together metaphysically, and that was what drew me to those maquettes.

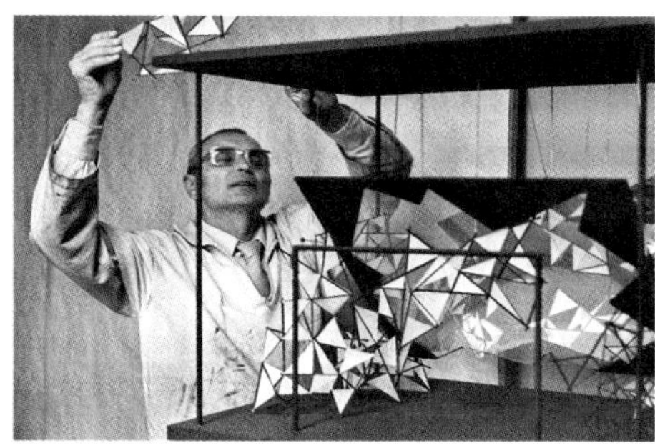

Fig. 5. Josef Svoboda, building maquette for *Juan* ballet, 1959.

In 1967 Ronaldo Tapajós, a friend who did theater, asked me to do the set designs for Ionesco's *The Lesson*. He had been asked to direct it as part of his end-of-the-year work at the university. Both of us were admirers of the Theater of the Absurd; we read Ionesco, Beckett, Sartre, and Arrabal, and we already had produced a few shows in our neighborhood. Theatrical texts, moreover, were especially interesting to me because as you read them they propose a spatial imagination of scenes.

<sup>AJ</sup> Right, because they are conceived for their materialization in space.

<sup>WC</sup> That production was also the first opportunity I had been given for a public work, in a real space. It was very stimulating, too, because I proposed a set design that altered the concept of time. I conceived of a lighting scheme that

6. Josef Svoboda (1920–2002) was a Czech set designer, active in Prague, and one of the preeminent figures in the world of the theater during the latter part of the twentieth century. He was the founder, along with M. Radok, of Laterna Magika and creator of a number of tools for the theater, including the multiscreen and other lighting apparatuses that have influenced set design around the world.

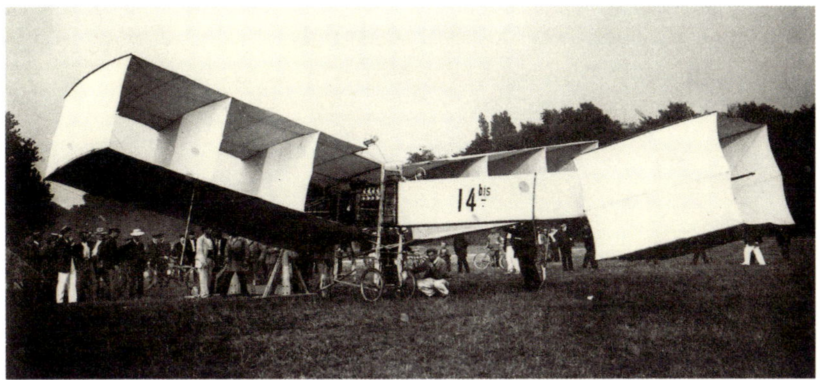

Fig. 6. Airplane No 14-Bis by the Brazilian pilot Alberto Santos-Dumont. Bagatelle, France, October 23, 1906.

changed as the play's main action unfolded, culminating in a murder. The lighting was planned and executed to slowly build tension, to make the audience's mounting sense of the impending murder, which doesn't happen until the very end, almost insufferable. I found it very interesting to associate the theatrical space with narrative time, since the action is ignited, in this case, after the progressive accumulation of tension over time.

It was quite serendipitous that I had been able to see Svoboda's set models in the context of a visual art exhibition like that biennial, which that year had been centered on fantastic art like Dada and Surrealism. Absorbing the presence of those maquettes provoked in me a dysfunction very similar to what I had felt as a child when I saw [Alberto] Santos-Dumont's airplane in the Rio airport.[7] It was a life-size reproduction of a strange object, a plane, a structure that invented the possibility of flight, and to have it right there in front of my eyes had a huge impact on me [Fig. 6].

AJ And yet, if I'm not mistaken, Svoboda's were maquettes in the strict sense of the word: objects made to scale, created in order to be executed on a larger but equally precise scale, while yours did not necessarily imply materialization on a different scale.

WC My maquettes were absolutely conceived to be built on a larger scale, just within a more utopian perspective. In an age when painters had such a hard time

7. Alberto Santos-Dumont (1873–1932) was a Brazilian aviator and forerunner of modern aviation; in Brazil he is believed to be the first person to fly according to a preestablished circuit. His feat was carried out on October 23, 1906, in the Bagatelle field, in Paris. It is for this reason that the national airport at Rio de Janeiro is named after him.

finding spaces where they could hang their work, it was absolutely unthinkable for a young artist to flirt with the idea of using a 200-square-meter space. But the maquettes expressed the desire to be bigger, despite the certainty that they were and always would be impossible to execute. You are right, however, on one point, which is that they function in the same way: they fulfill their function even at the scale of the maquette. They don't need to be built; it's enough for them just to be a hypothesis. Take, for example, *Noche* [*Night*], which is one of the first maquettes, from 1967 [Fig. 7]. It's like a place forgotten by the rest of the world. Two tiny houses, a vast night, on a street that could be anywhere. But the maquette is built in such a way that here, in this little corner, there is an interior sky, the universal night. It is an unspecified place, where nobody and nothing passes through. But at the same time, it has everything. The majesty of the universe in an almost intimate circumstance. Back in those days, I remember, there was this truck that traveled around Rio, and inside it had these landscapes that an artist had created on the heads of pins. You would walk into the truck and there would be a bunch of tables set up with microscopes, and you could just sit down and look at the landscapes the artist had painted on the heads of all those pins. The idea, the suspicion, that it was possible to paint something very large in a very tiny space impressed me tremendously at the time, particularly because I myself was looking for a way to produce those kinds of games with scale.

In another of those maquettes, which has since been destroyed, there was a house that was being absorbed by a hydraulic system that transformed it into a thick, black liquid, like oil, and then emptied it into a pool . . . and that reminded me—mental associations are so funny—that in those days I was also a reader of science fiction, and I remember one book that had a real impact on me. It was called *Way Station* [by Clifford D. Simak], and it's the story of a house and a little boy. The little boy is walking through a field and arrives at a lone house in the middle of the landscape. This is a house that, according to the description in the book, resides there in a strange way. It is slightly different from the other houses nearby, and this intrigues the little boy, who approaches the house to get a look inside. He sees that the house is hermetically sealed; he peers through the windows and believes that nobody is living inside. According to the descriptions in the book, in this house things seem to happen that don't happen anywhere else in the world. Little by little it becomes clear that this is, in fact, a kind of intergalactic station, a place on Earth where those who travel through the cosmos can stop for a while, and then continue on to wherever they are going.

I don't recall exactly how it happens, but I do remember that the little boy manages to get inside the house and becomes friends with the strange being that lives there. Then he begins to examine all the things left behind by the

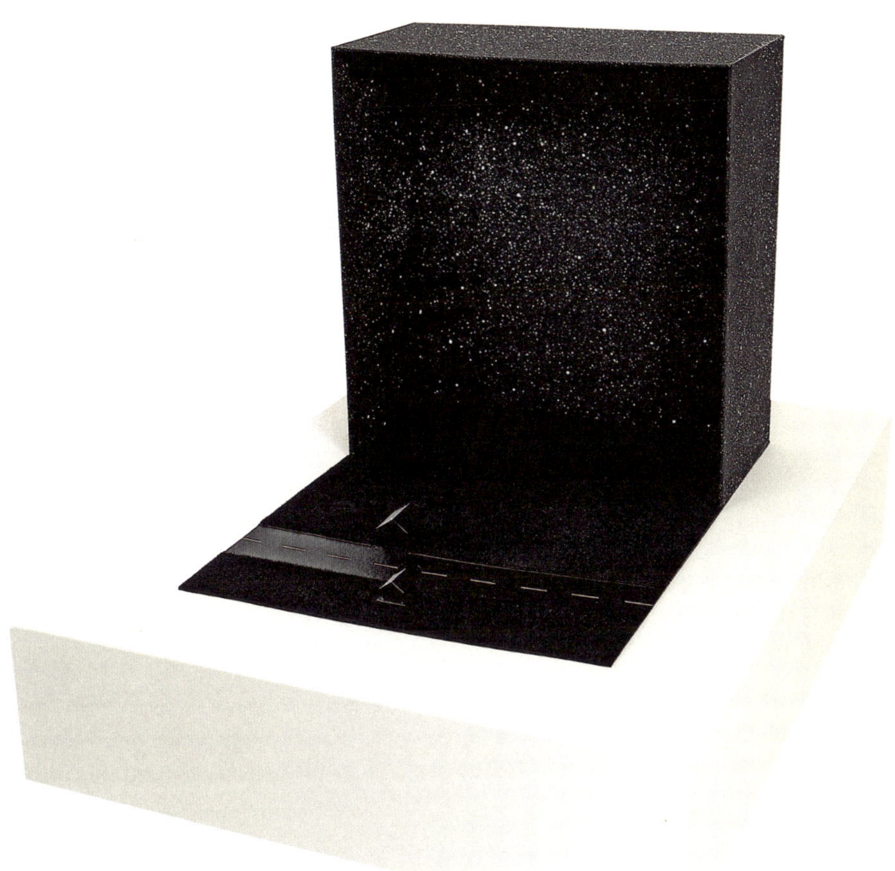

Fig. 7. *Maquette V, A noite* [*The Night*], 1967.

inhabitants of other galaxies. This writer's capacity for invention was incred-ible! I remember one thing in particular, a pyramid made of spheres that moved constantly, all oscillating around one another, without ever disrupting the very precise configuration of the pyramid. The author described four or five of the objects that forgetful travelers had left behind, and these images had a powerful effect on me. In that book I learned how to imagine objects that did not neces-sarily share the temperature, the materials, and the shapes of our world. And today, I can state that the closest thing to an art object is an unknown object.

I remember another similar story, this time by Jorge Luis Borges, one of those stories in which he describes inexplicable situations: a dead man is found at a border. Nobody knows where he is from, and the author suggests that he represents destiny. At the end of the story, even as his identity and where he had come from remain unknown, one thing was certain: there was a tiny cube in his pocket, a metal cube that nobody could quite identify. It measured around four centimeters on each side but, oddly, was so heavy that nobody could manage to lift it up off the floor.

I can safely say that these two references are a constant presence throughout my work. It's as if I were constantly pursuing the possibility of creating objects that may not raise doubts as to their recognizability, but are nonetheless capable of provoking unsuspecting tensions in our perception of them. This is why I care so much about the public's reaction to the objects I create, because it is very typical (and was especially typical in the 1970s) for people to declare that they, too, could make objects exactly like mine. They would say this, of course, because they did not recognize these objects as artistic productions, and that's why they thought that they could make them, too. I actually asked some of these people if they had understood what the objects meant, and they always answered that no, they had no idea what they meant or how they might be used. And I found this odd, to say the least; I really struggled to understand how they could believe themselves capable of building an object that they themselves couldn't decipher. How could they have envisioned and manufactured such an object? This is where the paradox resides, in the audacity of certain artists to conceive of objects that did not exist previously, but that are now there, here, right in front of us, like an invented reality.

AJ What the public often doesn't understand is that the complexity of a work of art—its importance, its beauty—does not reside in its material or technical execution, but in the fact of [the artist] having imagined the possibility of its existence. And that is what makes it so radically difficult to explain to certain people why Malevich's *Black Square*, which is so easy to produce materially, may be one of the most improbable works to have been made in the twentieth century.

WC Yes, and that it continues to be improbable despite the historical guarantees . . . because often what gets acknowledged as artistic production is insufficient for encompassing the dimension of wonder.

AJ That's why I insisted on drawing a distinction in nature between what one may observe in your maquettes from 1967 and those of Svoboda, because yours don't respond to an exact scale but rather to one that is evidently undefined. They are not maquettes in the utilitarian sense of the word.

WC No, of course not. Can we talk here about a hypothetical scale? I mean, what would be the exact space suggested by these maquettes? Would it be, in the end, one that they themselves would have engendered, invented? People often have said that my works seem to want to lend form to the space they occupy. And we are talking here about an artist working in a cultural moment that demanded more spaces for creative activity. Brazilian artists of that era created not only their work, but also, out of necessity, the cultural conditions for that work. In other words, all of us, an entire generation, were dedicated quite urgently to creating new spaces and new conditions. So ultimately, the need for a more open cultural atmosphere was actually also an attempt at aesthetic survival.

<sup>AJ</sup> And for that reason it's so lovely that those works have been envisioned as maquettes for a space that is possible, though not previously determined.

<sup>WC</sup> It's as if that space were utopian, but imagined and paradoxically possible. That's why I feel so comfortable nowadays when I make outdoor sculptures, because in some way that possibility was my desire from the very beginning, because even my outdoor sculptures have a surprisingly intimate quality about them. That's why I say that my large-scale sculptures are private rather than public.

<sup>AJ</sup> I think it's very illuminating to compare this way of thinking about space in your work with what one might observe in the works of Jesús Soto. When I would ask him, for example, what he found so interesting about the square, he would always mention a number of qualities, including the fact that a square doesn't have a fixed size. A tree, he would say, has a precise dimension—it can be one or several times larger than a person, but never infinite or microscopic— whereas a square can be envisioned at any size. It is not tied to a specific scale.

<sup>WC</sup> The image of the tree has a prescribed mental scale, as do so many objects we create. Nobody would imagine a book four meters high. Geometric figures are precisely the opposite: they are abstractions, they have no scale. There is an object in my *Manual da ciência popular* [*Manual of Popular Science*; 1982] that is called *Princípio de realidade* [*Principle of Reality*] [Fig. 8]. In the accompanying text, what I say about those objects that have no scale is that they can be made in any size. And if I call them *Princípio de realidade,* it's because I am amused by the relationship between the idea of reality and the lack of scale. And it reminds me of something Mondrian said, that the straight line is a curved line at maximum tension. As if he believed that lines are inevitably curves, including the straight line, which depends on the natural tension of a hypothetical horizon.

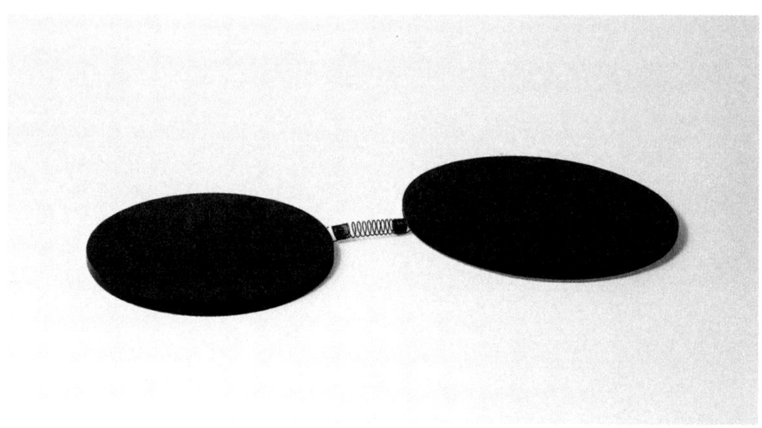

Fig. 8. *Princípio de realidade* [*Principle of Reality*], 1981.

<sup>AJ</sup> It's a provocative comparison, because Soto's entire body of work, and particularly his pieces from the 1950s, was conceived in this way, as fragments of an unthinkably larger reality.

<sup>WC</sup> Is there any other way to think of art, really? Meaning, as an impossible, constant, inevitable fact? Art would be destroyed if one day we could define it as something just barely possible. In a way, art is exactly that constant searching that alters the idea of the search itself, because it has no object; one is not looking for anything, and the novelty of what one might find is infinite.

<sup>AJ</sup> For that reason, what I find interesting in your written work, for example what you wrote in your book *Notas, (    ) etc* [*Notes, (    ) etc*; 2006], is precisely that clear determination not to complete the meaning of what is being said [Fig. 9].[8] As if, voluntarily, you challenged yourself to build a sentence to the point of almost saying something, just before the materialization of one of the meanings suggested in the text.

<sup>WC</sup> It's like looking at the ocean. The sea will never give us its true meaning, but it will give us back the imagination of our expectations so that we might elaborate on it a bit more.

*The best vision of a thing suggests*
*its unfinished future*

8. Waltercio Caldas, *Notas, (    ) etc* (São Paulo: Gabinete de Arte Raquel Arnaud, 2006).

 Phrases like these are crafted in such a way that they seem to want to tell me something, but it's something I can't quite decipher, something I have to complete. It's like facing the probability of meaning.

 Yes, but there's a little catch there: it isn't that they are trying to point out something. They speak, but what they speak contains no restrictive meaning. I wanted to arrange words in their maximum relationship with one another, so that each one might hold onto the freedom it had conquered through its autonomy. I didn't want to finish off the meaning in the conclusion, but in the possibility of a conclusion, as if I were trying to free myself from the affirmative quality of aphorisms.

 For this same reason, moreover, you called them phrases, because you didn't find it useful, or precise, to call them verses.

 I called them *Notas*. It took me some time to find a title for them, because one word wasn't enough. That's why I called them *Notas*, and then added an empty parenthetical and that *etc*, which lets you imagine something unknown. And it adds a third precipice, as if things, all things, were other. One element is known, it is temporal: "Notes." The second thing is suggested but unknown. And the third thing—that "etc."—is a shot fired into the unknown. I have such a hard time stripping down phrases.

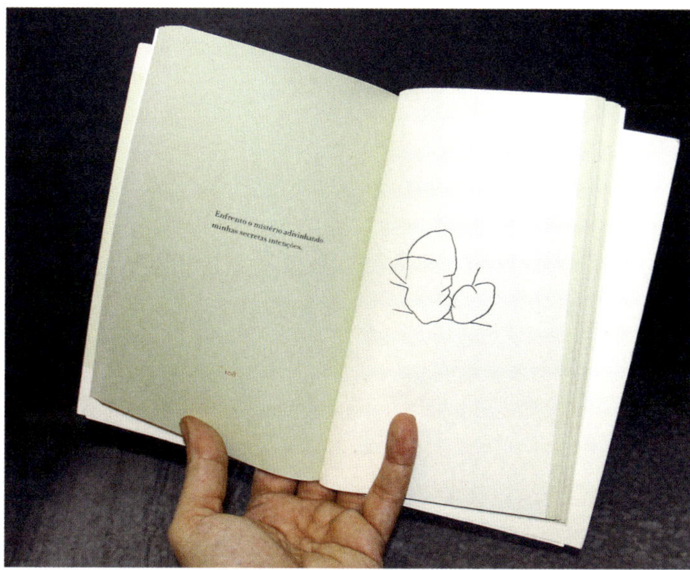


Fig. 9. *Notas, (    ) etc* [*Notes, (    ) etc*; 2006].

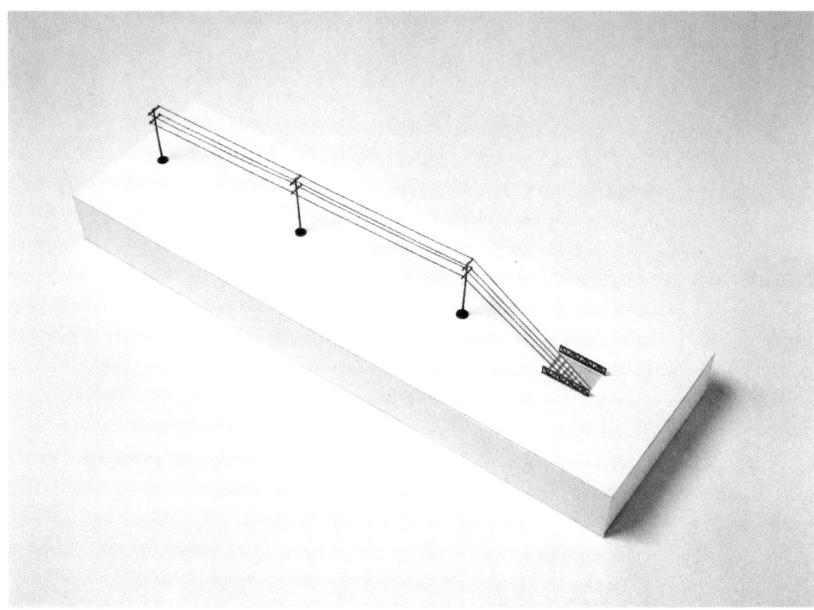

Fig. 10. *Maquette I*, 1967.

<sup></sup>

AJ There's something curious about them, it almost seems that those phrases approach the borderline of verse, without being verses exactly—not wanting to be verses, even.

WC It's as if they only wanted the poetry of their freedom . . .

AJ And at the same time, they sound like aphorisms.

WC All I want from the aphorism is the synthetic and circumstantial form.

AJ In that case we are dealing with, as [art critic] Ronaldo Brito put it, an art of boundaries.[9] And this is a quality we find not just in your books, in those phrases, but also in your objects and drawings.

WC Yes, it's like I only feel comfortable in art when I can imagine for it a dimension greater than what I myself am able to achieve or imagine.

9. Ronaldo Brito wrote: "The work is tied to the boundaries of art, and its requirement is to situate itself, from there, at the maximum extremes. More than conscience, the work has an obsession with boundaries. It breathes in that tension and elicits its strength from that ambiguity." In Waltercio Caldas and Ronaldo Brito, *Aparelhos* (Rio de Janeiro: GBM Editora de Arte, 1979), 11.

Fig. 11. *Condutores de percepção* [*Perception Conductors*], 1969.

AJ That's why I thought it was so telling when you said that you began by building objects (and not sculptures), and trying to build what you had not found in
other artists' work. It was almost a way of doing what you didn't see in them,
like opening up a space around their work, in that second nature of culture.

WC Yes, and that becomes more critical with age, because things you don't want
end up getting added, like works from the past, for example. And so you find
yourself feeling tempted to free yourself from your own history, and this creates a new situation. That's the moment when you learn how important it is
to leave certain works "open," because you know that you will need that little
point of entry in the future. And this, then, becomes an obsession. That freedom becomes an integral part of the works.

AJ Let's go back, again, to the 1960s, to talk about a series that I believe is an
important one, the *Condutores de percepção* [*Perception Conductors*], of 1969. It
seems to me that this series represents the clear beginning of what we might
call your mature practice. Yet if we compare it to some of your 1967 maquettes,
like *Maqueta 1*, for example, we see that they function in a very similar way
[Figs. 10, 11].

WC Both are conductors of energy.

<sup>AJ</sup> Clearly, they are both conductors, but conductors that are unable to fulfill their function.

<sup>WC</sup> I would say that blue doesn't have to be true to be blue. Art is concerned with suggestions—in other words, to propose what is not evident. Matisse dealt with this when he proved that blue could be utterly new, even when using the same blue he always did. The problem lies in the relationship between colors; and so the way the phrase is organized is what determines the meaning. The fact that I use recognizable objects in those first maquettes does not necessarily suggest that they ought to function as they do in reality. The problem lies elsewhere, and in my case an object is well used if it simply shows that it might still have the ability to become something else. A conductor does not necessarily need to conduct anything. It's enough to suggest the possibility that it could conduct something. There is clearly some artistic freedom being used in these suggestions.

<sup>AJ</sup> Of course, but I was actually thinking of something much more elemental: because they have been tampered with, those electrical cables do not deliver energy, yet they suggest the possibility that this thing might continue indefinitely in the directions indicated at either end, with the added mystery implied by the fact that one of the edges penetrates the ground in an unusual way.

<sup>WC</sup> That series came out of an attempt to push the limits of a relationship, in a way, between what the object is and what it says about itself. That's where you find the relationship not just between the title and the object, but between the word, what it expresses, and what it is. Clearly, those objects are not conductors of perception in the technical sense. But in the end, what could a conductor of perception really be? Now, it is also true that the word has the power to transform that object into a conductor of perception. So I use the word to define its function, naming it. I would say that they are works in which the perception of the object is, in reality, the suggested conductor. As if it were possible, for example, to execute the autonomy of an idea, using things and words, not necessarily adding one to the other, just juxtaposing them.

And it is out of that confrontation that a new kind of object emerges, one that is no longer just word or object, but rather an idea justified by the presence of the object. And perhaps because of that we might be able to consider this a third type of object, one that is more complex than it may seem at first. The complete series of these objects from the 1960s is made up of around ten or twelve works, all of which point out the borderline between names and things.

 The borderline that exists in our space of meaning, and those that our perception imposes.

 Yes, the boundaries that our perception attempts to impose upon them. For that, the object would have to be active. An active object does not surrender to the gaze; it forces us to look at it in a different light. Because you are not passive when you observe a work of art. Immediately the work calls out to you and invites you to play a game, and you find yourself inside that game. It isn't an object in which I can just deposit my authoritarian ideas, because the object disturbs the expectation I have built around it. You can even close that box and deny that confrontation, but it's been opened and we cannot deny what we see. What those conductors of perception can tell us is that, from this moment on, we are no longer the same.

 What you do between the word and the object, the relationship you establish between them, is similar to what the Surrealists sought to establish between two words in the same verse. Those objects function a bit like the verse described by Pierre Reverdy, when he said that the poetic image was the result of the clash between two different and distant words, and that the force of the poetic image was determined by the potency of that clash, by the sparks that might be set off in the coming together of two very different realities.

 After Dada and Surrealism nothing has been done without considering that inaugural possibility. What I think is essential there is the fact that something more than the known world can motivate artists. With them, for the first time, the subjective world could also be used as material for creating art. And from my perspective, this is the great freedom that the Surrealists gave us. There is something else about these objects that I would like to point out. In those days, some art led us to believe that it was possible, and even necessary, to manipulate the work of art in order to understand it better. But I never thought of this as a rule. Even though I admire the work of Lygia Clark, I think the artist's intent to have the viewer manipulate the work is just another property of the object, like color or material.

And so, in my box-objects, I was searching for one that didn't need to be manipulated, one in which the secret, or perhaps the hermeticism, would also be critical for its emergence. For me, as an artist who has always been concerned with the processes of deciphering the work of art, that difficulty was even more important. When I walk into an exhibition and I sense that the artist is trying to help ease me into the confrontation that all works of art invite us to take part in,

I almost feel offended, because the way I understand it, I am the one who must make the effort necessary to understand the meaning of the work, if I want to, if I am willing to try. For that same reason, I am never offended if people tell me that my work is difficult to understand, because that, to me, is a characteristic of art, just as it's a characteristic of the sky, the ocean, and nature itself. I mean, how do you understand a tree? Is there a right way to do that?

AJ I am very interested in what you are saying, because if you read what certain critics and artists like Lygia Clark wrote, particularly in the 1960s, it seems they had a desire to establish an opposition between the psychic density of those manipulable objects—which is real—and the purely optical relationship that, in their view, occurred between viewer and painting. And in doing this they forgot that it was never that way, that painting was and always has been a mental and cultural experience more than an optical one.

WC She has said (though I never heard her myself) that the brain is also guts. And maybe Lygia found, as any artist might after assuming that risk, that the relationship between viewer and painting was not enough. In that sense her attitude is more understandable. Tatlin found that the experience of art had its limits in his time, and so he tried to build an airplane. Each artist, at some point, feels that the art that has been created is insufficient, that there is no turning back from experimentation, it must move forward, because at a certain point, the only salvation possible is the movement that broadens the horizon. A point of no return.

This is a crucial moment for any artist, one in which the work of art is both destroyed and created at the same time and the artist feels unable to close the work, because closure can only occur with death. In this sense I give the Dada and Surrealist artists a huge amount of credit for having questioned the cultural morality of their time, and for having pushed the sleeping corpse of conformity to the edge of the abyss. Duchamp was the one who arrived and gave it a precise nudge, so precise, in fact, that it impedes the cadaver from coming back to life. The important thing here is the quality of that nudge, the spontaneous quality of that act, like all his manifestations, which always seemed to happen coincidentally, maybe even indifferently. This is how he ensured that the corpse would not rise from the dead. I don't mean to invoke "the death of art," either; I only want to point out the foolishness of believing in the guarantees represented by a definitive history of art.

AJ Most artists go through stages or periods in their output that can be classified chronologically quite precisely; by observing the palette used or the topic explored, you can discern the artistic moment a piece comes from. With you, the opposite is true. With you, it is often considerably harder to situate a work based on its material or formal specificities. The one exception might be the objects you have built. I would almost venture to say that, in your case, the exhibitions and books are what most clearly demarcate the crucial facets or cycles in your career. This is true, for example, of the exhibition that you put together in 1973 for the Museum of Modern Art in Rio de Janeiro.

WC It's surprising that such an early exhibition was envisioned as a retrospective. I had been working on my own since 1965, and some of my objects had circulated around two or three private collections, but nothing more. When the director of the museum invited me to show my work, I made a selection of what I had done over the previous five years. I didn't have any problems showing these pieces because they were objects that already had a certain connection. So what I did was organize the exhibition around two vectors. One was of the box-objects inside small glass display cases, and this also included the *Condutores de percepção*. I also exhibited, among other pieces, a work called *O louco* [*The Madman*; 1971], a long box that one would likely open expecting to find something inside, and what the public found was a little man walking down a street, in the immense space inside the box [Fig. 12].

The second vector consisted of drawings, installed in a separate room. With those drawings I tried to compose a kind of visual encyclopedia, almost like a catalogue of visual definitions for objects registered in that imaginary analogy. There was a drawing for an astronaut, a locomotive, a rocket, etc. The objective was for each drawing to represent the image of an object: tiny vignettes of an unfinished almanac. To give you an idea, picture a sphere drawn on a piece of paper, a small sphere, with a flock of birds flying out of it, which made it look like something huge. I called it *Ciência* [*Science*]. I remember another drawing of train tracks, in which smoke billowed out from above the tracks, but with no train. Then, between the smoke and the tracks there was a calculation, a series of numbers added up, like a mathematical non sequitur. I also showed *O colecionador* [*The Collector*; 1973] in that show; it was as if someone had collected the word *fim* [end], like the *fin* that appears at the end of a movie [Fig. 13].

AJ Right, it was about a collection that was in principle infinite, or at least of an indeterminate length and duration.

WC That was also the piece that I placed at the end of the exhibition.

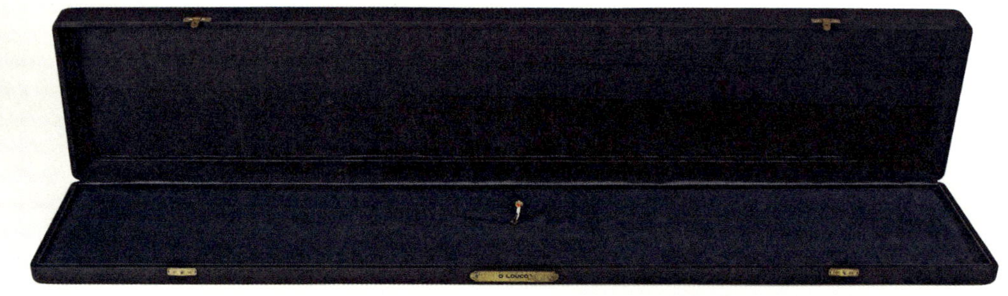

Fig. 12. *O louco* [*The Madman*], 1971.

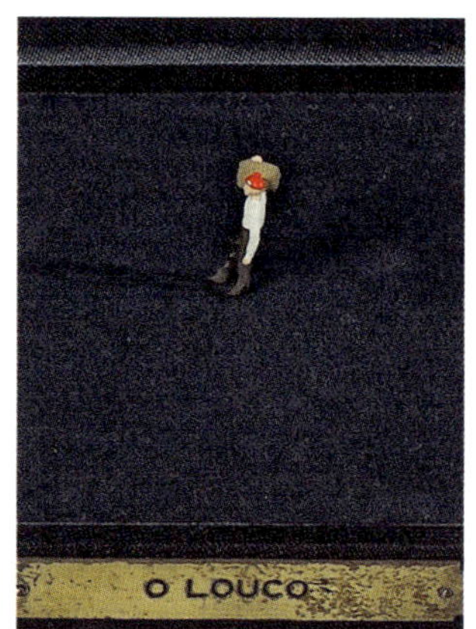


AJ  Those are clearly Borgesian objects. Your descriptions remind me of that Borges story about the ruins, 1:1 in scale, of a lost world that would have covered the entire planet. I remember it as a story in which real ruins became the scattered fragments of an imagined world that had disappeared completely.

WC  Yes, as if it were possible to perform a kind of archaeology of the collective human imagination, or something like that, right?

AJ  Exactly, but of a collective imagination whose fragments are scattered around the world. The fragments are real.

WC  That's the interesting thing, that art allows you to create works on a scale that are neither human nor inhuman. In that sense, art would be a third scale, a specific scale. I even created objects that I called "third objects," which we talked about before, around 1997. It's something that also has to do with the way I treat mirrors and how they function.

AJ  Which is a typically Borgesian topic, as well, and one of the great preoccupations of representative painting. Before going into the matter of mirrors, however, I'd like to talk about an exhibition of yours, one with a very suggestive title, *A natureza dos jogos* [*The Nature of Games*], held in 1975 at the Museu de Arte de São Paulo. What got you interested in games?

WC It was because I was having my first exhibitions, and the relationship between the works and the cultural environment sometimes, for me, took the form of a game. Between 1973 and 1975 I had my first contact with the whole issue of exhibiting, which for me could never be reduced to a simple collection of objects arranged in a space. Ever since my first show at the Museu de Arte Moderna in Rio de Janeiro, I saw that it was possible for the exhibition design itself to create another work of art, a new poetic condition for the pieces. Meaning that the solution was not just about placing the objects in a space; it was conceptual, and would depend on questions of scale, architecture, and narrative spaces within institutions, museums, and galleries.

AJ I think that for you, as for me, the exhibition is a kind of cultural gesture that you introduce into a larger space, which is the cultural medium in which you are doing your work.

WC Yes, but it's one thing to juxtapose known objects and to suggest new associations little by little. And it's another thing to confront an unknown object and

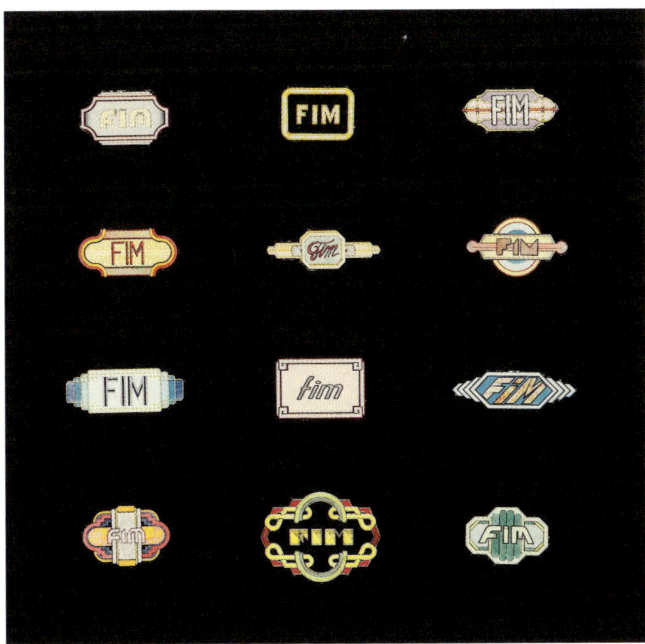

Fig. 13. *O colecionador* [*The Collector*], 1973.

relate it to another, also unknown, object. At that moment, the game falls apart and one finds oneself, yet again, lost in space [Fig. 14]. And that situation forces the viewer to rethink the relationships between all the pieces he or she has seen up to that point. And in a certain way, the works are going to demand that kind of reconsideration all the time, because if they are truly new, if they contribute something never before seen, for a time they will remain uncategorizable, strange. And then, little by little, an informative text and the technical descriptions on the wall will alleviate that strangeness, and the work will eventually become identifiable as part of a history. But that first moment of perplexity and nonrecognition is very important, and I think it is the most privileged moment a work of art can enjoy. My secret ambition would be to make that moment last as long as possible, because once you can identify or classify a work of art, you can no longer see it for the first time. You can only recognize it as something known. And to me that feels like a loss.

AJ That's how I see the work of the curator, as a person whose ideal function consists of eliciting the greatest potential of meanings from a work or collection

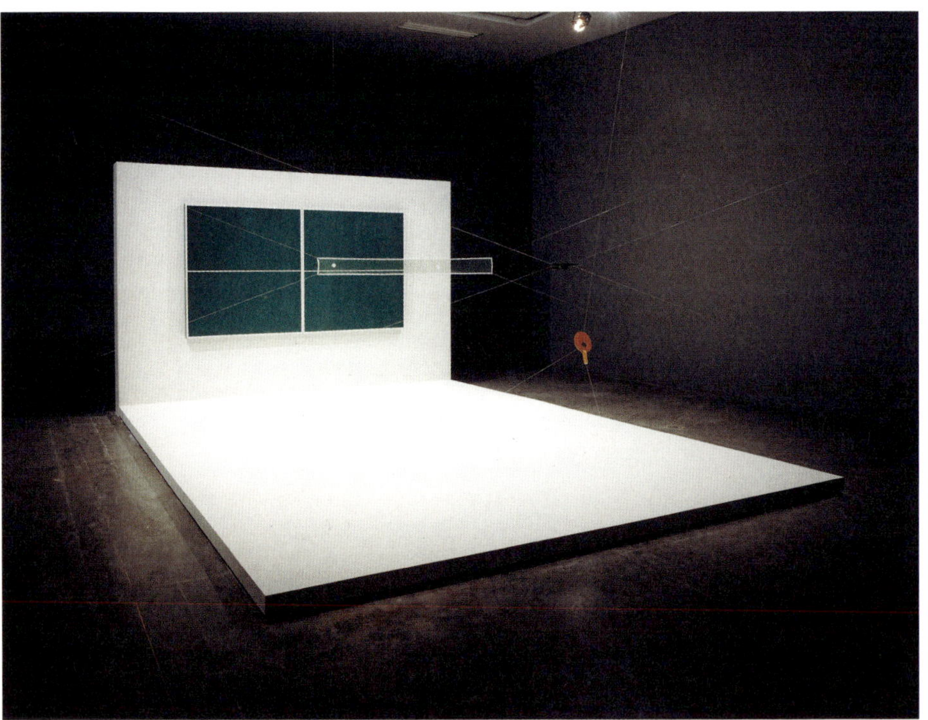

Fig. 14. *Ping-Ping, A construção de abismo no piscar dos cegos* [*Ping-Ping, Constructing the Abyss in a Blink of the Blind*], 1980.

of works. A curator is someone who produces meaning through his or her reflection on art. From that perspective, the curator can proceed in a number of ways, depending on the work or works in question. So, if we are in the presence of a new work, for example, the curator's job has to do with making the art interpretable for the contemporary audience, situating it as you say, or at least giving the public a few hints for understanding it. Now, for a work that is already perfectly inscribed in the history of art, the curator's function is more complex, because it consists of placing it in its historical context for the viewer, while also finding some way for that work to unleash its potential for contemporaneity. And this can only be achieved by restoring, at least partly, its original opacity, its capacity for inspiring wonder. A curator, then, is an individual who questions works from different points of view (those that are made possible by the historical moment) and who has the ability to reveal areas of opacity or unknown meaning in the work.

<sup>WC</sup> I would agree with that, but only when the curator is sensitive to the poetic proposal of the work, because that is the prerogative first of the work, and secondly of the curator.

<sup>AJ</sup> I would agree with that, too, as long as there is no confusion between that poetic proposal and any supposed meaning that is previously, definitively, and unequivocally inscribed in the work, making it impossible to see anything but what the artist has imbued it with. Because in that case, once the artist makes his or her interpretation known, the work is condemned to that version and that version alone. We could never speak of anything new in that case.

<sup>WC</sup> Perhaps that is why all artists were and continue to be contemporary, in a way. What I mean is that a Velázquez can be appreciated as an utterly contemporary work, and that enjoyment and appreciation may even be greater precisely because of the accumulation of information that the artist's own contemporaries did not have access to.

<sup>AJ</sup> And in that sense, the best and most important work for a curator would be to reveal a work's particular manner of being contemporary.

<sup>WC</sup> Maybe, but what happens today is usually the opposite, don't you think? So often curators try to impose characteristics upon contemporary works that ultimately limit them, by trying to force on them a facile, contemporary story to justify them. This is so typical that, for me, a well-conceived exhibition—we

are assuming that the curator has been competent—would be one that surpasses the expectations of the curator. Because if a work does not resist the curator's version and is incapable of saying anything else, something else, it will be insignificant.

AJ That's exactly right. A dense work is a work that exceeds the expectations of its creator and its viewer. But you can't expect that to happen in a single exhibition, in a single text. You can't say everything in one show, nor can you pretend to exhaust the potentialities of a work in a simple essay. Otherwise you run the risk of not communicating, not saying anything at all.

WC In that sense, one of the greatest virtues of all works of art is the capacity for resistance, the capacity to resist any explanation, even that of the artist.

AJ That is how I see the concerns you had following your first exhibition—when you sensed the importance of thinking about how your work would be received.

WC Yes, except the exhibition should be thought of as architecture. It's as though once the works were selected, I said to myself, "All right, now that I have the raw material, I have to do more than just arrange it." It is imperative to construct another poetic vision with the works, a poetic vision of spatiality, of their public presence. When I realized that, I understood something crucial for myself, which is that, contrary to what Hélio Oiticica and Lygia Clark were pursuing, my objects needed to maintain a kind of silent distance from the public. In that sense I have never created an object or a sculpture that pretended to establish an easy complicity with the viewer. I never thought of them as manipulable. My objects had to be physically concluded, and at the same time preserve an incomplete silence.

In general, visitors to biennials and large exhibitions do not pause for more than fifteen seconds in front of a work of art, and so it is extremely important to pay critical attention to those moments of contact. You have to establish a tension that produces meaning, between the viewer and the work, and also among the viewer, the work, and the gallery space. You have to think about the visual evidence of the physical spaces, a bit like Gaston Bachelard in his book *The Poetics of Space*. So I think of the museum space as a prolongation of my work, of my relationship with space.

AJ Like one more component in that game of meaning that emerges in and from the exhibition . . .

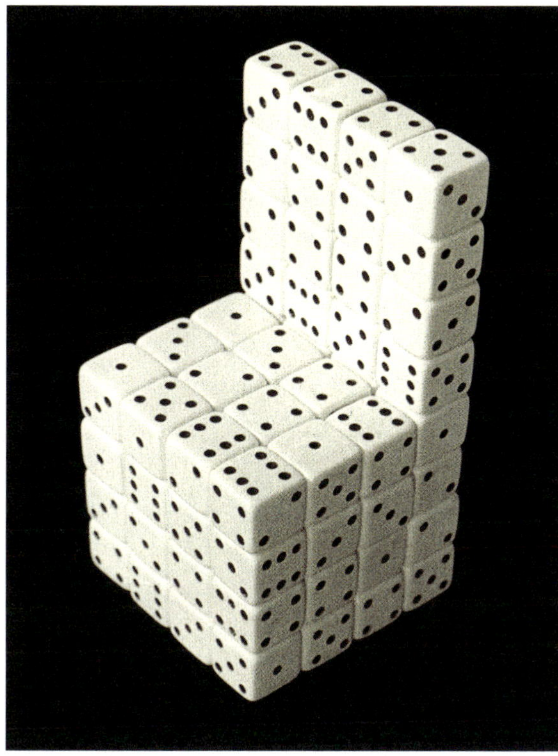

Fig. 15. *Moto perpétuo* [*Perpetual Motion*], 1973.

WC That's it. With *A natureza dos jogos* I understood that I could treat the exhibition as a game between the objects and the viewers.

AJ And did the objects refer to known games or were they based on a more general or conceptual notion of the game?

WC I would say that it was about a general notion of the game, of chance, of the referee. I used dice as a raw material [Fig. 15]. There, I showed *Leitura silenciosa* [*Silent Reading*; 1975], which was a reference to the teaching method by which the student is asked to read a text silently and then explain it. The goal is to ascertain how much the student understood what he or she read. In my case, it was about drawn objects, of course, and it was paradoxical to suggest to the audience that they "read" them in silence [Fig. 16]. The show also had conductors of perception and even the first light mirror, like the one that is in the Colección Patricia Phelps de Cisneros.

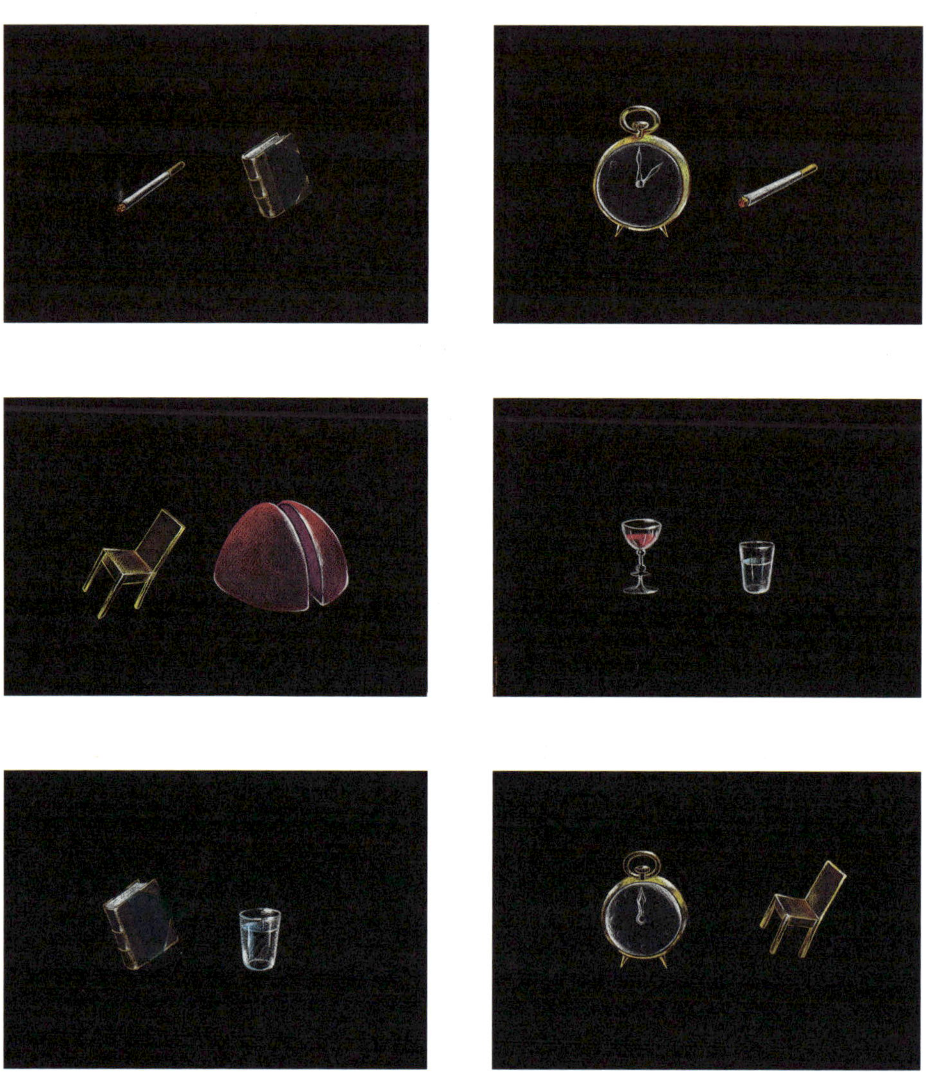

Fig. 16. *Leitura silenciosa* [*Silent Reading*], 1975.

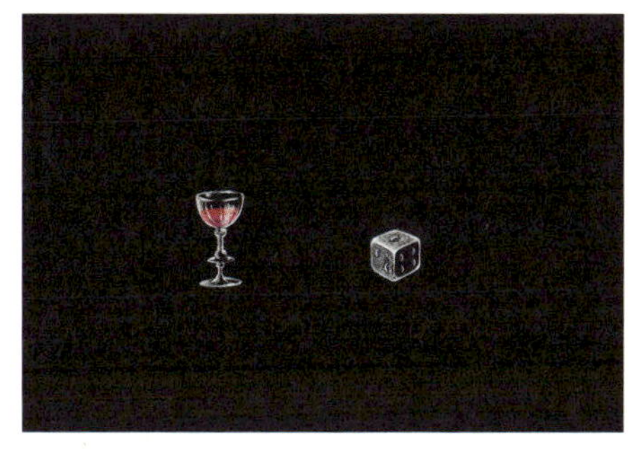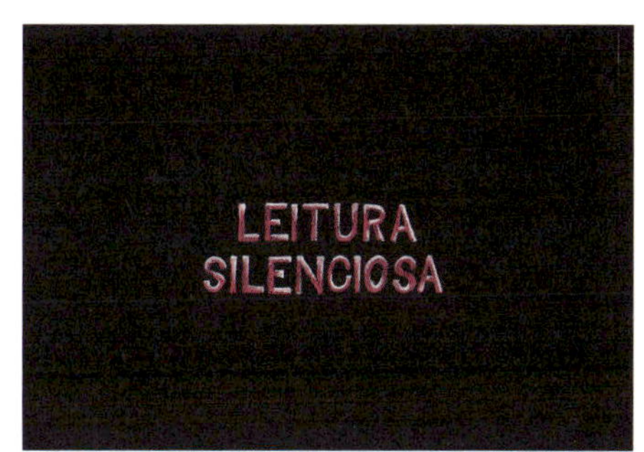

LEITURA
SILENCIOSA

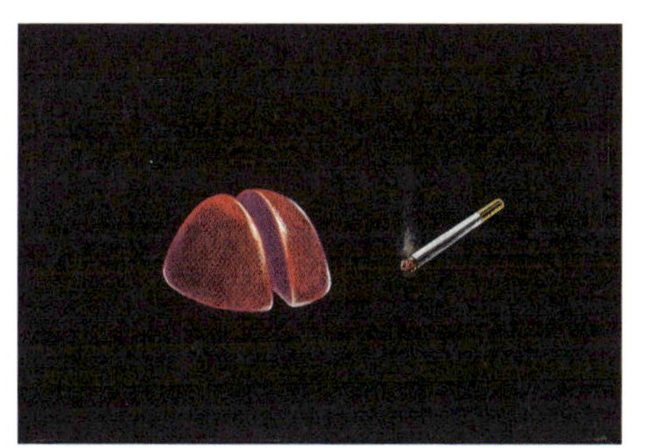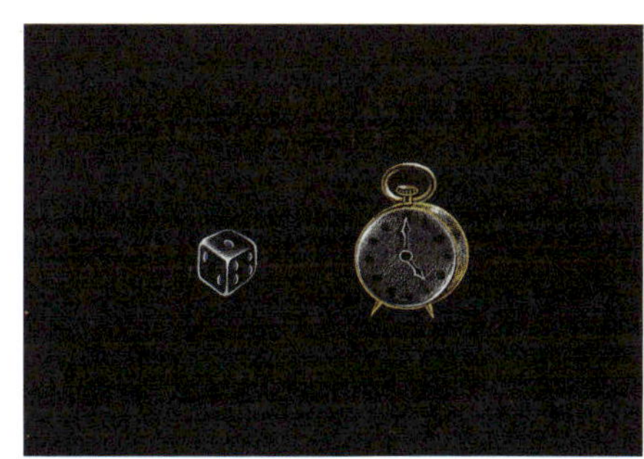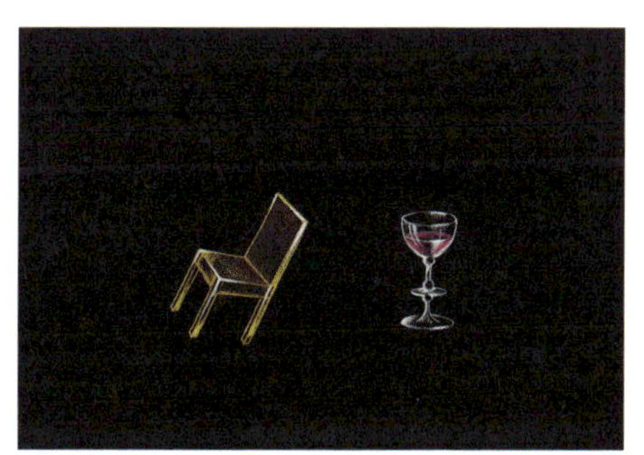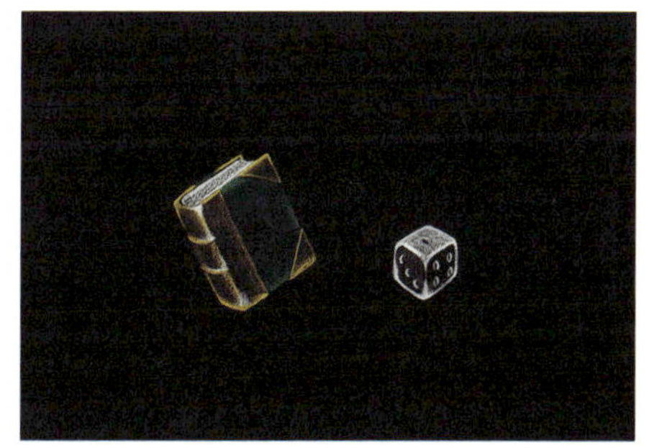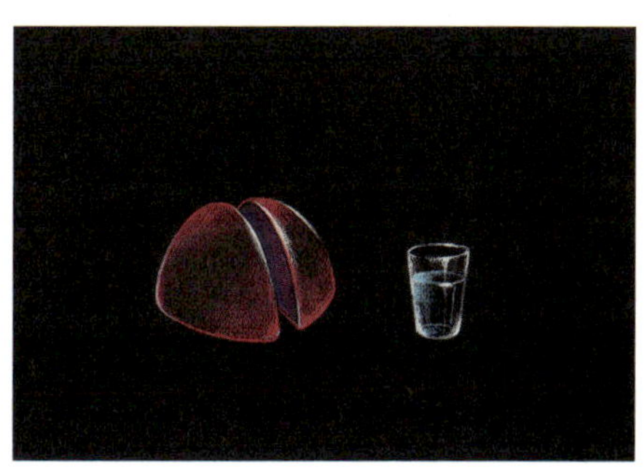

# THE INFINITE POSSIBILITY OF ENCOUNTER
## The point of no return

*At various points in our conversation, Caldas reminded me of how the second nature of art and its history, as well as the collection of works one created, was very much a burden for artists in general and for himself in particular. He knew this even as an adolescent, when he destroyed the huge quantity of drawings he had done between the ages of fourteen and twenty-one, to "free" himself from their oppressive presence. He also brought this up when he spoke of his first maquettes. At a certain point, the things we do begin to weigh down on us, to present their resistance. Style pursues us, and with it, habit.* "Does God have a style?" *Picasso asked Malraux.* "He made the guitar, the Harlequin, the dachshund, the cat, the owl, the dove. Like me. The elephant and the whale, fine—but the elephant and the squirrel? A real hodgepodge! He made what doesn't exist. So did I!"[10] *And Picasso carried that demand with him to the point of saying that an artist shouldn't draw in his own way (Ingres drew like Ingres, when in reality he should have drawn like the thing being drawn).* "Take, for example, a tree," *Picasso also said.* "Under the tree there is a goat, and next to the goat, a little girl who looks after the goat. Fine! You need a different drawing for each thing. The goat is round, the girl is a square, the tree is a tree. . . . And yet, we use the same drawing for all three."[11]

---

WC One tries to create what doesn't exist, to add to the known world something new, so that visions and senses may be surprised. In my case, as I already said, I began by making objects that I hadn't found anywhere else. That is, ultimately, the work of the artist as I understand it: to improve the quality of the unknown. But the objects we create add to the real and come to exist for us like all the rest of the world's objects, and at that point it becomes necessary to confront a different fact, because the reality of the things we make comes to modify the reality of the things we have yet to imagine. When a young person is starting to produce objects that surprise him, after a certain amount of time he begins to perceive what he has achieved. And so, little by little, those objects begin to impose their presence and change their own universe. That is when one has to cultivate a different stance in order to continue producing, in spite of oneself. Our past is no longer virgin. Today, for example, if I wanted to tackle the

10. Quoted in André Malraux, *Picasso's Mask*, trans. June Guicharnaud with Jacques Guicharnaud (New York: Da Capo, 1994), 18.

11. Quoted in Parmelin, *Picasso dit . . .* , 40.

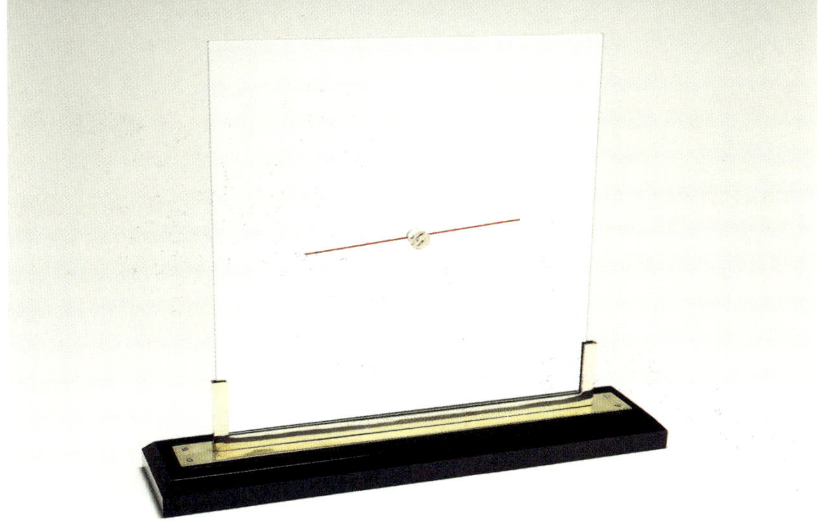

Fig. 17. *O limitógrafo* [*The Limitograph*], 1975.

issue of mirrors, I wouldn't be interested in revisiting what I had already done.
I could start with the mirrors that I conceived before, or work against them,
but I wouldn't want to repeat myself. Mirrors don't need to be duplicated any
more than they already have been. At a certain point, we have to fight against
our own body of work. Again, the point of no return.

<sup>AJ</sup> And when did that point of no return manifest itself for you?

<sup>WC</sup> Starting in 1975, and constantly ever since. If you compare the exhibitions of
1973 and 1976, you'll see a significant change. I go from the *Condutores de per-*
*cepção* to *O limitógrafo* [*The Limitograph*; 1975], which was a machine of sorts for
measuring boundaries. In it, a cork closes, or stops, a line in space [Fig. 17]. It is a
work of passage, which came about at a very significant moment, because then
came *Convite ao raciocínio* [*Invitation to Reasoning*], in 1978, and a variety of other
pieces along with it [Fig. 18]. So this was a period in which I really broadened
my possibilities, opened my borders, and I didn't want to be an artist with an
identifiable style. Mobility would be my freedom, my program, and I began
to expand my work in different areas and with a very diverse set of materials.

<sup>AJ</sup> Would *Espelho com luz* [*Mirror with Light*; 1975] be representative of one of these
areas?

<sup>WC</sup> At that moment it was very hard for me to favor one specific object over another.
Each object was created in a context in which I made four, five, ten objects at

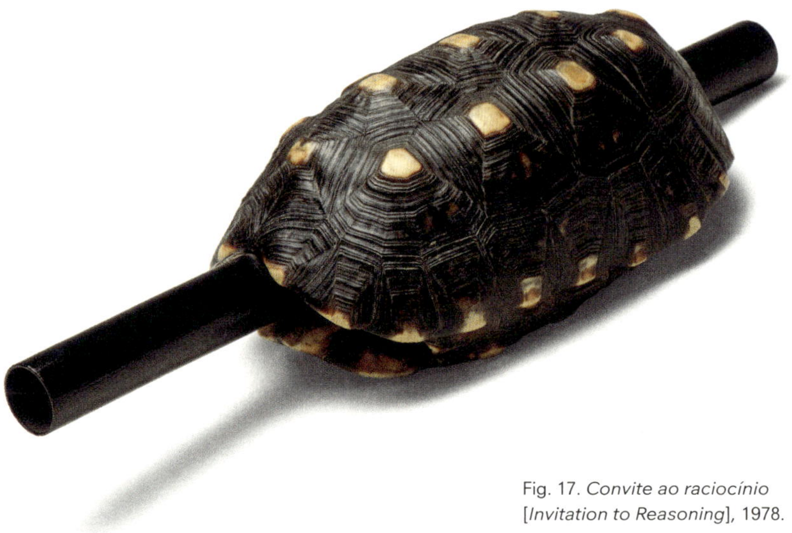

Fig. 17. *Convite ao raciocínio*
[*Invitation to Reasoning*], 1978.

the same time, and that diversity was what mattered to me. But something new was happening, and the pieces now came together through something invisible—an internal thread, absent and present at the same time.

AJ And would it be possible to define that invisible thread?

WC What I want to point out is that all those works, which were seemingly so different from one another, have one thing in common, and I came to the conclusion that I did not need, as I suspected, an identifying formality. The important thing was to create exactly the object I was imagining, the most stimulating one that would allow me to add new forms to that diversity. I once wrote that knowing my secret intentions was enough for me. I do always end up looking at certain recurrent themes in my work, and the only thing I can say is that we are all condemned to be who we are. And the thing in us that wants to change is our will to materialize the next thing.

AJ I understand, but that problem of style is always there, lurking over the artist. Even in the materials used, one can detect the manifestation of an identity, especially when you build objects that you yourself invented.

WC I think the word "style" tends to cause confusion. I would rather talk about a formal procedure that can end up trapping the artist, which has always been an issue, and there are a number of different solutions to that problem. One solution is what I see in Morandi, when he picks a single topic and discovers in it an infinite array of possibilities, just as Cézanne uses Mont Sainte-Victoire as a starting point for a number of canvases. The other solution is Picasso's, which involves constantly changing themes and processes even as he maintains a formal identity throughout that is distinguishable in any and all of his different phases.

When an artist like Morandi or Cézanne chooses to focus on a single topic, it is because the primacy does not lie in the topic but in the painting, in all the visual senses that unfold in the act of painting. So, if you transpose this to a more modest situation like my own, I would say that the range of formal possibilities, such as the use of a huge array of materials, is no small victory, not after Dadaism. And so what I aim for is a formal freedom that is dynamic enough to accept and absorb the most diverse variety of materials and attitudes. That, I think, is the most essential thing. Clearly, I have a preference for certain materials, and without a doubt that preference is meaningful at times, but I know that I have the freedom to change them and use whichever ones are most appropriate to the situation at hand. And in any event, I have a huge wealth of topics.

AJ Of course, but that freedom applies more specifically to the works in which you juxtapose different objects, objects that you yourself have not produced. As soon as it's you who has built them—the ladder, for example, or some mirrors—an identity inevitably emerges in your working method, and that identity inevitably becomes something of a style, a formal identity that is yours and yours alone.

WC Yes, but that can happen in other ways, like in those first drawings of mine, when I was interested more in the passage from one drawing to the next than in the content of any one drawing. It was that dynamic of passage, from one piece to the other, that appealed to me, far more than whatever formal identity might have existed among them. The same thing happens with my objects: the fact that there is a common mode of production is what unifies them in some way, and that might be the connecting thread we are talking about. That is fundamental, because it is up to me to preserve each work's freedom, which is not something you achieve once and forever. It's as if each new work had to break free from the past, from a possible formal relationship, and also lay down the conditions for the next work. And that effort is what justifies them, by generating new possibilities that emerge through an invisible thread that connects them.

AJ But even that mobility has moments that might be identified as characteristic.

WC Yes, they could be characteristic of preferences that emerge along the way. But every time that comes up, I do whatever I can to make sure it is not merely a matter of form. I have even come to think that I am a one-phase artist; I just try to make sure that the phase is always at the beginning. I am not looking to structure a program that I can then follow and develop further. What motivates me, precisely, are the new situations waiting to be discovered. And some artists might find that infinite even when operating within a very restrictive procedure. Morandi is an example of what I am trying to explain. Maybe it has to do with the way artists produced their work until, say, the 1940s. But after that, I think the "isms" become unconvincing, insufficient, limited. It doesn't matter anymore if something is abstract or figurative; that simplistic option no longer has anything to do with artists' interests, it's no longer related to matters of style. An artist can be conceptual or figurative, Pop, Surrealist, or Neo-figurative. In other words, at a certain moment in time multiple trends and styles began to coexist. And that is, perhaps, a sign of the time in which I began to work. The previous "isms" ultimately came to be seen as part of history. And in that maximum complexity of a whole range of trends, artists confronted and continue to confront the challenge of achieving a personal form of expression.

It's worth remembering, too, that I was a student of Ivan Serpa, who was fascinated by artistic processes and who experimented with various techniques all at once: abstraction, figuration, and even within abstraction he was sometimes geometric, sometimes not. And I think my work has evolved at a much more complex moment, during which we have begun to see intersections with other disciplines. There are conceptual artists who are concerned with scientific problems, others who focus on language and begin to reflect on artwork from the vantage point of writing, etc. I think my own search responds to a very real need to understand the world, because the insertion of works of art in culture also, ultimately, becomes an artistic problem.

In the end I don't feel the need to know what kind of art I will be creating a year from now. What interests me is walking on my own two feet; what motivates me is the path itself that produces meaning and generates situations that can eventually become things. And that's why each piece becomes nuclear, almost autonomous, as if only that piece is able to start and finish what was proposed. Proposing a formal or conceptual coherence to that diversity of objects doesn't matter to me; the work of conceiving and producing them, on its own, is what builds a link between them and reality.

AJ Yet those autonomous objects will be starting points for the configuration of the nuclei that characterize your work.

wc Of course, but it's something that occurs naturally, because from around 1975–78, when I chose to be an artist without any specific formal style and was striving for critical mobility, I still had yet to accumulate a body of work dense enough to make evident those nuclei of interest.

AJ To use an astronomical metaphor, we might say that the works are free bodies that will slowly accumulate into clusters that grow denser and denser, in some way obeying the laws of gravity. In other words, they will come together as larger and larger combinations on the basis of their private affinities. Those bonds are almost a force of gravity that brings them together, independent of when they were produced, constituting complete nuclei such as the mirrors. In the beginning we might regard them as Borgesian objects, but then it becomes clear that the nucleus of the mirrors begins to individualize, and one may even sense, as with the ladders, that they might break off to become another, independent nucleus.

wc Yes, definitely, these are not objects tossed out at the future, as the artists of the historical avant-garde might have conceived them, but bodies that orbit around concerns in the here and now. They do not respond to the kind of utopia that the avant-gardes generated. You know, I think the avant-gardes lose their relevance when we can no longer see in them a plan of action, when we turn them into a noun, a slogan. That passage from the desire to take concrete action upon reality, which was what characterized the avant-gardes, to their existence as objects, styles, movements is what some people identify as their failure. The fact that the transformation of reality has lost traction as an aspiration of artists and of people in general, to me, does not amount to a failure that discredits artists and relegates them to being simple producers of utopias.

AJ Of course not, because even though they might not have met the expectations they generated, those works did alter our world.

wc They altered it, all right, and they achieved a fair portion of what they set out to achieve. But it's also true that that productive utopia lost its way around the 1980s, and artists became more pragmatic, to put it one way, when they started to be concerned with inserting themselves in the market. I think that at a certain moment, the need to inhabit the real world, which artists defended so staunchly, ultimately found itself up against a kind of tyranny of the real world (like the demands of the market for example). Now, it is critically important to discuss the conflicts between art, the market, and the culture of entertainment.

o ( u ist ) o é

o ( r thi ) s is

# MIRRORS
## A mimetic machine

Today at the tip of so many and perplexing
Wandering years under the varying moon,
I ask myself what whim of fate
Made me so fearful of a glancing mirror.

. . .

I see them as infinite, elemental
Executors of an ancient pact,
To multiply the world like the act
Of begetting. Sleepless. Bringing doom.

— Jorge Luis Borges, "Mirrors"

*Around 1975 Caldas produced a number of objects that might be termed "Borgesian," which reflected a desire to escape that personal biological history that makes individuals act a certain way and prefer certain material and chromatic configurations. It was a desire, simply put, to escape style. At first these objects seemed isolated, the ideas somewhat circumstantial: some are the product of formal construction, such as his* Escadas *[Ladders], some are drawings, and others are simply the reorganization of elements taken from the surrounding environment—as in* O colecionador *[The Collector] of 1973—and feature no intervention at all from the artist. Other pieces, in contrast, are manipulated, like his* Espelho com luz *[Mirror with Light], from 1975, or organized in an unexpected way, as in* O pequeño príncipe *[The Little Prince], from 1978. Sometimes, moreover, the work is nothing more than a text or a collection of words assembled together in an enigmatic way. In certain pieces the artist uses photography, in others collage, drawing, or sculpture. We find here, quite clearly, a tremendous variety of approaches, techniques, and modes of operation, and it is virtually impossible to classify these pieces into truly autonomous nuclei or clusters, even when the repetition of certain obsessions, of problems more than themes, begins to suggest the possibility of independent clusters. The mirrors represent only one of these obsessions, though it is one that has captivated the minds of artists since practically the beginning of time. [Fig. 19]*

 Mirrors are clearly a recurring, almost obsessive theme in your work. I don't think we can put off talking about them any more.

 This is a topic I would like to discuss very carefully, because it is complex and vast. Even though I have made a number of mirrors, I still feel that I have only scratched the surface. In the first mirror I ever made, I etched the word *fin*, and the viewer saw him or herself through that word. The second one I did was *Espelho com luz*, which is in the Colección Patricia Phelps de Cisneros [Fig. 20].

 Now, putting the word *fim* on the mirror leads me to two possible interpretations, and one of them has to do with the theme of the *vanitas*. Perhaps it is telling us: "This is your ending."

 I'm not sure . . . my mirror doesn't have the morbid quality of the *vanitas*. I think of it more as a satirical, humorous object. I could explain it a little better with the example of the mirror I made in 1976. It was done in painted metal, and it is an object in which one element is projected out toward the viewer and another is fixed on the plane of the wall, as if one were the reflection of the other [Fig. 21]. In this way, a mirrored environment is created without necessarily using polished glass surfaces. For me this was a real revelation,

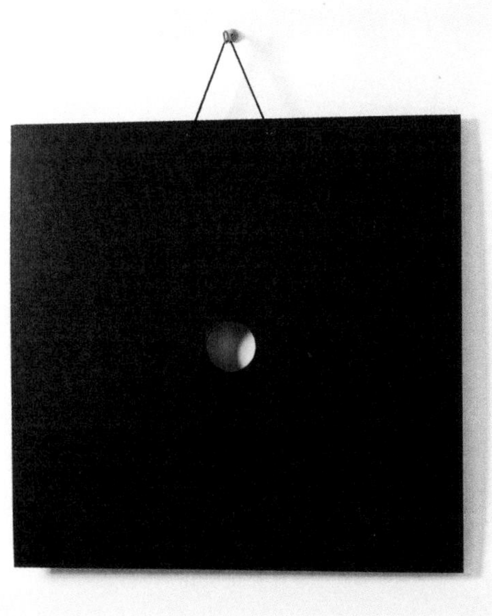

Fig. 19. *Espelho* [*Mirror*], 1975.

Fig. 20. *Espelho com luz* [*Mirror with Light*], 1975.

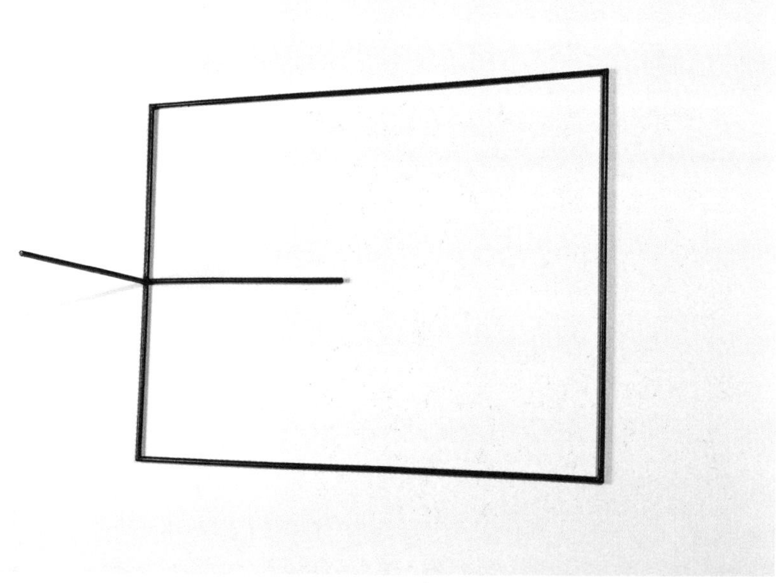

Fig. 21. *Espelho* [*Mirror*], 1976.

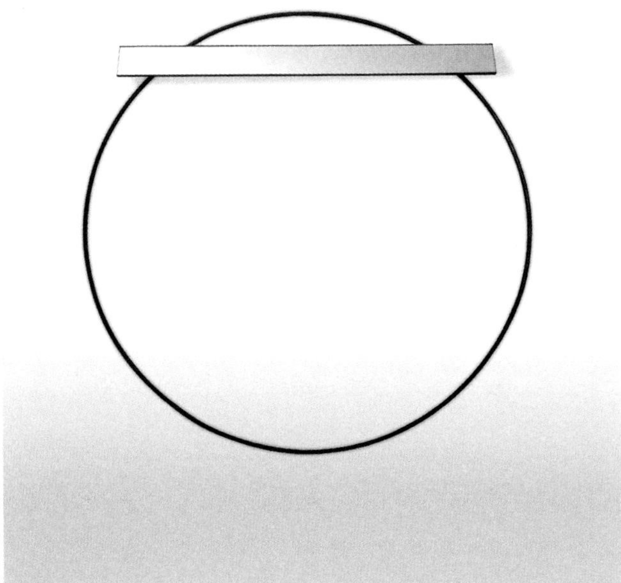

Fig. 22. *Circunferência com espelho a 30°* [*Circumference with Mirror at 30°*], 1976.

because I didn't have to use the object of the mirror as we know it; I was able to isolate just its mimetic function. Then came *Circunferência com espelho a 30°* [*Circumference with Mirror at 30°*; 1976], which paradoxically shows what you don't see and, moreover, doesn't show what you expect to see—yourself, looking into it. The viewer faces a complete and total void, which is that circle, and while the viewer may wish to see a certain image, the mirror reflects another dimension, presents an unexpected response [Fig. 22].

AJ Mirrors clearly present an infinite array of issues. Could you try to define what it is that most draws you to them?

WC To tell you the truth, I don't really know why they interest me. I could tell you that they come close to being something like a metaphor of representation, that they possess, in their operation, a kind of mimetic secret that I try to reveal. But I have to say that the mirror as an object seduces me far less than the desire to build it, and even less than the possibility of producing an artifact that functions the way mirrors function, that questions what mirrors do in such a banal way.

<sup>AJ</sup> Right, you end up producing an object that questions the idea of the reflection, but does so only once. What I mean is that what attracts me to those nonreflecting mirrors is that they seem to materialize a kind of idea, in the Platonic sense of the term. In other words, they produce the idea of mirroring without reflecting any object in particular.

<sup>WC</sup> What you just said is very important, as if this occurred "only once." I think you could sum up my entire oeuvre in those words, because the visual fact is stated on the basis of an initial appearance. In other words, if we could characterize a specific moment, it would be one in which the operation already contained the very nature of the instant—the certainty that something just happened. That's how those mirrors work, in a way; they are objects that reveal what happens in front of our eyes, as it is happening. One thing that made a real impression on me, for example, was visiting the Museum of Natural History in New York and seeing the first Aztec mirrors. They're not shiny at all, and they're not made of reflective material, either. They're made of polished black stone. The pseudo-transparent quality of those mirrors confirmed my suspicions about the other side of mirrors. I have never believed in their seeming ability to reflect. Mirrors are cruel; they make us believe that they hold the truth of what we see, when in reality they are a trap that we accept . . . I don't know how else to put it . . .

<sup>AJ</sup> A subtle trap?

<sup>WC</sup> No, I think they are actually rather arrogant. As if they possessed a fictitious truth that, in reality, is produced not by them but by what we expect to see. In a way, art could be a metaphor for this disillusionment, in the sense that it never quite matches what we know of the world. Sometimes it is insufferable how art shows us more than what we want or expect to see. That's why some of my works attempt to deal with the functional dismantling of the mirror. I always wanted to demonstrate that idea by building a primordial mirror, one that might react in the most inexplicable way, as if it had a divergent idea of itself.

There is something else interesting in what you said, related to Plato's idea that things are conclusively where they are supposed to be. Meaning that, for him, we grasp the correct places of things through our perception, whereas the type of mirror we are talking about takes the world out of its place. It makes us doubt the idea of place. In *Espelho com luz*, for example, the image is not just a reflection, it is a transparent membrane that functions, wouldn't you say? The mirror suggests to us that its activity is more important than what it reflects. That mirror gives us some very basic information about the purpose of art—

that the art object is something else, that it inhabits a space that is not exactly ours. We might call it an object of the third kind, a third object, that does not fulfill our expectations and is of no known species. If there is such a thing as objects that are not natural, they would be mirrors . . . and works of art.

What intrigued me about the Aztec mirrors is that when you see yourself in them, you perceive only the strongest lights. I couldn't see any low or medium tones, just the illuminated parts of the face, while the shadowy areas would get lost in the darkness of the stone. The mirror we all know offers us every bit of light imaginable, because it reflects it all in the very best way, but the Aztec mirror denies all but the strongest light. That was how I came to understand why Aztec sculptures possessed exactly that same quality: when sculpting a face in a stone, an Aztec artist emphasized the parts that were lit up and buried the shadowy or less illuminated parts of the face in bas-relief.

I have another work in my book *Aparelhos* [*Devices*] that is also a mirror, but it doesn't reflect anything. It was made of paper, not metal, and it seems to exist just to be penetrated by someone's gaze. Really, I have so many mirrors, I could practically put together an entire exhibition around them. If I did that, I would definitely include that metal mirror, and the cardboard one, too. I would also add *Espelho com luz*, as well as *Circunferência com espelho a 30°, Miroir b* [*Mirror b*] [Fig. 23]—the one I made for Borges—and one that was in the show at the Gulbenkian Foundation [Lisbon], *Espelho C* [Fig. 24].

 What is the difference between mirrors *A*, *B*, and *C*? Are they from different series?

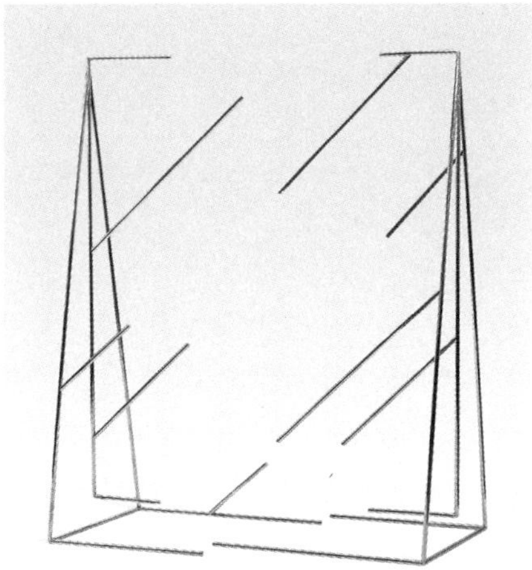

Fig. 23. *Miroir b* [*Mirror b*], 2005.

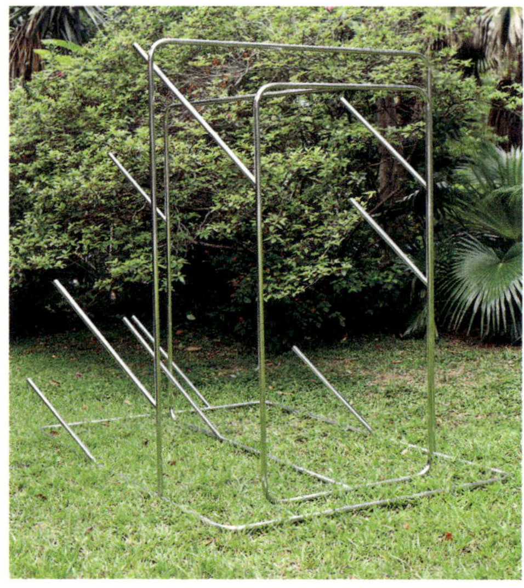

Fig. 24. *Espelho C* [*Mirror C*], 2005.

WC No. First I made several mirrors, all flat, until one day I made *Miroir b,* the one for Borges, which emerges completely from the plane. *Espelho C* would be a mirror of the third kind, three-dimensional. In that mirror I tried to isolate the problem of its internal thickness. It's like a door, a threshold where you can enter because the scale allows you to.

AJ There is something about that three-dimensional mirror that is very interesting to me: it seems to open out into space in layers, like a stratified object, just like in Clark's *Counter-reliefs* and Oiticica's *Spatial Reliefs.* Might there be some kind of connection between these processes?

WC I don't think so. My works have always opened out into space, ever since the beginning. It's just a thematic coincidence in this case.

AJ Yes, but why do you think of the mirror in terms of different layers or strata?

WC That's a good question. I don't know, maybe the reflection, for me, has its origins in the transparency of volumes. Think of Narcissus and his lake.

AJ I have always thought that the reason many artists (as is the case with Soto, Oiticica, and Clark) open their work into space through superimposed strata is because, in some way, they regard space through a pictorial tradition. Painting has conceived space precisely as a succession and superimposition of transparent layers.

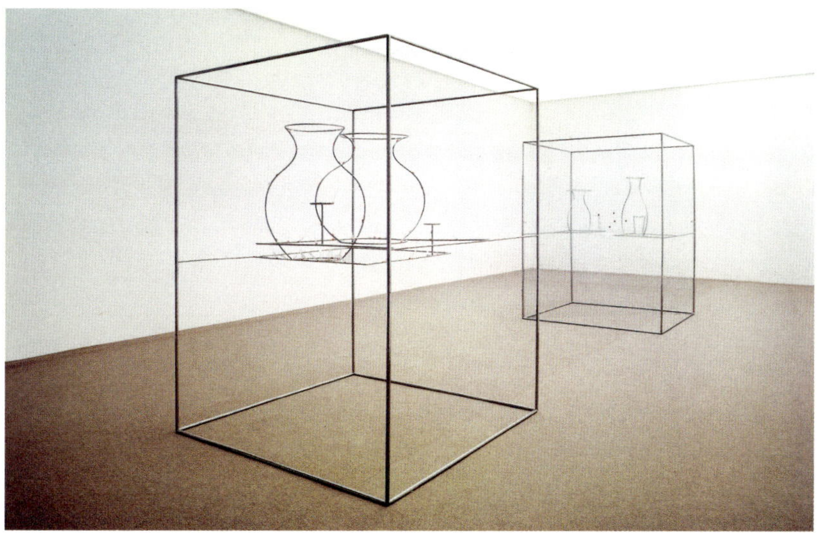

Fig. 25. *A distância entre . . .* [*The Distance Between . . .*], *Série Veneza III* [*Venice Series*], 1997.

<sup>WC</sup> But that's another problem. It would be more interesting if there were different layers or strata in the image, which is not exactly impossible because the strata of an image are imaginary, though in painting you can certainly think of stratified images.

<sup>AJ</sup> The strata of painting are also imaginary . . .

<sup>WC</sup> No. In paintings they are real. For example, if you take a pair of binoculars and scan the landscape, you clearly see how the binoculars cut off the planes of the image. The most important characteristic of binoculars is the way they transform images into strata. I have always thought that binoculars "Morandize" images, because Morandi has this curious quality of ascribing the same pictorial value to the foreground, the mid-ground, and every other ground, which transforms the image into a dense, opaque film. And that's why his objects seem more real, because they are not subjected to the illusion of perspective. When you talk about some artists who open their work up to space through stratified objects, it's as if everyone were emerging from pictorial toward sculptural information.

<sup>AJ</sup> By using pictorial strategies . . .

<sup>WC</sup> I'm not so sure, because pictorial strategies to me are very specific, and it is still possible to build a sculpture in planes or strata [Fig. 25]. It's not necessarily a

pictorial issue. Moreover, I think that sculptural heritage is older than pictorial. I believe that humans worked with stones before colors. When cavemen began to deal with images, they embedded them on the walls of a cave, perhaps to explore the three-dimensionality of the wall in the darkness.

<sup>AJ</sup> And yet I feel that your sculptures, if we can call them that, are marked by pictorial and even drawing-related issues, because they are born from them, or simply related to them. Many of your *B* and *C* mirrors, for example, seem like drawings in space.

I find *Circunferência com espelho a 30°* curious for another reason we haven't brought up yet, which is that it has clear parallels with the use that the mirror has been given in Catholic iconography. I am not a religious person, but I find that religious painting is forced to invent all sorts of mechanisms to speak about the very thing that can't be seen, that transcends space and time—in other words, the divine.

<sup>WC</sup> Definitely. You know, someone once said that theology is the most fantastic branch of knowledge, the fantastic realism of human understanding. This is the source of religion's cunning as well as its cruelty, in the way it transforms metaphysical problems into overly pragmatic solutions.

<sup>AJ</sup> Maybe, but what gets under my skin is that this mirror at thirty degrees functions like the mirror of the Virgin Mary in Catholic iconography. This is a mirror without reflection. And that's why, whenever one of these is placed in a church, very great care is taken to place it at just the right angle so that the visitor cannot see what it reflects, or at least sees nothing more than the reflection of the cupola of the church as a metaphor for the infinite, the celestial dome.

<sup>WC</sup> I tried to do something similar in *Espelho com luz,* though for different reasons. When you stand before a mirror, you almost feel a certain critical distance between you and the image, as though it were somehow exposing your inner self in a public space. I was just recently able to confirm this, when my mirror was on exhibit for a few months at MoMA in New York: people who know me would send me photos of all types of things, but never of themselves in the mirror. So they would send me pictures of a Calder reflected in my mirror, which was a bit of a distance away, things like that. They seemed to feel the need to avoid the typical relationship with the mirror.

AJ  That's why I found it interesting that you, reflecting on the mirror, would also resort to that artifice to obtain one that cannot reflect us.

WC  It's like an attempt to let mirrors start at the beginning, as if it were possible to build them from point zero, which is partly my obsession with them. It's what makes me think of them as machines, because if you try to envision them from zero . . . what would a mimetic zero look like? It brings up a huge number of questions that, in the end, have a lot to do with art.

AJ  Now, would it be possible to conceive of an object that might be only potentially reflective?

WC  Perfectly. *Espelho C* is that kind of object, as is *Miroir b*. More than objects that want to reflect something, they are objects that want to be mirrors. In other words, the final adjustment that would transform them into mirrors is deliberately absent.

AJ  So would the function of that button in *Espelho com luz* be to activate it?

WC  No, in that case the purpose of the button is precisely to achieve its negation, or at least to negate, partly, its representative certainty. That button is there for the opposite reason: to criticize the arrogance of appearances.

*Talking about mirrors inevitably brings us to the question of painting, even when in the case of Caldas this is a very distant topic from a technical point of view. In the West, at least, and in particular since the Italian Renaissance, it is impossible to speak of painting without considering the fascination that this curious mimetic machine has held—and continues to hold—for artists. Perspective came into existence, in part, with the support of the mirror (as was the case with Brunelleschi), incorporating it somehow into painting. When artists wanted to test the veracity of a work, they would turn it to the mirror. This was, at least, what Leonardo da Vinci recommended. The mirror was judge and jury for the painting, and it is no coincidence that one of the greatest efforts of representative painting, Las Meninas [The Maids of Honor] by Velázquez, was born, as well, as a kind of challenge that the painter posed to the mirror.*

AJ  I suppose your personal interest in the mirror is what prompted your fascination with this masterwork of Spanish and Western painting.

<sup>WC</sup> That painting, *Las Meninas,* very closely examines the mirror, and Velázquez undertook this with the absolute awareness that its mimetic function needed to be exposed. In this work I see the artist's clear intention to put the matter of reflection to work. And not just in this painting, either: this also comes up in a painting from thirty years earlier, *Cristo en la casa de Marta y María* [*Christ in the House of Martha and Mary*, c. 1618] [Fig. 26]. It is a work in which Velázquez anticipates what is going to happen in *Las Meninas.* In it, Mary gazes straight out of the center of the painting, and Jesus is reflected in the mirror in the background, to the right. This stratagem allows us to understand that she is gazing out at a space that is behind us.

<sup>AJ</sup> As if we might just possibly be able to see Christ, if we simply turned around.

<sup>WC</sup> More than that, even: it's as if we were inside the painting. As far as I know this is the first time the gaze of the viewer is treated internally by the work. But it's even more ingenious than that, and in a certain way it negates us physically. Notice how Mary is not even looking at us; she's looking just slightly to the left, toward Christ, who is behind us. Seeing her makes us transparent.

<sup>AJ</sup> But at the same time it integrates us into the scene.

<sup>WC</sup> Barely, with the gaze. These may be the reasons Velázquez is considered a painter's painter, because he deals with problems that turn most painters into victims, whereas he elucidates the essential operation implicit in the act of painting a picture. There is another interesting detail here, too, which in an artist like Velázquez cannot be considered coincidence: the edge of the mirror coincides with the border of the painting, as if he wanted to underscore the relationship between the painting and the mirror.

<sup>AJ</sup> This brings us immediately to your 1994 book on *Las Meninas,* and to the pieces you have created based on Velázquez. In fact, one of your metal constructions seems to reproduce the basic scheme of that painting [Fig. 27].

<sup>WC</sup> That series is called *Los Velázquez.* I transferred the title of *Las Meninas* to *Los Velázquez,* as if there existed various Velázquezes, one of whom painted the backgrounds and the action of the paintings, and another one who depicted the royal characters, for example.

<sup>AJ</sup> At the same time, it seems that you conceived that painting as an empty mirror, before reflecting the characters Velázquez painted.

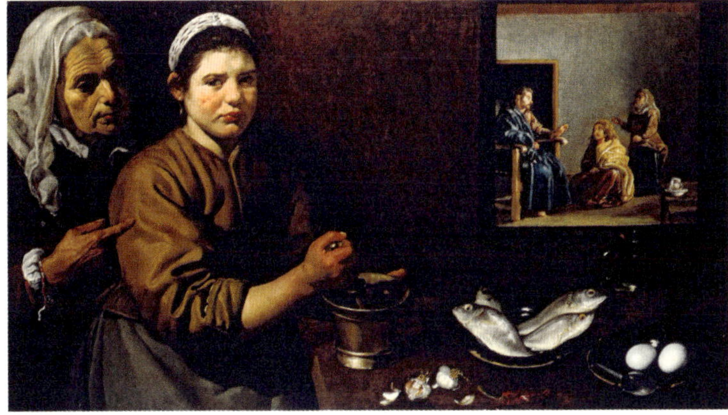

Fig. 26. Diego Velázquez (1599–1660), *Kitchen Scene with Christ in the House of Martha and Mary*, c. 1618.

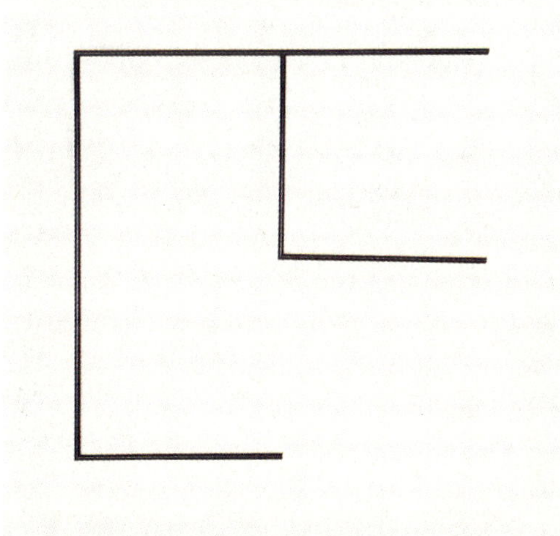

Fig. 27. *Ferro pintado* [*Painted Iron*], 1978.

<sup>WC</sup> Yes, that too, but in *Las Meninas* the pictorial surface is envisioned as a skin, as if the object of the mirror had been painted. Velázquez paints the actual operation of the mirror. And he does it by creating double situations, like when he paints the mirror in the background and to the side a door of the same size, a little opening into the background. So he places a mirror that reflects the space in front, and a door that opens up an empty space out toward the back. In some way, these two parallel rectangles play off each other. The device of the door adds another layer of spatiality to the work, three-dimensionalizing it. To say nothing of the fantastic solution of the light cast into the room through the windows at the right; thanks to this last window just enough light falls in, allowing us to see the king and queen in the mirror. In my book, this was the only oil painting I made. The others are computer-generated reproductions [Fig. 28].

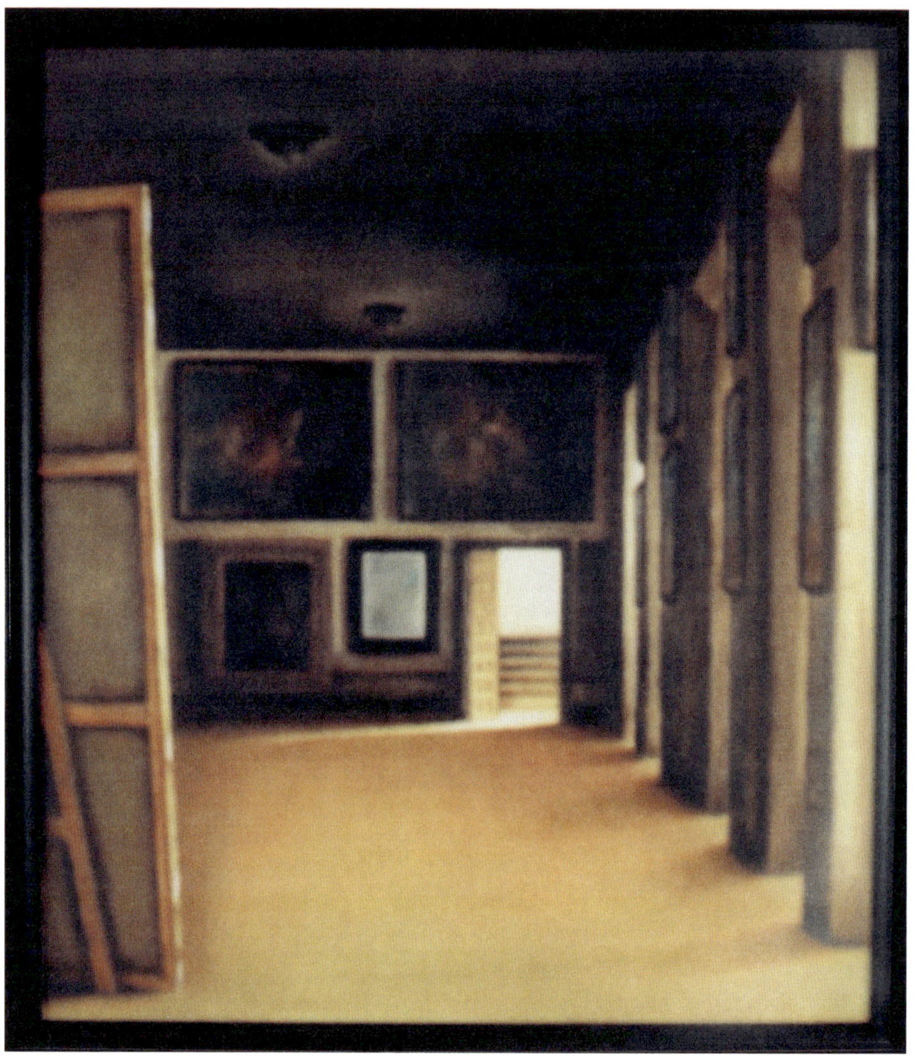

Fig. 28. *Los Velázquez* [*The Velázquez*], 1994.

AJ But it has a glass in front of it, as if you were aiming to make manifest the pictorial theory that, starting in the Renaissance, equated the canvas with a transparent sheet of glass.

WC But here, the glass is not transparent, it's not absent. In the painting we are talking about, which was done three years before making the book, I used a milky, semitransparent glass to bring the image out of focus and take it out of the painting. With that glass the image seems to float; it's no longer restricted to a flat surface. In my project that painting becomes an object with frame, glass, and volume. Then I took a photograph of that object, and from there I made the larger versions that were reproduced mechanically. In other images in the book I didn't use glass because I thought that the reproduction itself created a supplementary layer. What I did was emphasize a detail from the door and the mirror to show the importance of that parallel in the painting.

AJ Now, tell me something: is this publication the retouched replica of an existing book or is it a book created entirely by you?

WC This is a book that I created on the basis of reproductions of Velázquez, precisely as if it were a publication about the artist's work. But I think, because of this doubt you have raised, that you are actually thinking about another issue: the deliberate disauthorship of this book. If we could put the text back in focus, it would read: *Libros y espejos en Velázquez* [*Books and Mirrors in Velázquez*]. I only went out of focus with the chapter titles. For the text that went along with the images I did something different, because when I took a block of text and tried to reproduce it out of focus, the image that I generated didn't seem right. It was the one figure that felt alien to the book, like a microbe colony. This forced me, ultimately, to create a very specific stain that looked like an out-of-focus text.

AJ Many painters have said precisely that—that the artist often has to deform what he observes to achieve a more plausible image of the real.

WC Yes, but this text thing wasn't a personal whim; it was a Velázquez-inspired problem. I think he might have been the first artist to paint books exactly as he saw them. The painters in his age painted them so falsely that you could read them on the canvas. Velázquez understood that this simply couldn't be true, that nobody could read a book from the distance that lay between the artist and the model. And he painted them exactly as he saw them, with the gray blots of

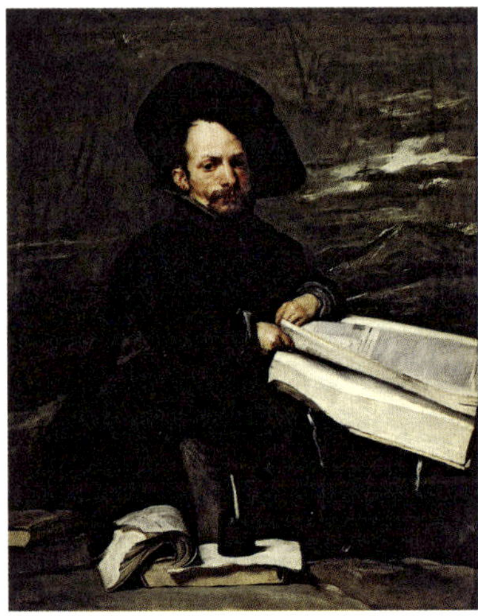

Fig. 29. Diego Velázquez, *El buffón Don Diego de Acedo "El primo"* [*The Jester Don Diego de Acedo "The Cousin"*], 1644.

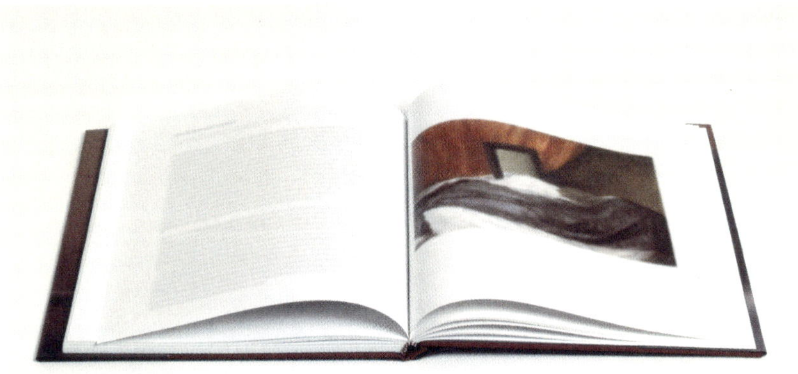

Fig. 30. *Velázquez*, 1996.

the text that he could make out from a distance [Fig. 29]. In my book, the texts are faithful to that decision Velázquez made [Fig. 30].

AJ The fantastic thing is that this anticipated the central matter taken up by the French Impressionists; this was exactly what they were aiming to do: paint the world as it appeared, in the way it appears before our eyes, not on the basis of what we know or think we know about it.

WC But Velázquez listened to his mentor [Francisco] Pacheco, who stated this problem with the remark, "I don't paint a rose, I paint a stain that looks like a rose." And this is part of what Velázquez learned with Pacheco, that the painter paints smudges that look like things.

# INTIMATE SCENARIOS
## Books and exhibitions

*If* Los Velázquez *reflects on the mirror, it is no less true that what we are dealing with is indeed a book: not a book about art, but an artist's book. In other words, a book about a specific way of working, of creating art. The thing we call culture is, more than anything, what Malraux said: the living presence of the past in each of us, the constantly renewed life of that universe of meaning in which we live, immersed, as fish in water. This is how every work of art and every human gesture derives its meaning: by the way in which it builds upon or renews the past by inscribing itself in it. This is how it always has been, and yet never before has that past been quite as present as it is now for those who wish to add their works to the age-old history of human inventions. It is clearly for this reason that, from his earliest days in Serpa's classes, Caldas felt summoned to think about his inscription in the annals of time, and to do it through the kind of cultural inventions that, like the book or the exhibition, could be a mise-en-scène of the artist and his ideas. Progressively, these two representational devices became for him much more than the documentation of what he had produced. They became a crucial aspect of his artistic concerns, as if both were a very particular kind of mirror in which he might see himself and think about himself, through his reflection.*

WC For me, the books and the library have become something of a machine for meaning. They work like Captain Nemo's organ in his *Nautilus:* a privileged place where I can establish new links between things—connect events, follow certain paths, and, absolutely, pick the type of plot that interests me. How could I find my way in this forest of meanings without their help? I read poetry, technical books, literature, art history, philosophy, and it is from that diversity that connections often emerge, in a way that I couldn't achieve through any other means. Parallels between writers and their themes, texts and illustrations . . .

This is why, from a very early age, books have been a part of my life; they are even the theme of a number of works, like *Matisse, talco* [*Matisse, Talcum;* 1978] [Fig. 31]. I have never wanted to publish a conventional book about my work. I remember when GBM Editora invited me to do *Aparelhos*, in 1978. In those days in Brazil, publishing a book was like assembling a kind of historical document that ultimately immobilized an artist's career. That kind of publication made the artist's work even more difficult, because it considered the artist from a prematurely historical perspective. And that's why I think that *Aparelhos* represented a real challenge, both for me as an artist and for Ronaldo Brito as the writer [Fig. 32]. Neither of us was motivated by the idea of doing another book about art. We wanted to create a dynamic experience, through which we could explore issues concerning art and not necessarily be obliged to summarize an artist's career. Our objective was not to show what I had done, but to turn that book into an experience that made the reader wonder what was going on at the time, and what might happen with art in the future.

AJ This is what you identify in *Manual da ciência popular,* which is more an editorial work than a book about your work [Fig. 33].

WC *Manual da ciência popular* was essential for me, because in that book I brought together a number of specific issues that were inherent to my working process. This happened two years later, when the Fundación Nacional de Arte [Funarte] invited me to make a book. Funarte was publishing a series of books on Brazilian artists; but because I already had done *Aparelhos*, I told them I didn't want to do another general book about my work. I wanted to do something thematic, in which I could explore what interested me at the time. That's how the 1982 *Manual* came about.

The book proposes, with a good deal of humor, a series of artworks that the reader can make at home, with materials and tools found in the domestic

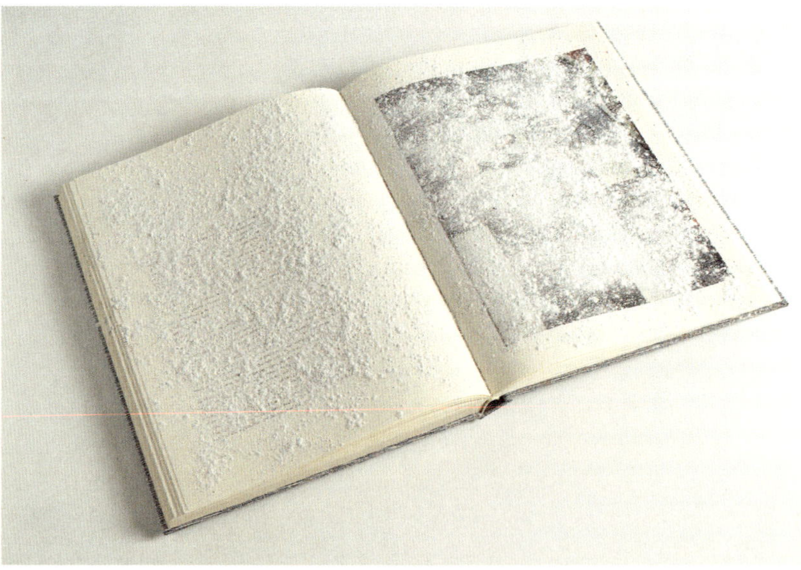

Fig. 31. *Matisse, talco* [*Matisse, Talcum*], 1978.

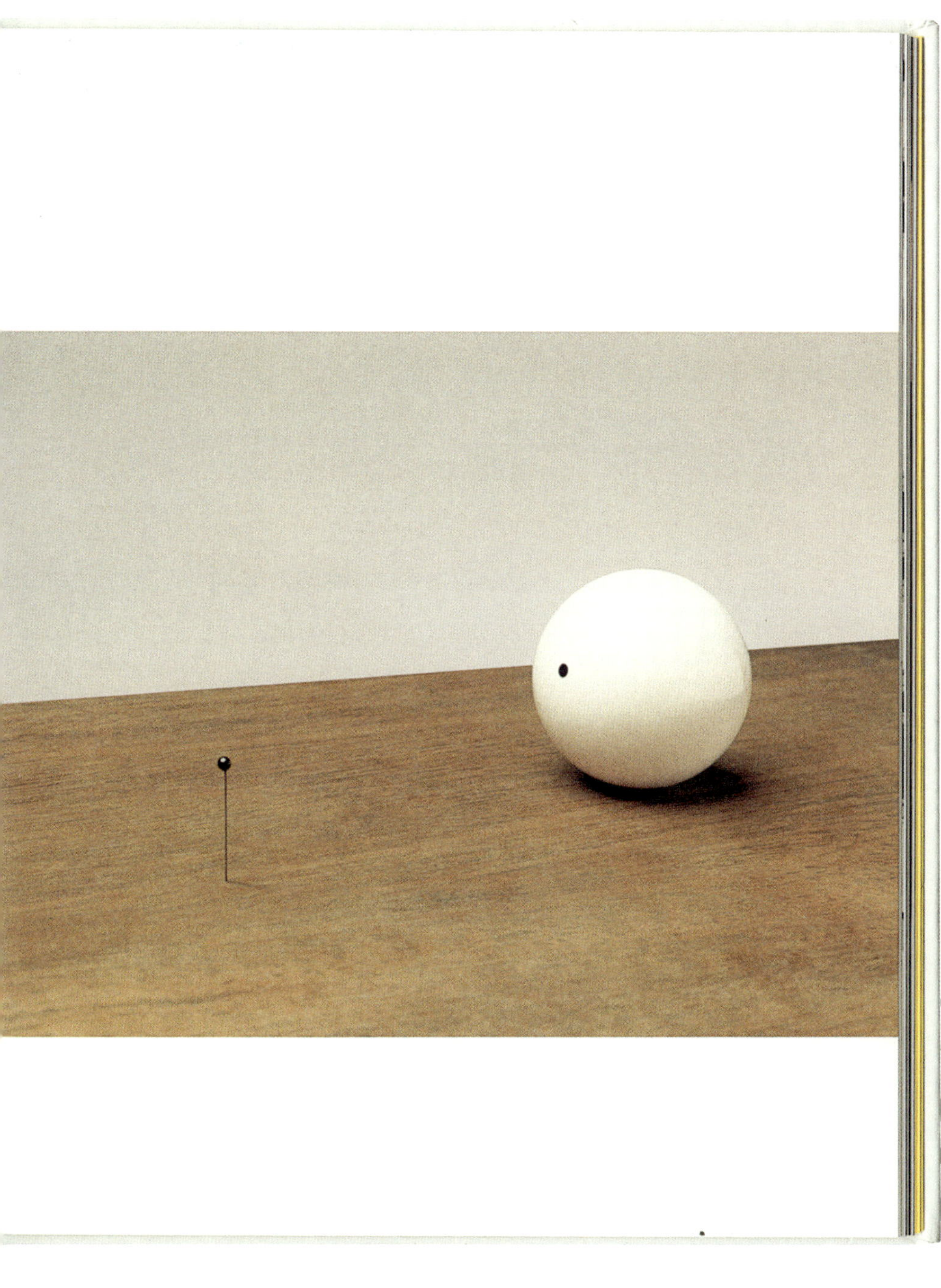

# Waltercio Caldas Jr.
## "Aparelhos"

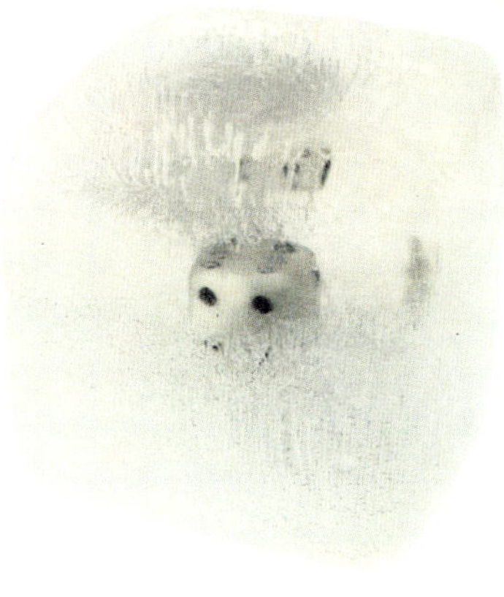



Fig. 32. Cover of *Aparelhos* [*Gadgets*], 1979.

environment. I used some images from *Aparelhos* and added some works I had recently finished, suggested by the new situation, some of which were conceived especially for the book around the Do-It-Yourself notion, as you find in many technical manuals. One of my objectives was to introduce the reproduction of artworks as part of the artist's prerogative. The experience with *Aparelhos* allowed me to see that certain qualities of an artwork undergo modifications when the work is reproduced. From there I realized that reproduction should be one of the components of visual language, and not just a simple footnote added to a work after completion. I was trying to find a way to incorporate reproduction as a new interest, something that was already implicit in *Aparelhos*. That deliberation is present on the cover of the *Manual*, which is the image of the book itself.

At the same time that I was dealing with integrating reproductions into the works I made, I also wanted to reflect on the inclusion, at some point, of everyday and ephemeral objects as works of art. The introduction I wrote focused on that; I said something to the effect that the reader should not be fooled by these objects, because after they are used as art they will return to their normal state.

AJ  What seems evident in your case is the absence—if not total, at least quite notorious—of a recognizable formal quality, of a totally characteristic style and palette that would help trace your trajectory over time (or at least your desire to

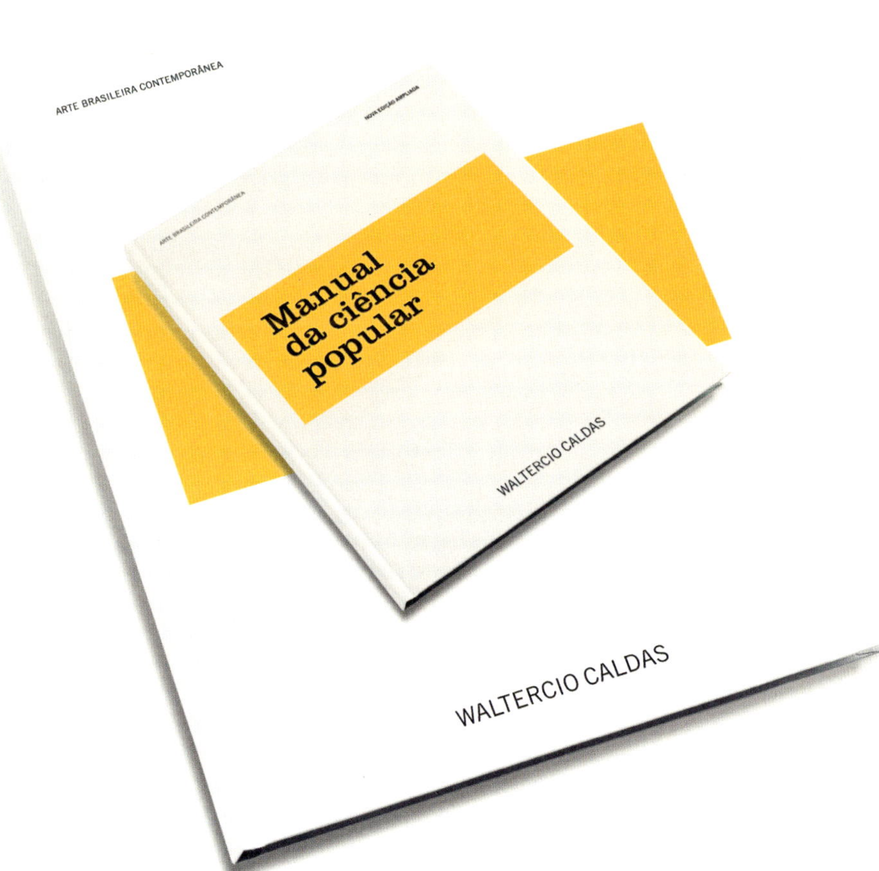



Fig. 33. Cover of *Manual da ciência popular* [*Manual of Popular Science*], 1982.

avoid the emergence of a specific style). And in that absence, the book begins to function not just as an integral part of your work, but as a work that possesses the peculiarity of building a gaze on the processes that make it possible.

WC  Hearing you say these things makes me think that my palette could be defined as the relationship between things, all things. Each book, each drawing, each exhibition, represents a different way of dealing with those connections. Each one of them is incorporated into my production not as a document or report of something that has happened, but as a production, as another work of art, as if at that moment my materials were, in fact, graphic matter and the reproduction itself of an object. In that sense, I turn my effort into the raw material of my artistic activity. When I put together an exhibition, the same exact thing occurs. Each exhibition is a declaration, a statement, and the relationship among the different objects and sculptures selected for an exhibition interests me as much as the articulation of that exhibition with others. I would say, moreover, that this occurs with each work of art as well, because each piece is connected to all the others. Each one is a passage between what was and what will be, and will introduce an important modification to the whole. That constant movement is the poetic vision of my work.

AJ All of this is extremely interesting, because I feel that the difficulty I experience each time I try to wrap my thoughts around the structure of these conversations is precisely the same difficulty that is an integral part of your work, of your way of functioning, and, to a certain point, of a heightened consciousness of the context of meaning to which you belong. What I mean is that when an individual integrates exhibitions and books as part of a device for meaning, and even a temporal device for reading, so to speak (your refusal to read it chronologically), it is because he has become aware of the fact that what we call the truth of a work of art is just a construct, because the genesis of meaning is something that never ends.

WC Yes, because that is the only way to break away from a programmatic imposition that would destroy it. I think that freedom to connect parts, independent of their chronological commitment, is critical. A visual object is not limited to just what you see; it is also what you cannot see. It's as if I had two personalities: one visible, which would be demonstrated through objects, and another invisible, present in the connection established between the two of them. Then, the tension between those two aspects also constitutes part of the work, and I think that new horizons always open up from there.

For example, right now I feel the need for another nucleus, one that I never perceived as such, and that would be present in the various different approaches I take when I draw. I myself have preferred the presence of objects to that of drawings, and now I realize that, through them and their evolution over time, I can find surprises. I have to correct that distraction.

AJ Yes, but that only becomes viable when the collection of drawings has achieved the density needed to establish its own force of gravity.

WC As if only now they were able to generate the necessary complexity to justify an independent interest, with which they might have a gravitational effect (to build on your metaphor) on the previous collections. The important thing, for me, is the guarantee that these nuclei will always be possible in the future, because they are created by the very movement of my work.

*The possibility of grasping the work produced by an artist from his or her internal connections, free of the tyranny of chronology, is doubtless seductive and stimulating. Even so, to programmatically deny the eventuality of a chronological reading could become a veil that hides part of the work, or its processes. In the end it is impossible to deny that works came about at specific moments in time. To use one example,* Miroir b *and* Espelho C *are unthinkable before the first metal mirror, done in 1975, because they are the consequence of the environment of meaning opened up by the first work. Their emergence and evolution over time are also part of the work. There is no point in replacing one tyranny with another. The important thing is to acknowledge, and integrate into our artistic experience, the fact that there does not exist a more privileged approach, that the genesis of meaning never ends, and that each new interpretation will enrich the work of art that captures our gaze and, with it, our life.*

# WORDS AND THINGS
## To make, to name

*"In the beginning was the Word, and the Word was with God, and the Word was God." So begins the Gospel according to John, and there is no doubt that for us nothing exists that hasn't previously been verbalized, described, named, by the word. And of course our vision of the universe is marked by the belief that there exists a real world out there, in which we are immersed as participants, that same world whose appearance we have tried to capture with art and describe with language. But it is no less true that the word and the image with which we try to capture it are not the world itself but a human creation, a parallel fact that we add to the real. If there is one thing that seduced me in the poetry of Ferreira Gullar, with whom I have had the fortune of publishing one of these conversations,[12] it is the constant struggle it raises between the word and the inescapable opacity of the world. The almost painful awareness that the word is just another object, never an analogical trace of the real. And so the modern artist, and especially the contemporary artist, cannot simply ignore its presence, its power. This is, at least, what has happened for a significant portion of the twentieth century, in particular for those artists who, in the wake of Duchamp's achievements and work, have wanted to add gray matter as another color to the palette.*

AJ　When and how did language appear in your artwork?

WC　Words have been part of my work from the start for several reasons. First, because my immediate references were movements that regarded the word as something important. And I'm not talking about Cubism or Dada, which already had used the word, but Pop, Arte Povera, and Conceptual art. Second, titling my work was always, for each piece, a very complex decision, because I always saw a significant relationship between names and objects. The first time this happened was in the *Condutores de percepção*, in which the title physically becomes part of the work.

AJ　The inscription of the title on a plaque is almost what makes that object work.

12. *Ferreira Gullar in conversation with / en conversación con Ariel Jiménez* (New York: Fundación Cisneros / Colección Patricia Phelps de Cisneros, 2012).

 What makes it work is, precisely, the unexpected connection between what can be read and what can be seen. And in those works I find that, in some way, words propose a new dimension of the object, they make it depend on reading. And on the other hand, the strangeness of those connections also robs the words of their explanatory power, because the object, at the same time, undermines the language being used. It's almost as if an empty space were created between what we see and what we know.

 Despite the fact that visually, its physical presence predominates.

 Yes, and I would say that even the operation of opening a closed box is fundamental to the situation that is created. Opening it means revealing the content suggested by the words, which immediately transfigures the object. It's like adding time to the work. In *Centro de razão primitiva* [*Center of Primitive Reasoning*; 1970], the title is as immediate as the needles it contains; without it, the suggestion needed to activate it is not unleashed [Fig. 34]. And that's not because the title is an explanation of the object—it's the opposite, in fact.

 Language is a material, another ingredient.

 Exactly, and the situation of the title that activates the object is so curious that when I make a piece of art in which the title is a tautology, as in *Talco sobre libro ilustrado de H. Matisse,* the audience gets even more lost.

 Of course. That redundancy between the title and what you see only obscures the object even more. That, in some way, is the function of the tautology in Conceptual art: to restore the opacity of the real.

 Yes, because the description of an object is not its title, and it doesn't even explain it, nor could there exist a verbal version of that object. And I perceived that dysfunction when I found myself going through the discomfort of having to talk about my piece, explain it to people. What I had proposed with *Condutores de percepção,* that ambiguous articulation between the object and its title, now applied to me, or to the relationship that was established between me, my works, and the public. Talking about my own work became a challenge of language confronting the autonomy of the works.

 In a way, when people asked you to explain one of your pieces, you found yourself obliged to translate it to spoken language.

WC And I began to ask myself if the artist could be a translator of his own work. The exercise needed to be one of generating a new situation for that other who was now speaking. And this implied a different problem, because when you create a work of art, you cannot help but be the author of a deliberate event, and when you speak about that event, you're almost forced to become a different, more distant person than the one who made it.

AJ What the public sometimes fails to understand is that an artist's own interpretation of his or her work is just one more among many possible interpretations, one that is of course very close to its conditions of creation and that is, as such, particularly indispensable. But in no way does it necessarily determine what that piece of art might awaken in others. The vision of the artist is one that speaks of the circumstances of production, not what it is capable of eliciting from those who are in dialogue with it.

WC It is just one interpretation, and not necessarily the most authoritative one, because I find that a piece actually achieves the most when it manages to resist its own artist's interpretation. That, quite simply, is the moment when the work of art becomes a problem, an object of examination for the artist himself. As such, it is important to consider the right language to use when speaking about that work, to establish a connection between the two, because then you are working not just with what is said about the work, but also with the way in which it is said.

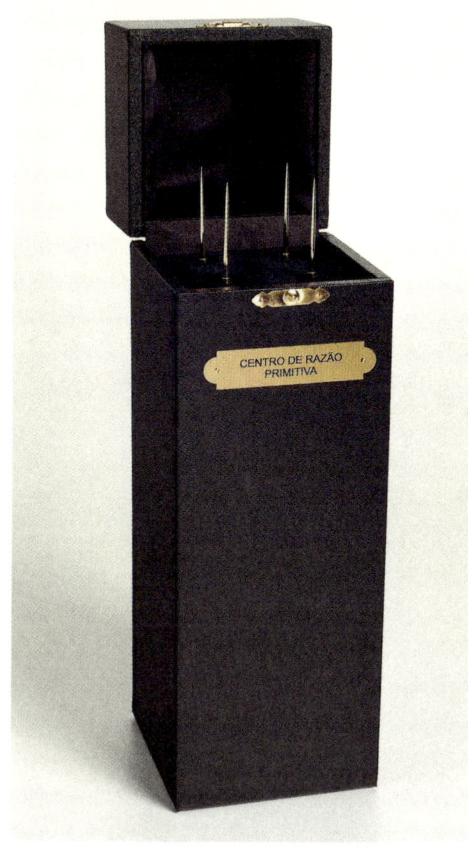


Fig. 34. *Centro de razão primitiva* [*Center of Primitive Reasoning*], 1970.

AJ And then the discourse about the work becomes an occasion to produce work.

WC Exactly, and with words. By producing tensions between the word and the object. Afterwards I realize that the object of my language is my own object. At that moment I begin to consider a specific way to deal with that issue: rather than a mere translator of the work, through language, I become an author.

<sup>AJ</sup> The worst thing, then, must be when people ask you to explain a work that is already the result of that clash with language.

<sup>WC</sup> In fact, that is an issue that artists have to face all the time, because it is about the self-sufficiency of artworks. And that's why I find it so puzzling that artists are required to give explanations for what they do. Never before were artists so solicited to decipher their works—and to make matters worse, never before were their explanations accepted so meekly.

<sup>AJ</sup> As if the artist's opinion were the exact, irrevocable translation.

<sup>WC</sup> And that need for a translation becomes as problematic as the work that the translation is trying to explain.

<sup>AJ</sup> I absolutely agree with you on that. Recently, in a conversation with Gullar about this, he told me that in his poetry from the 1950s he wanted to conquer the opacity of the world, and he did so by searching for language that seemed to come about at the very same moment as the writing. In my opinion, what happened there wasn't the victory over that first opacity of the world. What happened was that art ended up creating a new opacity, and this other opacity of art, of human creation, confronted the opacity of the world. And that's why, when you try to explain your work, you only produce another object, a verbal object that is different from the one you were trying to describe, and so in that act you add yet another layer of meaning to the work.

<sup>WC</sup> You end up in a justification that is actually a trap, and that becomes a vulgate of different versions. Sometimes the public is satisfied by a simple description of the art object, as if that could be an explanation. It was while thinking about that need of the public, and its desire to see artworks translated into words, that I did the book *Cronometrias* [*Chronometries*; 2012]. The book repeats an image that changes each time it appears, and these images are accompanied by poetic prose with suggestions that are related to time and space. The effort of writing about such abstract topics showed me that descriptions do have unexpected advantages.

There are points of contact between visual arts and written or oral language, and between these fields and music. The three fields can generate images, can't they? One can create mental images while listening to music, reading a book, or gazing at a work of art, it's just that those images will be generated in different ways. In *Cronometrías,* I asked myself some very ambitious questions. For example, I wondered if the existence of a clock that measured space instead of time was possible. In those cases the relationship between text and image is not one of content and illustration, but rather of something more complementary.

AJ Listening to you speak, I am suddenly reminded of some pieces from the *Série Veneza* [*Venice Series*; 1997] in which, I think, there is an illustration and even material evidence of the difficulty one faces when trying to make the object and the word coincide. These sculptures are built of metal pieces, with perfect, industrial finishes, yet the way in which you join the texts together is pretty clumsy, as if the operation of attaching a word to an object cannot be achieved with the same perfection as when joining two metal pieces, simply because they each belong to two different realities [Fig. 35].

WC And those words are names of artists, and if we look closely, it almost seems that the names of the artists have a history separate and distinct from that of their works—that the names somehow became detached from their original content. Many people know them without knowing anything about their work. The other day I read an interview with Luciano Fabro in which he said how surprised they [he and his fellow Arte Povera artists] were by the public use of the word "poor" to describe their art, which they truly felt was naked and unadorned, but never poor. Or then you'll find designers using the term "minimal" to justify a trend characterized by qualities they believe come from Minimal art, when in reality what they're doing is totally allegorical and phony. Some terms seem to take on a life that is totally independent of their meanings. In the case that you mention, the *Série Veneza,* something definitive occurs: I refer to several artists, but none of their names is used in the form of a citation.

AJ Of course not, because it is impossible to find a relationship between those names and the works to which they are attached.

WC Exactly, and that's why I love what [curator] Paulo Sérgio Duarte wrote in his text "La duda feliz" ["The Happy Doubt," 2001], about how the names of the artists are happier in that piece than in books. I thought this was really important, the fact that the names were there, in a sculpture, a freer, more welcoming space than the publications about those artists and their work.

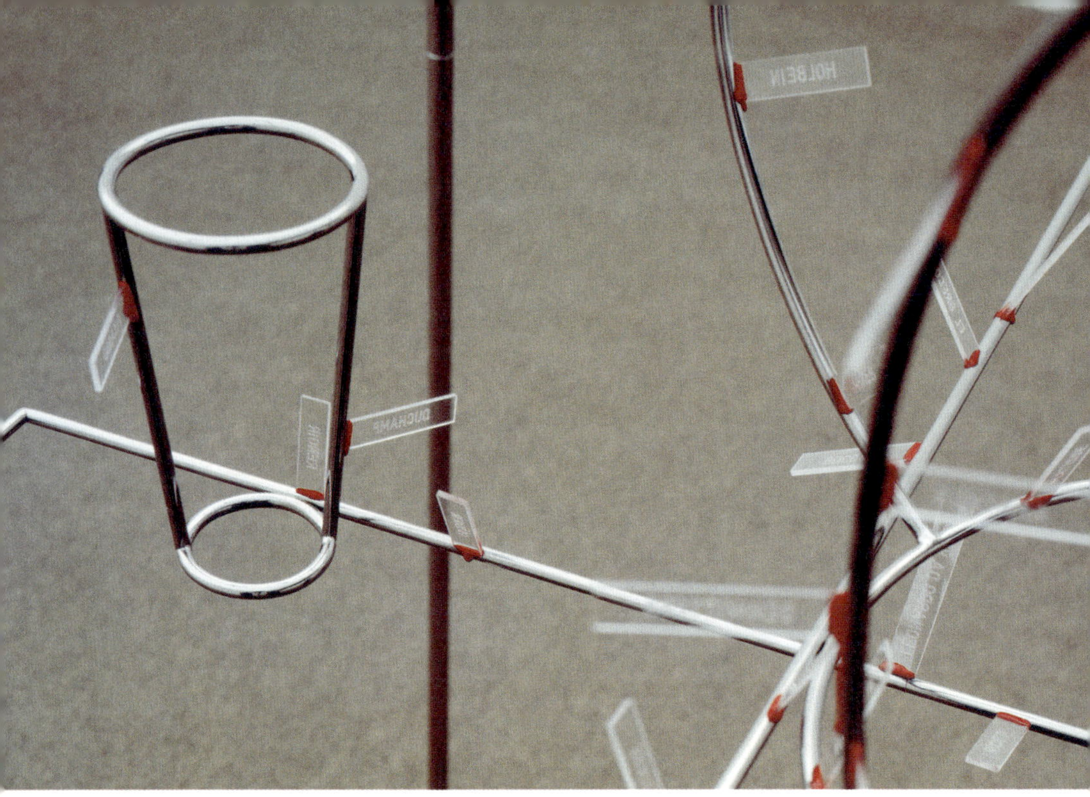

Fig. 35. *A distância entre . . .* [*The Distance Between . . .*] (detail), *Série Veneza III* [*Venice Series III*], 1997.

<sup>AJ</sup> What surprised me, on the contrary, was how hard it was for those names to find their place in the sculptures you aimed to associate them with.

<sup>WC</sup> Well, both things happen, really. The adaptation and the confrontation speak of the same situation.

<sup>AJ</sup> Yes, but to give an example: I would read the name Matisse, and then I would try to envision some relationship between his name and the work to which you had applied it. Then I would read the name Giorgione on that same sculpture, and the relationships I could build were really contradictory. And then it seemed to me that even the way in which those names were affixed to the sculpture, in an openly artificial way, was not entirely insignificant.

<sup>WC</sup> But the objective was not to connect the respective styles of those artists, not with one another, nor with my sculpture. The link was produced exclusively between the name-things. What interests me is the idea of pointing out the distance between art and art history, because it often feels to me as if history

configures a version of art that is completely separate from the practice of art. Each object in its concrete reality is one thing; art history's explanation of that object is something else entirely. And that is what prompts me to give words a physical existence. That's why, when I do a book on Matisse or Velázquez, only someone who believes that he or she is seeing a member of the royal family in that image could be thinking that I am talking about Velázquez. In reality I am talking about illusions in print. About how an image becomes a book, how a book becomes art, and, moreover, how a reader comes to regard a page with figures as a reliable account of fact.

In that case, the artist Velázquez interests me insofar as he dealt with similar problems in his own painting. My book, then, is an attempt to respond to the problems of representation that he proposed, but I have added some more layers. The layer of history, of the multiple Velázquian versions, of reproductions of his work in publications from different time periods, and other historical developments. And today, one of those layers is the difficulty involved in actually seeing what is in reproduced paintings, even in high-quality art books.

AJ In a way, what you are thinking about is the function of the book itself. For example, when you sprinkle talcum powder on a book about Matisse, you restore the opacity of the work that the book aimed to eliminate by explaining it. Right?

WC And Matisse, in a way, does the same with *L'Atelier rouge* [*The Red Studio*; 1911]. When he painted the entire studio and all the objects in it a dominant color, what he wanted to do was restore painting's chromatic opacity. He was aware of the fact that he was painting not a chair, but rather the imagination of a chair.

> *Matisse functioned according to the modern aesthetic of invention. His task
> was not to offer us an effective simulacrum of the world, its pictorial double,
> but to give the world a different reality: the reality of painting. Caldas, on the
> other hand, like many contemporary artists, operates within the logic of
> Borges: a mode of materializing, of lending a tangible body to the complex
> world of meaning in which we are all immersed; layers and layers of meaning
> that pile up, one on top of the other, successively, in a movement that knows no
> end, as in the library of Babel that Borges envisioned—the infinite reality of
> culture, the specular image of our intellectual universe and sole truth.*

# WORKING IN THE CITY
## An intimate horizon

*From his earliest maquettes in 1965, Caldas aspired to the architectural in his
work, wanting to give body to imaginary spaces, as if he himself were a kind
of Borgesian architect. At that time, however, it was naive to think that a
young man scarcely twenty years old could hope to build structures measuring
200 square meters in the middle of the city. That was an order of utopian
proportions. Now, that youthful utopia has become reality.*

AJ At a certain point in our conversation you told me that you felt comfortable
working on an urban scale because from the beginning of your career your
work aspired to that dimension and because in some way all of your pieces,
even those of architectural proportions, retain a kind of intimacy. And that
ostensible contradiction interests me, because it isn't always so easy to move
from the object produced in the studio to the scale that the city demands.

WC Charlie Chaplin said something that, I think, fits this situation very well: "If
what you're doing is funny, you don't have to be funny doing it." What matters
isn't whether you build something big or small; what matters is building it the
right size. In my case, placing a work of art in an urban space always seemed to
be an issue of creating a dialogue with the scale of that place. I don't necessarily
see sculpture as a decoration. I've never seen it as something that comes from
the outside, from the world of culture, to impose itself on the urban milieu.
In the case of the sculpture I did in Rio de Janeiro, in 1996, I placed it in a space
that people really didn't care much about, a traffic island in the middle of a
street [Fig. 36].

AJ That was possible, too, because you were able to pick the space for your
intervention.

WC I picked it, yes, because my intention was not to make a sculpture but to build
a place. It was like giving an imaginary solution to a relatively unknown corner of the city, a place that was almost invisible to most people. And that's
why, for me, the notion of "use" doesn't quite tell the full story in a situation
like this. And when I talk about finding an imaginary solution, I am talking
about the fact that the main disadvantage of creating a public work is that it is

excessively visible, and all the time. The public does not choose to see it or not see it; it's always there, always present. This is why I feel convinced that such work should not shout, but rather whisper, because all urban landmarks—buildings, for example—already possess eloquence as a result of their size, their façades, the very presence of their architecture, the way they reflect the sun, etc. To say nothing of the symbolic value that many of them possess; nowadays there are so many tall buildings that are truly iconic. My work, in contrast, comes from a softer form; it speaks in a whisper. Its eloquence lies in the evidence of its presence.

<sup>AJ</sup> That's what I like about the Rio piece. Each time I see it I feel that it is the materialization, in real space, of two points on a map, do you know what I mean? As if that had been your only action: to point out a place in the city from a map.

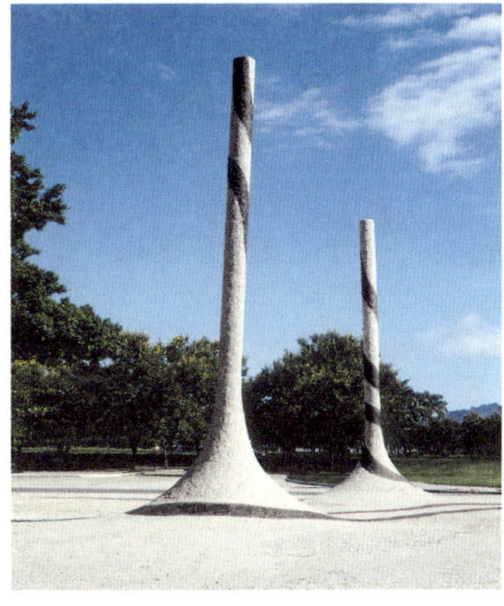

<sup>WC</sup> And in a way, that's what I did. It's one thing to place an object there, and another thing to establish a relationship, a tension between two elements of the same work, which is what happens there. The consequence of that tension is that the space between those two forms becomes a third element.

<sup>AJ</sup> From the beginning, one feels the need to compare them.

Fig. 36. *Escultura para o Rio* [*Sculpture for Rio*], 1996. Located at Av. Beira Mar, Rio de Janeiro, Brazil.

<sup>WC</sup> And then one finds a single line that envelops both, and it does this as if taking off from the ground, from that cobblestone street that is like the city's skin. What I wanted to do was create a sculpture that, despite its size, could radiate a kind of lightness, and that could lend that place a visual autonomy.

<sup>AJ</sup> Because, in fact, one doesn't perceive it as just some object deposited on that particular spot in the city; it feels like an anomaly that somehow occurred there. And in that sense, I think this is one of your most accomplished pieces.

<sup>WC</sup> There are others that also seek to create a place, like *A passagem* [*The Passage*; 2009], in Santiago de Compostela [Fig. 37]. Belvis park, where I envisioned it, is in the middle of the city, but at the same time it is a neutral space. In Santiago

de Compostela, the mystical and the religious are present on every single corner. This is why, when conceiving this piece, I imagined it as something located inside a chapel for those who have no gods, a chapel where people could, quite simply, reflect on everything, because I always remember something Paul Valéry said, about being a mystic without God. So what I did was deconstruct a chapel, but without any specific symbolism. The place that emerged was related to the nature of the city in which it was located.

The construction comprises one level of stone and a wall, the basic elements of any architectural structure, and there is a door that's always open, and a space where you can see a higher floor, but completely dispossessed of any mystical character. And this occurs, at least partly, because this is an open house in the middle of the landscape. There is a construction-related detail, too, which is that part of the piece is made in dark marble, reflecting the visitor as a mirror might. That reflecting wall is accompanied by another, more defiant wall, which passes by, reflecting an essential quality of Santiago: that of being a city of transit. At the same time, I don't think there's any doubt that we are talking about a work that occupies that site temporarily, as if it were a kind of inhabiting-of-place.

The relationship that is established between any structure I build and the landscape it occupies is always of paramount importance to me. When I was invited to create a sculpture in Norway, in 1994, I was given the chance to do interventions in several cities. I visited some of them, a trip that allowed me to identify a new quality that justified my intervention: I observed that, unlike Brazil, which is an immense country with huge cities situated at great distances

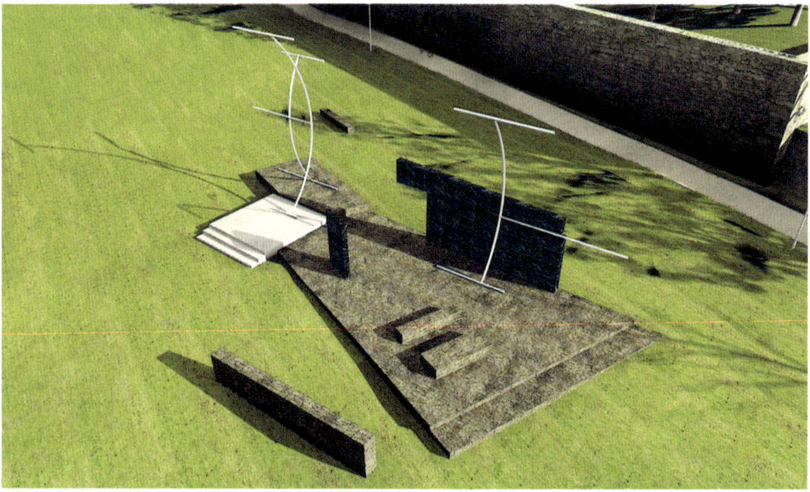

Fig. 37. *A passagem* [*The Passage*], 2009 (digital maquette).

from one another, Norway has many small cities in very close proximity to one another. Sometimes, the distance between two cities is fifteen kilometers, so that from an airplane, at night, you can see lights everywhere. And yet, I also felt that the distances between houses in those cities were surprisingly greater than the distances between homes in Brazil.

At first I had to wonder how it was possible that, with such tightly packed cities, people's dwellings could be so spread out, but after living with these people for a few days, I understood that in reality they lived as close together as they could. That difference between living far apart in contiguous cities opened me up to a whole new notion of scale. It was a scale of emotion, and it helped me to see that they had found a balance between the proximity of their cities and the intimacy of their homes. So what I did was to take into account that scale I was discovering rather than the one I had brought with me.

AJ And so that was the factor that made you decide to situate the work between two cities?

WC Yes, exactly, and moreover *Omkring* [*Around*; 1994] is installed on a precipice from which the sculpture projects out into space [Fig. 38], as if I had incorporated the cliff where it is located as one more characteristic of its placement. The place is a crag, and when you look at it from the side, the work seems very large and long, but when you look at it head-on, it seems to be much closer. So the notion of scale is different from two different sides of the work and recalls the relationship I perceived between the distances that separated the cities and the distances between people's homes. And furthermore, the dimension you experience with the body is different from the dimension you experience with the gaze. It is a sculpture with many points of view; almost a device for perspective projected onto the landscape. On one side, vertigo, and on the other, abyss.

*Espelho rápido* [*Fast Mirror*; 2005] is the same kind of public artwork. It's in Porto Alegre, on the banks of the Guaíba River, which flows quite slowly in that spot. And so the work is in dialogue with the water's movement. That is how I came to envision an imaginary transversal mirror able to reflect in every direction: horizontally, vertically, and in depth [Fig. 39].

AJ Could we consider it a mirror of the third kind?

WC Yes, but you have to have a certain aloofness when it comes to my mirrors, because they don't function mechanically. If I speak of type B mirrors, it's not because there necessarily exists a type A. In reality there is no such thing as a

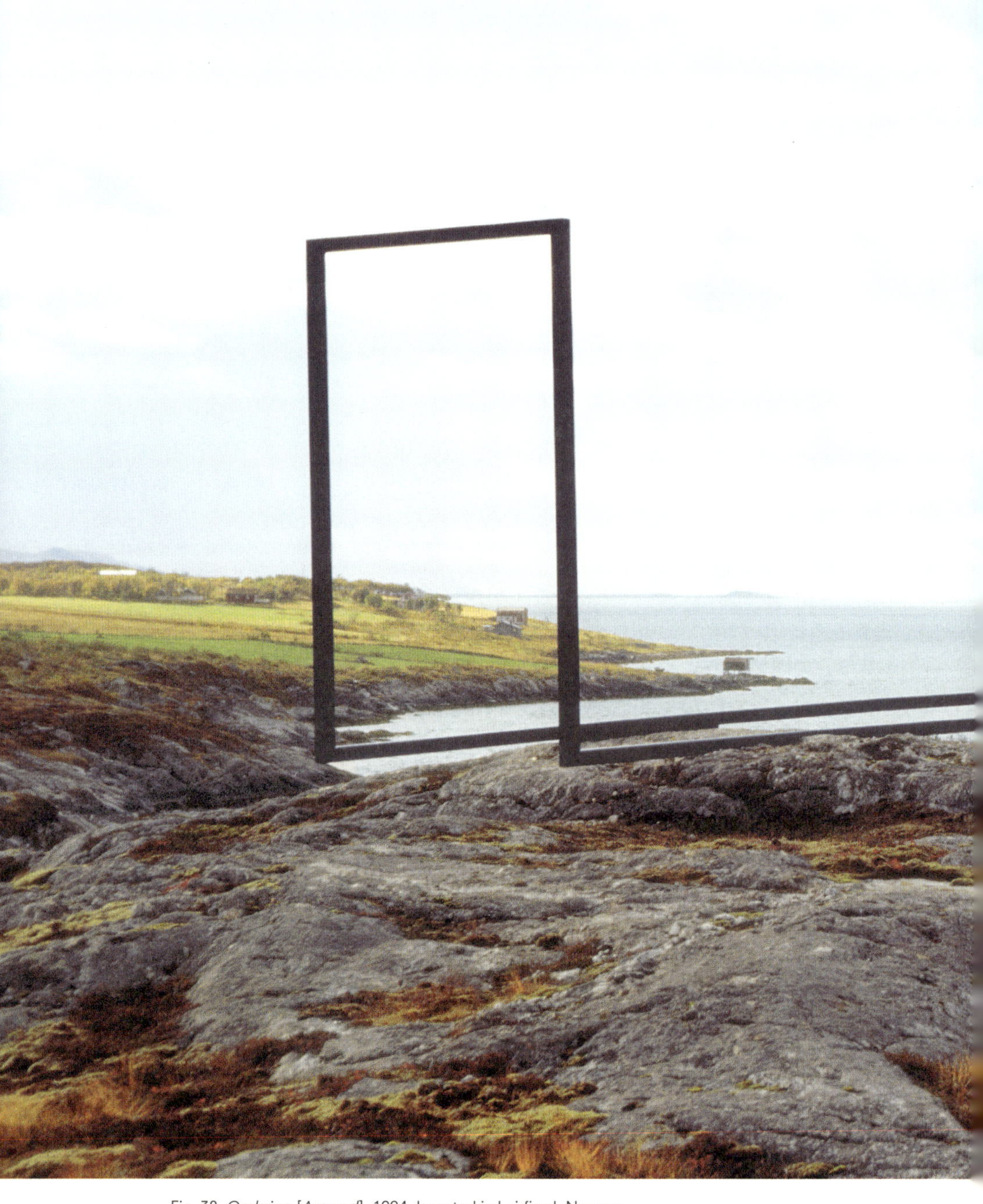

Fig. 38. *Omkring* [*Around*], 1994. Located in Leirfjord, Norway.

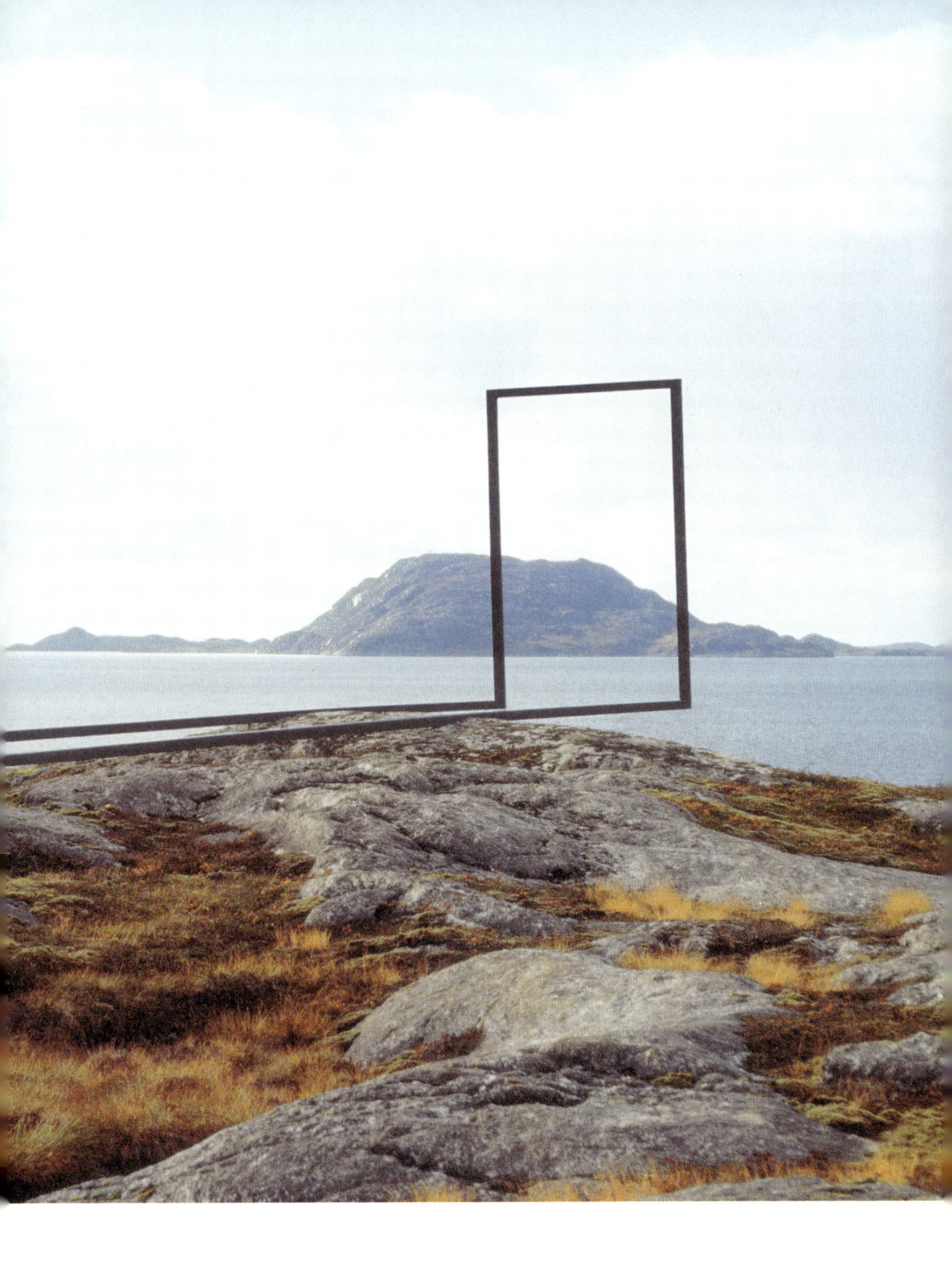

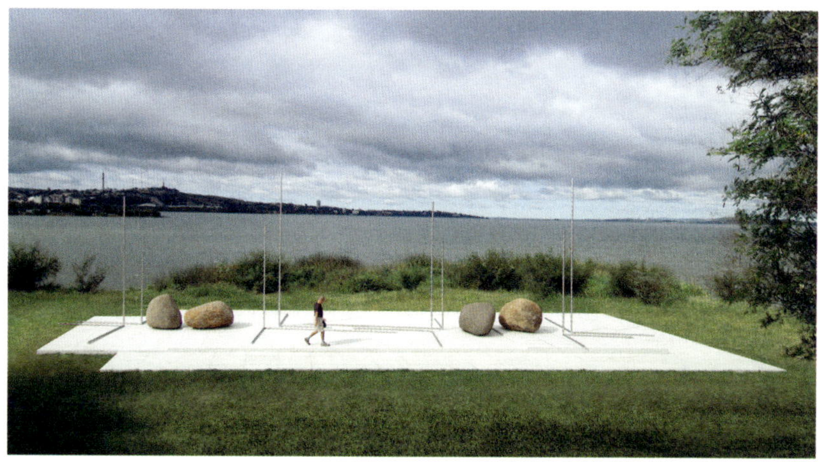

Fig. 39. *Espelho rápido* [*Fast Mirror*], 2005. Located in Mauricio Sirotsky Sobrinho Park, Porto Alegre, Brazil.

type A mirror. All I mean is that you can have other kinds of mirrors, or mirrors that operate in a different way. It's like saying that the mirror is not just an object but various types of objects. The black mirror, like the Aztecs' mirror, for example, has an atypical way of reflecting, because what happens in that mirror is very different from what we may observe in transparent mirrors. Its answer is of another order. But there are other mirrors, still, like the ones Borges described, that function in special ways when nobody sees them. Borges suggests that very late at night, when nobody is in the room, inside the mirrors you can hear the sound of weapons. What I like about those descriptions is the possibility of imagining a different function for mirrors. I always ask myself, it is possible to build a mirror if we have only partial notions of what mirrors really are?

AJ Or just verbal notions?

WC Yes, and even those mirrors that, when reaching the end of their lifespan, begin to function in a different way—like those old mirrors that no longer reflect anything but that people put in their homes as a kind of decorative element.

AJ They continue to be called mirrors and retain their external appearance, but no longer work as such, they no longer work at all.

WC That makes me think that mirrors are metaphors for the art object—a mirror that denies viewers their own reflection, returning their image with a surprising answer. I did another mirror that was turned around to face the wall. It was a black sheet, made of cardboard, with a hole in the middle, exposing the wall [see Fig. 19]. That mirror brought the wall into the foreground in two different ways: first, by creating the wall in its own image, and second, by hanging on the wall. And the mere presence of a support suggests that it ought to be hung in order for it to fulfill its reflective function. As if we could activate and deactivate it, and in doing so see ourselves in different ways.

AJ Let's talk now about *O formato cego* [*The Blind Format*; 1978–82], which is the first urban-scale work you did. It's important for us to talk about because, of all that we've seen up until now, that work seems to be the closest thing to what we might call a sculpture, an object in space, and not the creation of a place [Fig. 40].

WC What happens in this case is that it's located in a very windy spot. Because of this I wanted to build a sculpture that would offer very little resistance to the wind—a mass filled with nothing more than the edge of the space. What I was aiming for with the title was to suggest that it wasn't the object itself that interested me, but its format, its function.

AJ And yet, when you read "blind" in the title, you tend to think of this structure as an eye, or a lens.

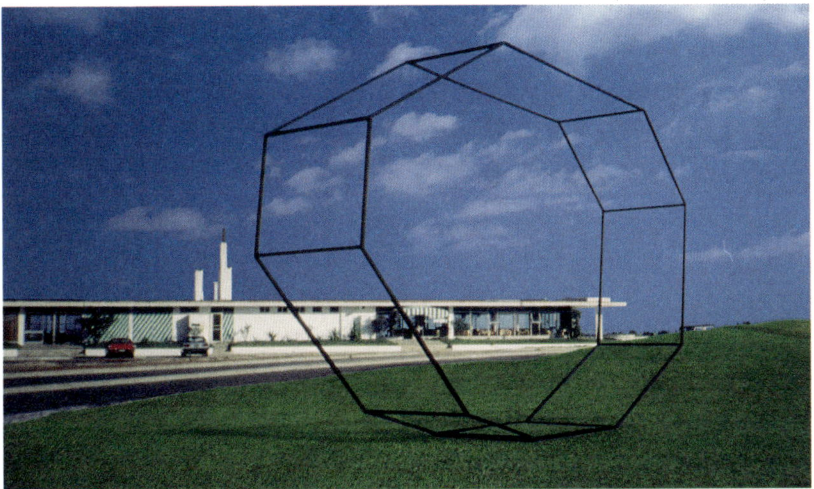

Fig. 40. *O formato cego* [The *Blind Format*], 1978–82. Located in Paseo de Las Américas, Punta del Este, Uruguay.

<sup>WC</sup> Maybe, but what motivated me was the formal dissolution of the object, its disappearance or its reduction to a simple functional mechanism. I have always been intrigued by the issue of blindness, the fact that blind people cannot see black. Borges said that he felt nostalgia for black, because people who cannot see live submerged in a kind of gray fog. In his letter about the blind, Diderot told the story of a man, blind from birth, whose sight was restored when he was an adult. What most surprised me about this testimony was that the blind man was very surprised to discover that his room was much smaller than the world. Might blindness possess its own space and scale?

<sup>AJ</sup> That's the path that takes us to language, because for a person who learned to see, read, and speak at the same time, the shape of a cube and the word *cube* go together. But for someone who learns the word independently from its visual aspect, things don't necessarily happen like that. And that was one of the questions that Diderot posed: he wanted to know whether or not a blind person, when presented with a cube, would recognize the appropriate word for naming it. He wondered if by touching a cube a person could know the appropriate word to describe it.

<sup>WC</sup> Listening to you I suddenly remembered something that Francis Ponge once said, that the word *sculpture* ought to be banished from all dictionaries. The idea that it is easier to speak about what a sculpture is by believing in empty spaces is very interesting, and maybe more true, too.

# INITIAL ASTONISHMENTS
## Responding to the stimuli of the world

AJ We have talked about your work as a collection of objects that come together in nuclei, seemingly bonded together by a secret affinity to form little planetary systems. Those planets or nuclei of meaning, however, do not rotate around a central axis, but rather slowly configure a multistellar structure that is variable and, more important, always open to the possibility of new nuclei forming and gathering, modifying the general configuration of the whole group. The system works, at least in your case, to explain the relationships that are established between your individual works, beyond the analogies of form or style that hound you, above and beyond even their chronological order. And yet there are times when I become convinced that many of these problems share a common origin. For this reason I would like to circle back and go a bit deeper into the early years of your education, because I sense that they are the source of the experiences that define this mode of operation, the obsessions that in some way force you to tackle certain topics and that definitely connect back to the early experiences of an individual confronting the world.

WC The earliest memory I have of what might be called an epiphany has to do with the discovery of the reproduction, to scale, of the first airplane created by a Brazilian, Santos-Dumont. That replica, installed around 1954 or 1955 in the hall of the airport of the same name, had a huge effect on me. Perhaps at the time I did not understand why this object moved me so deeply, but I think now I do. It wasn't just an object with angles, cords, wheels, made of fabric, with an engine; it was also the creation of a function. In reality this was the object that invented flying, or the possibility of flight [see Fig. 6].

AJ But that is clearly a retrospective gaze. At the time you couldn't possibly have understood it, much less formulate it in these terms.

WC No, I couldn't understand it, of course not. But in some way that encounter had such an impact on me that I built several airplane models in my house. I made them out of paper, balsa wood, and cardboard. I would say that I spent a fair portion of my childhood building and rebuilding that model. But it had an additional influence on me, because it showed me that I could make my own models. I remember, for example, once making a television camera—a type of machine that impressed me very much, because it was such a huge contraption, with wheels, and the person who handled it had another huge apparatus in the front. From this cardboard camera I moved on to a miniature television studio, with sets and furniture. And now I look back and think that the maquettes I made in response to those major events helped me to reproduce how I felt when I saw them. And maybe that's how and why I discovered the possibility of responding to the stimuli of the world. If what I wanted was to understand the world, maybe this was the first inkling I had that I could understand it through models and representations. Making something was like a new creative and personal freedom. And that's why I say that when I was given the chance to work in an urban space, I really did feel quite comfortable, because it was like going back to an initial sense of wonderment.

AJ And surely as you did the work, you tried to understand the impression that object had made upon you.

WC The child responds to things in a very pure, objective form, with no speculation of any kind. He is always, as Rilke would say, facing the open. But now I am certain that something in this invention of flight, created by an object that our own hands can manufacture, changed my life.

AJ I wonder, even, if the discovery of a machine capable of taking off and freeing us from the land on which we live didn't become for you a kind of metaphor for liberation—one that was more general, historical, like the freedom of breaking out of that anachronism that has weighed so heavily upon our collective historical imagination.

WC I don't know if, as Latin Americans, we all share the same desperation that comes from anachronism. I believe that our desperations are different. Each country has its own idiosyncratic way of responding to those problems, and its own time, too. Some days ago I was listening to an interview with Ferreira Gullar about the days of the dictatorship, and he mentioned something that I think is especially important. He said that unlike the dictatorships in Chile and Argentina, which began as aggressive tyrannies from the very start, the Brazilian dictatorship took four years to reach the same level of aggression, with its repression and tortures. We seem to have had significant differences in the way we reacted to difficult times. I don't know, either, if I could express very well what I felt during that time.

In any event, what I do think is true is that I was incorporating, by then, the idea of creating my own artistic expressivity. As an adolescent, I wanted to express myself—I needed to—and art gave me a new possibility for that, and a facility for expression. It was difficult to be an artist in Brazil; there were very few opportunities for us, and we had very few models to serve as references. This was why, as we discussed earlier, each of us had to invent his or her own idea of the artist. And maybe the encounter with Santos-Dumont's plane, its elaborate configuration with bits of fabric and wood, made up of those ordered cubic forms, intrigued me to the point that I really wondered how it was possible that such an object could actually take flight. What I'm saying is that its strange configuration is what I was so drawn to. Yet clearly that concern with escaping anachronism was present; it was and continues to be fundamental. And you could sense this in artists like Oiticica, Clark, and Serpa.

Another factor that had a strong impact on my aesthetic education—all of these things occurred simultaneously, by the way—was that Brasilia was under construction, and my father, who was an engineer, spoke endlessly about this new city. And also, of course, I recall the visits to his studio, where I could see models of modern buildings. There were also many designs of modern homes on his desk, and I would almost say that he spent his entire life leaning over his drawing table, calculating those structures that supported what he called "modern audacities." He almost seemed to believe that the job of the engineer was to lend structure to those delusions. It is no coincidence that one of [Oscar] Niemeyer's architects was the great poet Joaquim Cardoso.

Also, there is the fact that the house we lived in, which my father built, responded to or incorporated some of the principles that he considered to be modern: the house was distributed over the available space rather than occupying the center of the parcel of land it sat on, and you reached it by way of a ramp. So this home responded to certain characteristics that, today, I identify as forming part of modern architecture.

The construction of Brasilia was meaningful for a whole generation of us, and I, at the age of eight, lived and breathed that "modern" spirit. The famous quote by Mário Pedrosa, that "Brazilians are condemned to be modern," was a reality. We were all witness to the first strains of bossa nova, a music that was completely different from the samba we were accustomed to, because it had a new, fresh kind of spatiality, almost as if it had been dreamed up to be played outdoors. If you think about it, any piece at all by Antônio Carlos Jobim always produces that agreeable feeling of having been made for someone who wants to play music outside, looking out over the landscape, the horizon.

AJ A transparency?

WC A transparency, yes, with the presence of shadows and fresh water, in a way. When I am in a restaurant in New York, for example, and they put a bossa nova samba on, I sometimes feel that enclosed space suddenly opening up, maybe because I have experienced that feeling before. So we always live with that feeling of wide open borders, broad horizons. Le Corbusier said that Brazil was the only country that had an intimate horizon. On the other hand, we also lived with the sensation that Brazil was constantly under construction. Meaning, we had not been given a finished country, but one that we had to constantly remake.

AJ That's very interesting, because if there is one thing that is key to modern and contemporary art, it is precisely that way of being open to the possible . . .

WC Yes, it's just that *our* possible has always been more surprising, more unknown. But there is still another curious thing that may well have influenced some of my first pieces in the 1960s: the almost weekly visits I would pay to a fakir. He lived inside a huge glass box, atop a bed of nails, with some snakes inside. He was called Silk, and if you think about it, this was a very comical name because he lived with so few comforts. I asked my father to take me once a week to visit this fakir. He was on the first floor of a movie theater that showed 3D movies, the kind you needed special glasses to watch. He hardly moved at all, his gestures were very slow, and I was very taken with all that [Fig. 41].

Maybe one day I will understand why this had such an impact on me, but the fact is that I constantly asked myself how this man could live like that, all alone (or almost), because in fact he was protected from the public not by a thick, opaque veil but by a transparent sheet of glass. So he shared his intimacy, his destiny with the public. And they would silently watch this quiet figure go without food for one hundred days. And I saw this fakir as a metaphor for the man who manages to survive any circumstance at all. It was incredible to me that a man could survive such extreme conditions. Santos-Dumont's airplane, a city built for the modern future, the 3D movie theater, and that fakir—they are all scattered fragments in my mind's eye. There are so many other things I have forgotten, and I don't know why these have stuck and others have not.

AJ Don't you think there might be a metaphor there for your historical situation in the Brazil of those days? In my mind I can't help but see in that fakir the image

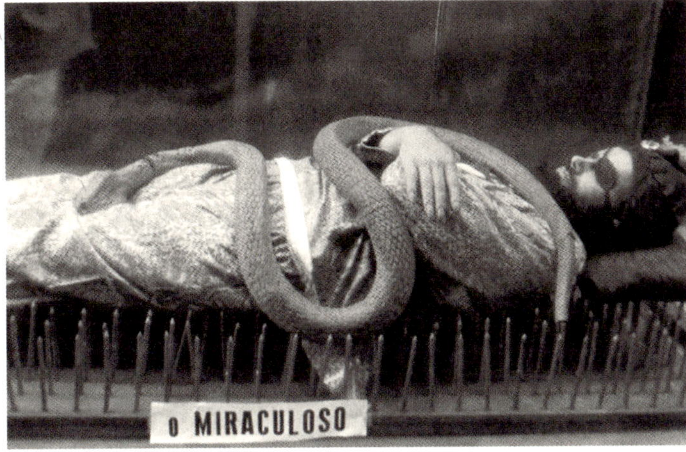


Fig. 41. Silk, fakir in the central zone of São Paulo, n.d.

of someone being trapped inside a hostile reality, and in Santos-Dumont's air-plane and the construction of Brasilia, images of liberation.

wc Absolutely. Looking back now, it all seems so coherent to me, but at the time I was so young—and I think art is not exactly a prerogative for children. Art emerges from an adult need for language, when you need to invent a destiny for yourself and respond to the world by changing it. Perhaps I have learned that we will always see what we still don't see, and that process is something that never ends.

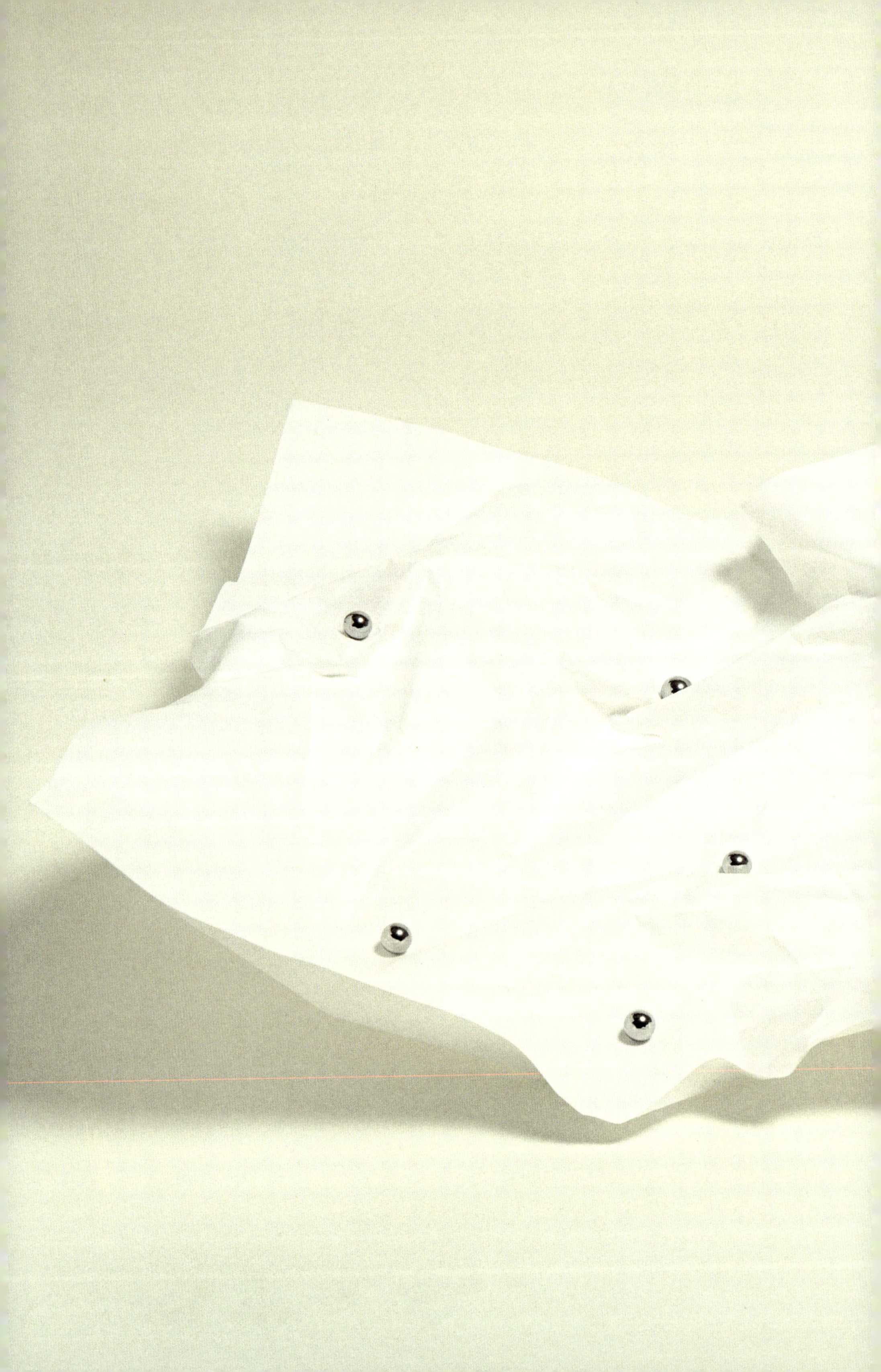

# INTRODUCCIÓN

Quien haya tenido la fortuna de conversar con Waltercio Caldas se habrá dado cuenta enseguida de su excepcional don para expresarse verbalmente. El lenguaje es en definitiva uno de los temas centrales en su práctica artística, tanto como metáfora de la comunicación en general, como, más concretamente, en la incorporación de las palabras en su obra. Los títulos que le atribuye a sus trabajos a menudo son muy poéticos y sugerentes, y el formato de libro ha sido uno de sus predilectos durante décadas. Por ello, producir un libro con sus palabras sobre arte es una labor tan apropiada como desafiante. Por mucho que Caldas aprecie el lenguaje, es muy consciente de los riesgos que implica usar la palabra para intentar explicar o sustituir la experiencia visual de los objetos en sí mismos. Conoce bien el peligro inherente al uso del lenguaje para tratar de esclarecer una obra cuando en realidad suele ser un sustituto mediocre de esa magia que solo el ojo puede percibir.

Los temas cubiertos en estas conversaciones entre Caldas y Ariel Jiménez van desde espejos y maquetas hasta música e historia. Nos hablan de pasiones por Velázquez y el jazz, el encuentro temprano con una maqueta del primer avión en el aeropuerto de Río de Janeiro, y de su fascinación con un faquir indio. Por amplios que sean los intereses de Caldas, podemos observar cómo ha surgido cada uno de ellos y los ha incorporado a su obra durante su larga y prolífica trayectoria.

Los títulos en la serie Conversaciones / Conversations suelen seguir un orden cronológico, de la infancia de cada uno de los artistas al presente. Sin embargo Caldas se resistió a esta estructura desde el inicio, pues el desarrollo de su carrera artística se puede entender mejor como una suerte de espiral más que una línea recta, con muchos intereses y propósitos que reaparecen cada cierto tiempo, creando así una compleja red de conexiones. Por ello este volumen sigue un eje más temático, explorando las preguntas recurrentes del artista a lo largo de varias décadas.

Para esta publicación Caldas ha diseñado una serie de intervenciones como un guiño a su frecuente uso del libro como un medio artístico. El lector se encontrará con imágenes y páginas que irrumpen ligeramente nuestra expectativa sobre cómo una publicación presenta información sobre un objeto visual. Los gestos son sutiles, pero el argumento que subrayan –que las fotografías de los objetos no sustituyen al objeto mismo– es explorado de distintas maneras durante su carrera, desde el *Manual da ciencia popular* hasta *Velázquez*.

Estamos sumamente agradecidos con Waltercio Caldas por su compromiso y su voluntad de participar activamente en todos los aspectos de esta publicación y su producción. Ariel Jiménez demostró una vez más ser un interlocutor generoso y riguroso, ofreciendo una profunda comprensión del proceso intelectual de Caldas sin dejar de desafiar muchos de los lugares comunes sobre la abstracción y la forma que frecuentemente aparecen en la historia del arte brasileño. Estamos particularmente entusiasmados con el ensayo introductorio a este libro de Guy Brett, pues él fue uno de los primeros y más perceptivos entusiastas del trabajo de Caldas, e introdujo su trabajo a una audiencia internacional.

Patricia Vasconcellos proporcionó un invaluable apoyo en todas las etapas del proyecto. Del equipo de la CPPC me gustaría agradecer a Ileen Kohn y Donna Wingate por su cuidadosa coordinación editorial, y a Lucia | Marquand por sus excepcionales estándares de diseño y producción. Una vez más, Kristina Cordero realizó una excelente traducción para este volumen, como también lo hizo Mariana Barrera Pieck con el ensayo de Guy Brett, y mi agradecimiento para Michelle Piranio y María Esther Pino por su detallada corrección de estilo.

*Gabriel Pérez-Barreiro*
*Director y curador jefe, Colección Patricia Phelps de Cisneros*

# TOMÁNDOSE LIBERTADES

"Las cualidades características del trabajo creativo de Waltercio Caldas –inteligencia, precisión, prolijidad, su ironía fina e impecable ejecución– están presentes en cada pieza sin excepción alguna".[1]

La generosa valoración de Frederico Morais ciertamente suena acertada. A esta lista yo añadiría "refinamiento", y también "humor", el cual en ocasiones muestra cierto parentesco con el de Marcel Duchamp. La paradoja es que a estas cualidades ha llegado por un proceso de negación. Lo negativo puede ser una gran fuerza creativa, particularmente en el trabajo de Waltercio Caldas. Tal como lo expresa Paulo Venancio Filho, en el texto *NO,* uno de los más bellos ejemplos que yo conozca de la integración de las formas de un artista con la palabra escrita. Se mezclan perfectamente. Van las primeras siete líneas del texto:

### "NO"

*El trabajo insiste persistentemente en ser una frontera. Insiste aún más en reducir la frontera que es. Quiere borrar sus bordes, su constitución misma. Borrarse a sí mismo y, de nuevo, borrarse a sí mismo, que es el dispositivo mismo. De esta forma, puede seguir ignorando todo lo que sugiere definirlo. Su definición se expresa cada vez más en negativo. No es ni esto ni aquello. Quizás no quiera ser, pues su existencia está al lado de su no existencia. "No" es la palabra que representa el trabajo.*[2]

En este libro de entrevistas y conversaciones con Ariel Jiménez, un interlocutor muy perspicaz, Caldas describe la evolución de su trabajo. Su tono es profundo y honesto, percibe su camino hacia adelante como una experiencia personal y trabaja con sus propias reglas. Nunca es rígido ni dogmático. El proceso de inventarse a sí mismo como artista no estuvo motivado por la búsqueda de un *estilo,* "sino estimulando la necesidad de comprender lo que pasaba en las cosas que producíamos".[3] "Porque ahí reside la paradoja –de acuerdo con

---

1. Frederico Morais, *Aberto Fechado: Caixa e Livro na Arte Brasileira* (São Paulo: Pinacoteca do Estado de São Paulo, 2013), p. 82.

2. Paulo Venancio, "NO," en *Transcontinental: Nine Latin American Artists*, trans. Florence Eleanor Irvin (Londres: Verso, 1990), p. 66.

3. *Waltercio Caldas in Conversation with/en conversación con Ariel Jiménez*, p. 31. A menos que se indique lo contrario, todas las citas de Caldas han sido tomadas de estas entrevistas.

Caldas–: en esa osadía de los artistas para concebir objetos que no existían, pero que ahora están ahí, delante de nosotros, como una realidad inventada".[4]

La primera vez que vi uno de dichos objetos fue en 1986 en el departamento de Waltercio Caldas, en el entonces nuevo "desarrollo" de grandes torres que trastocaban la campiña y playa del sur de Río de Janeiro. Caldas adoptó irónicamente este estilo de vida aspiracional y consumista, al tiempo que mantuvo vivo su apego a la negación como un instrumento de libertad. De acuerdo con mis notas en el diario que mantuve durante ese viaje, el departamento era "una suerte de no–lugar suspendido" y las obras ahí creadas eran "cosa y no cosa, objeto o sombra, ninguna forma, auto–negación. . ." El objeto que Caldas me mostró era un bloque de granito de 30 × 24 × 10 centímetros, con las esquinas de arriba y abajo redondeadas, y estas últimas funcionando como patas, como en una caja o un mueble. Estaba casualmente colocado en el suelo, y recuerdo que una parte cubría la alfombra persa que Waltercio tenía en sus habitaciones. El bloque era elocuente y mudo a la vez. Quizás por eso siempre lo recuerdo como un enigma. Lo veías en un instante y después desaparecía. Lo volvías a ver constantemente. Esta es la clase de objeto que no es bueno observar por mucho tiempo, que se mantendrá en el instante preciso en el que fue observado por primera vez.

Caldas se burla sutilmente de las expectativas del espectador. Como Duchamp, genera "un nuevo pensamiento para el objeto". Ambos usan objetos ordinarios como vehículo para sus ideas; sin embargo sus sensibilidades son muy distintas. Caldas alcanza una pureza excepcional. Sus objetos son siempre sorprendentes y, en ocasiones, de una simplicidad devastadora, como en el caso de la obra temprana *Prato comum com elasticos* [*Plato ordinario con ligas*, 1978; Fig. 1], la cual consta de dos bandas de goma estiradas sobre un plato blanco. Este objeto, incluso la fotografía del mismo, transmite una sensación indescriptible de espacio. Aunque hay un elemento de sátira social en esta y otras piezas de ese periodo, Caldas parece estar buscando la gran expansión de la naturaleza, el espacio en el sentido cosmológico.

Un rasgo característico y notable del arte de Caldas son sus libros. Son muchos y sorprendentemente diversos. No parecen ser una subdivisión de su producción artística sino la continuación de sus ideas sobre el objeto. Son libros–objeto. Detrás de la diversidad de materiales empleados se encuentra la perspicacia de Caldas como el apasionado coleccionista que es. Durante una de mis visitas a la casa que había adquirido en Río me mostró su biblioteca con orgullo,

4. Ibid., p. 46.

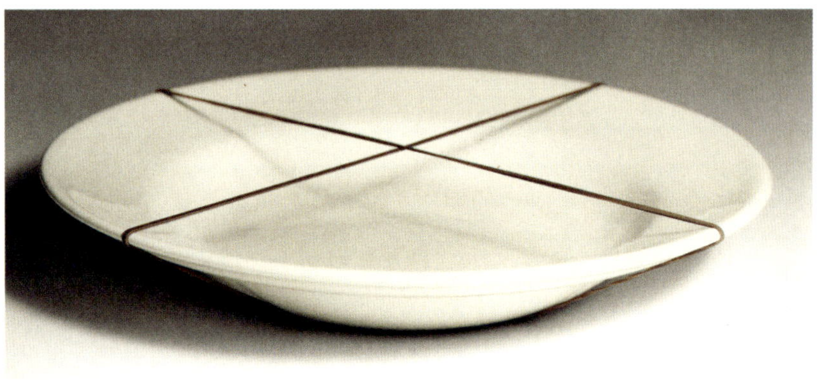

Fig. 1. *Prato comum com elasticos* [*Plato ordinario con ligas*], 1978.

la cual incluía su colección de fotografía brasileña temprana, impresiones de revistas satíricas de Brasil y literatura de vanguardia europea.

El formato de libro resultó especialmente fascinante para los artistas brasileños en las décadas de 1950 a 1970, porque generaba un clima de cuestionamientos de carácter fuertemente interdisciplinario. Este fue interpretado por figuras tales como el físico Mario Schenberg, quien adoraba la obra de Mira Schendel y escribió elocuentemente sobre ella, el crítico de arte y teórico político Mário Pedrosa, cuya comprensión y apoyo fueron esenciales para Lygia Clark, Hélio Oiticica y otros, Haroldo de Campos, pionero de la poesía visual y estudioso de la literatura, y Ferreira Gullar, poeta y activista, quien describe muy bien sus luchas artísticas e intelectuales en otro libro de la serie Conversaciones/ Conversations.[5]

Los libros–objeto de Waltercio Caldas ciertamente pueden enmarcarse dentro de ese clima de cuestionamientos, cuyo espectro era enorme y abarcaba, por ejemplo, la versión en libro de Lygia Clark de su obra participativa *Livro-Obra* [*Libro-Obra*; 1964–83], así como el *Livro de carne* [*Libro de carne*; 1978–79] de Artur Barrio, en el cual las páginas son sangrientas rebanadas de carne. Este trabajo de Barrio se exhibe como tres impresiones fotográficas y un texto. La dicotomía entre el carácter participativo y práctico del libro de Clark y el de ciertos artistas, Caldas en particular, cuyos libros–objeto no pueden ser tocados, persiste. De hecho ambos producen un cambio en la apreciación de lo que puede ser un libro: tocarlo constituiría trastornar su balance estético. Esto lo trasmite sutilmente en el libro–objeto *Matisse, talco* [1978] [véase p. 198], una de las obras más conocidas de Waltercio, en la que el talco, esparcido sobre las páginas abiertas

5. Ariel Jiménez, *Ferreira Gullar in conversation with/en conversación con Ariel Jiménez* (New York: Fundacion Cisneros, 2012).

de un libro de arte sobre Matisse, puede percibirse como muy susceptible a ser perturbado. Uno esperaría poder manipular los libros, pero los de Caldas son puramente visuales: abiertos a doble página como regularmente se muestran en museos y exhibiciones en bibliotecas (el libro *Velázquez* [1996] [véase p. 196] es una excepción, debe ser visto página por página y sin embargo exhibe un estado constante, una sola decisión perceptiva).

Al encontrarse con *Matisse, talco,* el espectador experimenta el desconcierto de conjugar dos cosas que tal vez nunca antes se habían puesto juntas. Esto genera un tipo de humor particular basado en la incongruencia y la fluidez de significado. El procedimiento es familiar al Surrealismo "hermoso como el encuentro fortuito de un paraguas y una máquina de coser sobre una mesa de disección" (Comte de Lautréamont), y recibió un impulso en la era del Conceptualismo ("se puede hacer arte de cualquier cosa", o "un gran artista puede hacer arte con tan solo mirar" (Robert Smithson).[6]

A mi parecer, *Matisse, talco* es una reflexión sobre los materiales en general, y el modo como estos se usan en el arte. El talco está presente en todos los niveles, desde cubrir por completo el libro abierto hasta varias formas de atisbar la página impresa. El artista esparce el talco de manera distinta cada vez que la obra se exhibe. Se establece un vínculo con el momento del modernismo occidental en que el color se suspende en el blanco monocromático. En el proceso, el polvo se vuelve un instrumento gráfico sumamente refinado.

Una serie de principios de la década de los noventa lleva el intrigante título *O ar mais próximo* [*El aire más próximo*]. Estas piezas se elaboran quizás con la menor cantidad de recursos que cualquier otra obra de Caldas: simplemente hilos que configuran grandes curvas que flotan en el aire de la galería. Una vez más, el mínimo de material físico revela el máximo de energía espacial oculta, lo cual afecta profundamente nuestra definición de "la obra", tal como afirma el crítico de arte Paulo Sérgio Duarte: "La obra no está en donde pensamos que está: ni en las ideas que la alimentan, ni en la forma en que se materializa visualmente, sino en la tensión transparente que se genera entre lo que se me ha dado para ver y lo que se me ha dado para pensar".[7]

Dos desarrollos en la producción de Waltercio Caldas han cobrado fuerza en los últimos años y me parecen de particular importancia. En primer lugar, su profundización de la "exposición" como un conjunto compuesto, elaborado a partir de una selección de piezas individuales de distintas fechas, cada una con un significado como parte de un todo. El segundo es el constante incremento

6. Robert Smithson, "A Sedimentation of the Mind: Earth Projects", 1968, en *Robert Smithson: The Collected Writings*, ed. Jack Flam (Berkeley y Los Angeles: University of California Press, 1996), p. 112.

7. Paulo Sergio Duarte, *Waltercio Caldas* (São Paulo: Cosac Naify, 2001), p. 200.

del alcance de sus estructuras al aire libre, y sus relaciones y diferencias con obras concebidas para el interior. En la práctica, las obras al aire libre comienzan a incrementarse gradualmente, luego de que fue capaz de generar fondos suficientes para producir sus primeras dos esculturas exteriores: *O formato cego* [*El formato ciego*, 1978–82] [véase p. 217] en Uruguay, y *Jardim Instantâneo* [*Jardín instantáneo*; 1989] comisionado para un parque a las afueras de São Paulo.

A partir de allí, se inicia un diálogo fascinante en su trabajo entre el exterior y el interior, un proceso lleno de paradoja y transformación. *Jardim Instantâneo* se parece a una tarima, con vistas a un valle y unas colinas lejanas. "Un lugar invisible", según Caldas. También definió "la relación de mi obra con la línea del horizonte, la línea que no está en ninguna parte".[8] La mayoría de sus obras al aire libre se orientan horizontalmente (la excepción más notable a las obras de Caldas al aire libre alineadas horizontalmente es una comisionada para las calles de Río de Janeiro, *Escultura para o Río* [*Escultura para Río*, 1996] [véase p. 211]. La mirada es dirigida hacia arriba por un poderoso –y lúdico– vórtice que atrae hacia sí mismo todos los elementos del pavimento urbano, como un torbellino solidificado. La energía de la ciudad es devuelta con humor a la energía cósmica de la naturaleza). A pesar de que los materiales y las formas de estas, frecuentemente, son los mismos que los usados para su obra interior– plataformas, muros, tubos de acero, piedras–, la escala de estos elementos es radical pero sutilmente ajustada, no para dominar a lo humano o al paisaje sino para exaltar la respuesta emocional al lugar, al aire libre.

Son dispositivos de artificio inconfundible, que hacen referencia a la cultura y la construcción humana y sirven para acentuar la libertad y la apertura de los espacios al aire libre. Esta libertad espacial se siente fuertemente, incluso en las fotografías de la obra *in situ*. Una inserción particularmente audaz es la de cuatro figuras con forma de "jarra", su favorita, elaborada con tubos de acero sobre una plataforma de mármol ligeramente elevada en un hermoso valle cerca de Río de Janeiro, *Espelhos ausentes* [*Espejos ausentes*, 2003; Fig. 2], que responde perfectamente al deseo que Waltercio expresara alguna vez de hacer un objeto "con la máxima presencia y la máxima ausencia".[9] La apariencia de jarra se representa como un contorno de algo que en realidad no tiene contorno, mientras que el acero, al ser reflejante, otorga fluidez al contorno artificial mediante el reflejo de la luz. Los tubos condesan el azul del paisaje y el cielo circundante, y el continuo movimiento y sonido del río adyacente. El recipiente está vacío, precisamente, para poder llenarse de la naturaleza que lo rodea.

8. Guy Brett, *Transcontinental: Nine Latin American Artists* (Londres: Verso, 1990), p. 71.
9. Ibid., p. 70.

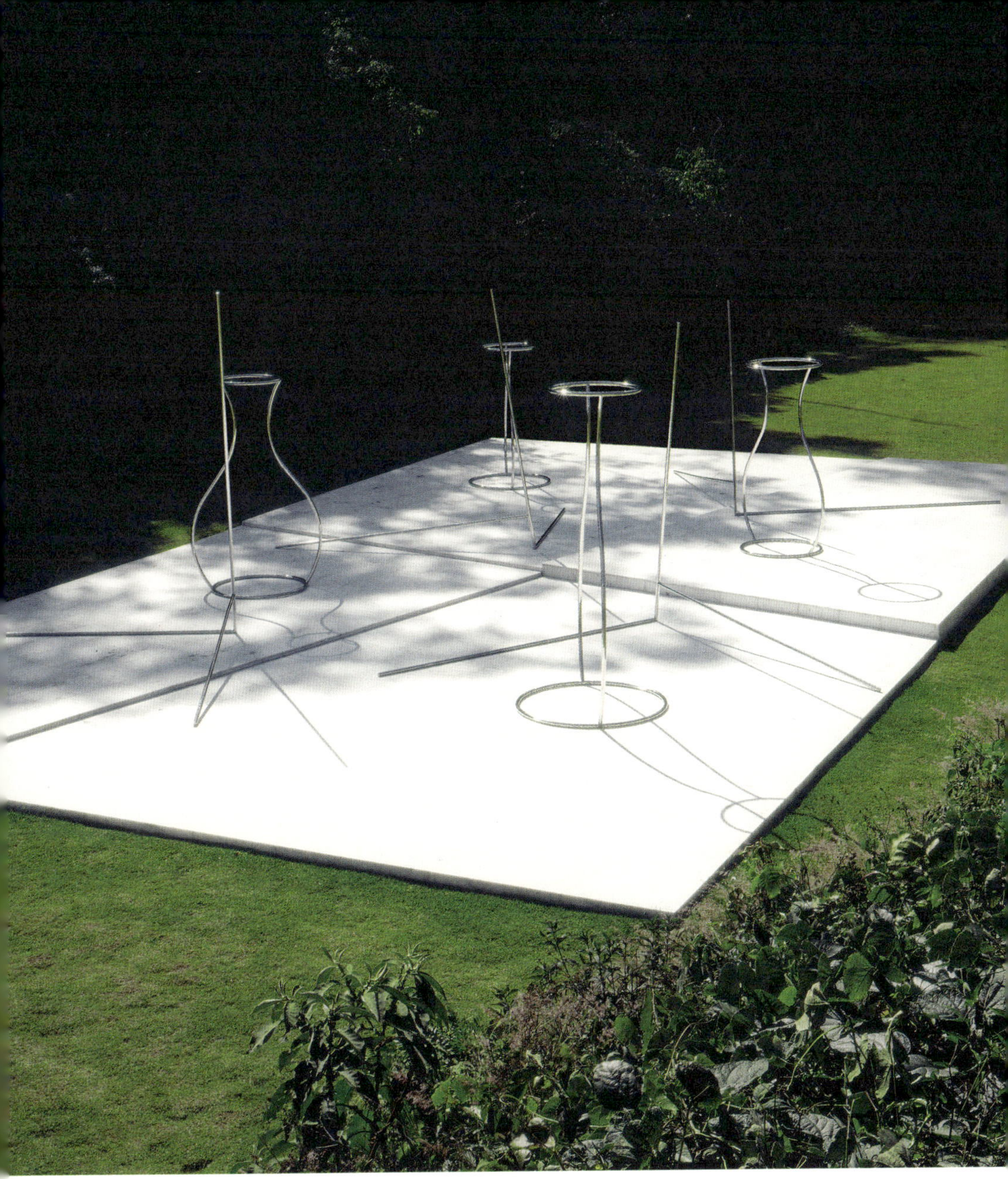

Fig. 2. *Espelhos ausentes* [*Espejos ausentes*], 2003.

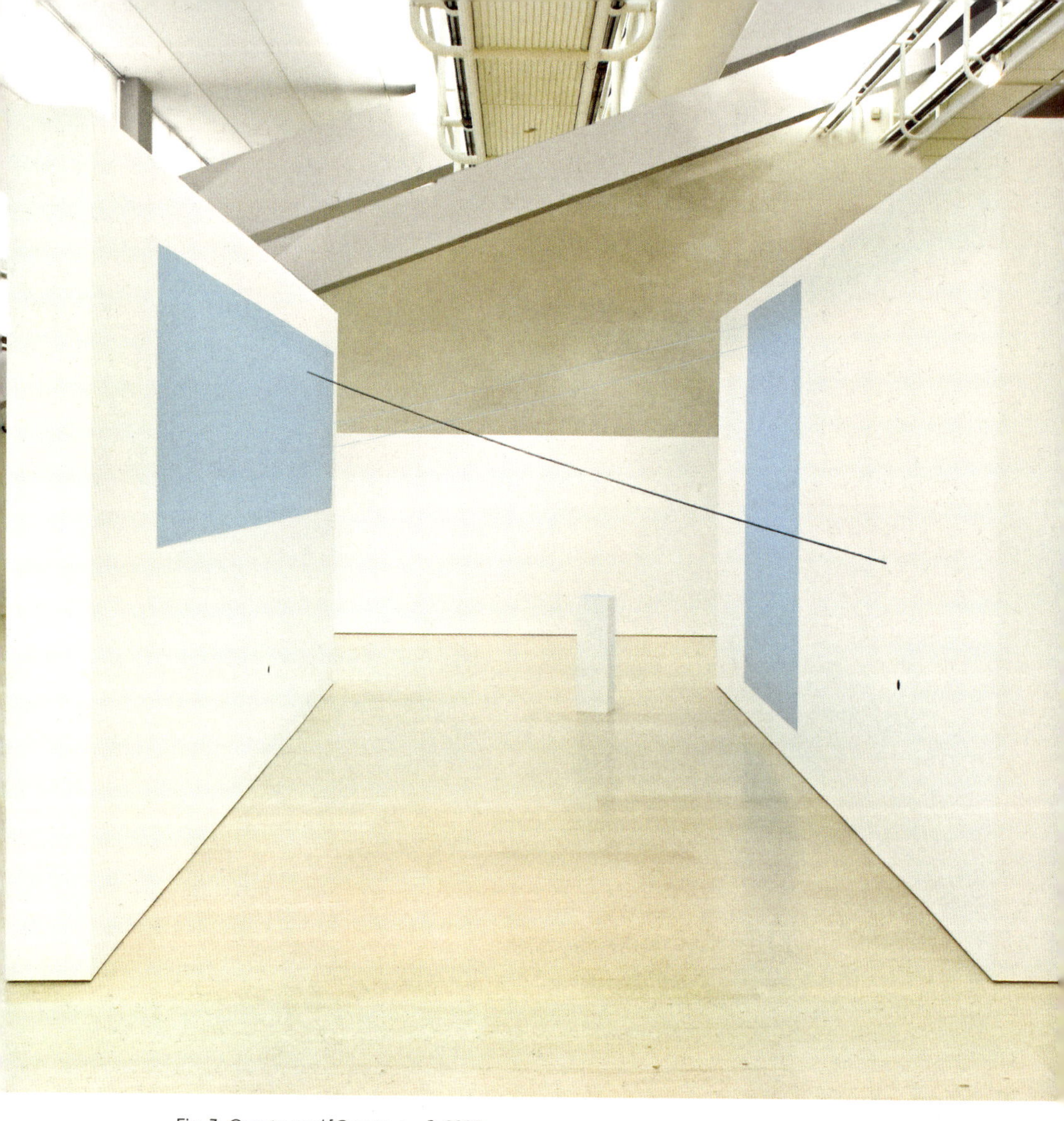

Fig. 3. *Quarto azul* [*Cuarto azul*], 2007.

En 2008 tuve la fortuna de visitar una de las exposiciones dispuesta por Waltercio Caldas para ser "transitada" en la Fundação Calouste Gulbenkian en Lisboa. Su título es *Horizontes*, una serie de habitaciones que, de maneras muy distintas, evocan el profundo espacio del universo, una mezcla entre lo doméstico y lo cósmico. Después de verla le escribí a Waltercio muy emocionado:

*¡Tu exposición es realmente hermosa! Es una de las exposiciones más hermosas que he visto en mis cuarenta años en el mundo del arte. Te vas a reír cuando leas esto pero es verdad. Mi alma entera se elevó en cuanto entré en tu espacio.*

Quien haya seguido el trabajo de Caldas desde la década de los setenta habrá notado que continuamente se mueve hacia la abstracción. ¿Qué clase de abstracción es esta? Es una que incorpora una gran cantidad de espacio vacío, o "silencio" como Caldas lo llama, y juega mucho con la transparencia [Fig. 4]. Su espíritu evoca nuevamente la posición de Mira Schendel influenciada por el Zen ("Yo diría –Mira me escribió en una carta a mediados de la década de los sesenta–, que la línea, frecuentemente, solo estimula al vacío. Dudo si la palabra estimular sea correcta. Algo parecido. En cualquier caso lo que importa en mi trabajo es el vacío, activar el vacío").[10] La sensibilidad y la modestia frente a la inmensidad y ferocidad del universo de Schendel se refleja en la actitud de Hélio Oiticica ante la naturaleza, expresada en estas hermosas líneas: "La obra nace de apenas tocar la materia. Me gustaría que la materia de la que está hecha mi obra permaneciera tal y como es; lo que la convierte en expresión no es más que un aliento: un aliento interior, de plenitud cósmica. Más allá de esto no hay obra. Un toque es suficiente, nada más".[11]

Nada más que un aliento. . . La rueda ha dado una vuelta completa y nos conecta de nuevo con la metáfora de negación que ha jugado un papel tan importante en la evolución artística de Waltercio Caldas, en la búsqueda de lo que él mismo ha denominado "una espacialidad nueva, fresca".[12]

*Nota del autor: algunos pasajes de este ensayo se han incorporado de textos existentes, cuando sentí que no podía mejorar lo expresado originalmente.*

---

10. Mira Schendel, extracto de la carta a Guy Brett, en *Mira Schendel, No Vazio do Mundo,* ed. Sonia Salzstein (São Paulo: Galeria do Arte do SESI, 1996), p. 57.

11. Hélio Oiticica, Nota en su diario de septiembre 6, 1960, en *Hélio Oiticica: Painting Beyond the Frame,* trans. Stephen Berg (Río de Janeiro: Silvia Roesler Edições de Arte, 2008), p. 84.

12. Jiménez, *Waltercio Caldas,* p. 111.

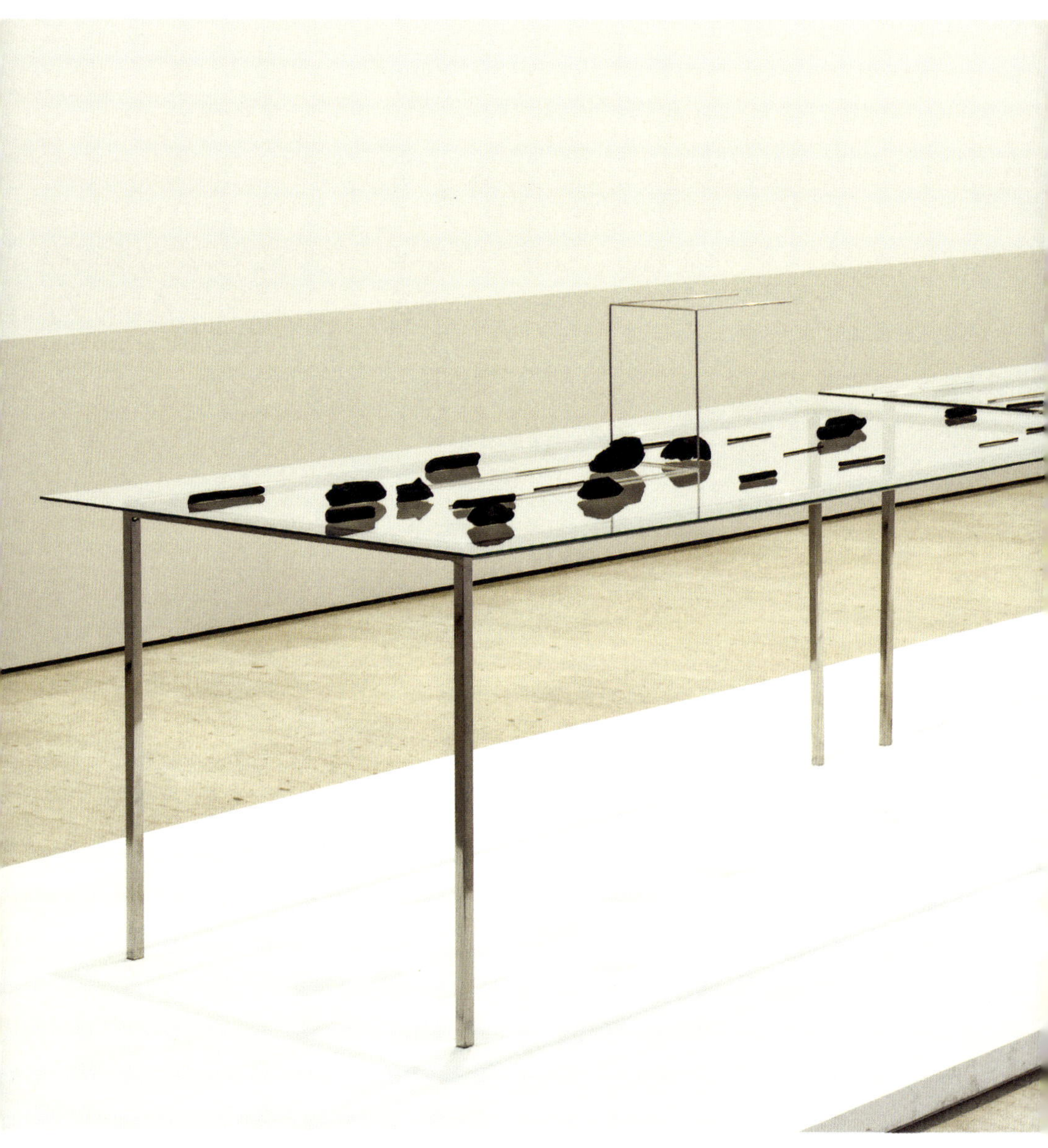

Fig. 4. *Anda uma coisa no ar* [*Hay algo en el aire*], 2002.

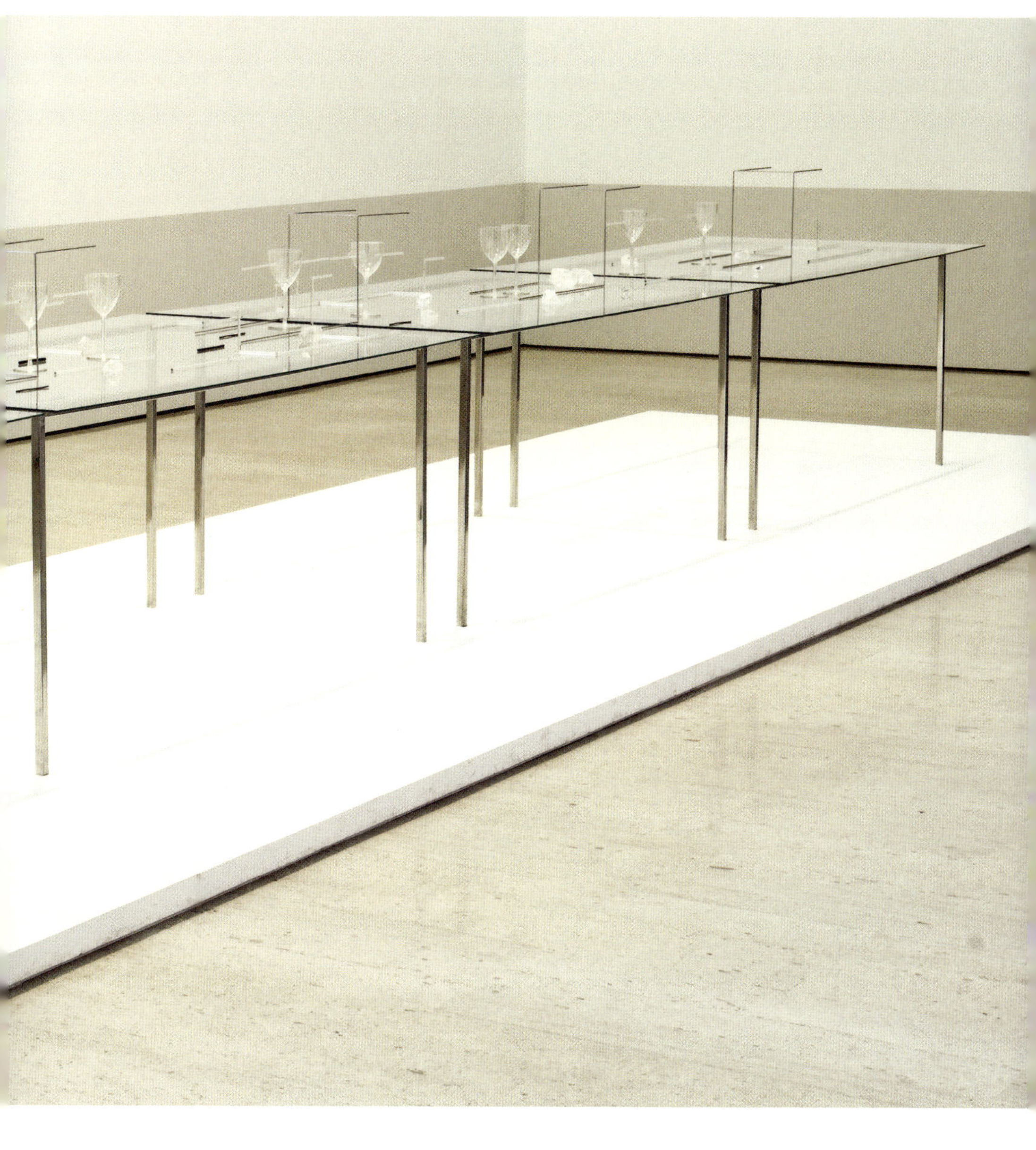

WALTERCIO CALDAS

EN CONVERSACIÓN CON

ARIEL JIMÉNEZ

# DEFINITIVAMENTE INACABADO
## Liberarse de sí mismo

*La eclosión, durante el siglo XIX, de eso que hoy conocemos como arte moderno, está en parte unida a la manifestación cada vez más importante de una cierta incapacidad para cerrar la obra de arte; esto es, para dotarla de una estructura discursiva completa, capaz de ser leída sin resto o, como decía Cézanne, para realizar un arte como el arte de los museos. Toda obra moderna posee una tendencia a lo inconcluso, a lo abierto, y lejos de ser una flaqueza que pudiera achacársele a un artista o a una generación en particular, como quizás lo hizo Zola con Cézanne y los impresionistas, se trataba en realidad de una característica general de ese mundo abierto a lo posible que estaba entonces construyéndose. Más aún, esa peculiaridad es quizás una de las pocas que hoy siguen vivas y forman parte esencial del pensamiento y del arte contemporáneos.*

WALTERCIO CALDAS  Es cierto, y en mi caso, por ejemplo, me enfrenté a ese fenómeno desde muy temprano, sin saber por supuesto lo que me sucedía. En los años sesenta dibujé muchísimo, y no hacía un solo dibujo, sino treinta a la vez, uno detrás del otro. Hacía un primer dibujo, y luego uno segundo que partía del primero, y el tercero del segundo, y así sucesivamente. Y ese encadenamiento era en realidad lo que me interesaba. Era el pasaje de uno a otro lo que me estimulaba a seguir [Figs. 1 y 1a].

ARIEL JIMÉNEZ  Es muy significativo ese sentimiento de que algo se te escapaba en el dibujo que acababas de hacer, y que solo otro lograría definirlo, quizás atraparlo. . .

WC  Sí, y tal vez intuía que aquello, fuera lo que fuera, no tendría fin. . .

AJ  Ese concepto de lo inacabado es central en el pensamiento moderno y contemporáneo, y no solo en las artes plásticas. La conciencia de que el mundo en el que vivimos es una realidad en constante evolución, como lo muestra Darwin, y de que nuestras teorías son incapaces de explicarlo en su complejidad, halla un paralelo evidente en esa apertura de la plástica durante los dos últimos siglos; en esa obra siempre incompleta o que, como en el caso de tus primeros dibujos, incluye en su estructura misma la conciencia de una carencia. Era ya el tema del *Chef-d'oeuvre inconnu* [*La obra maestra desconocida*] de

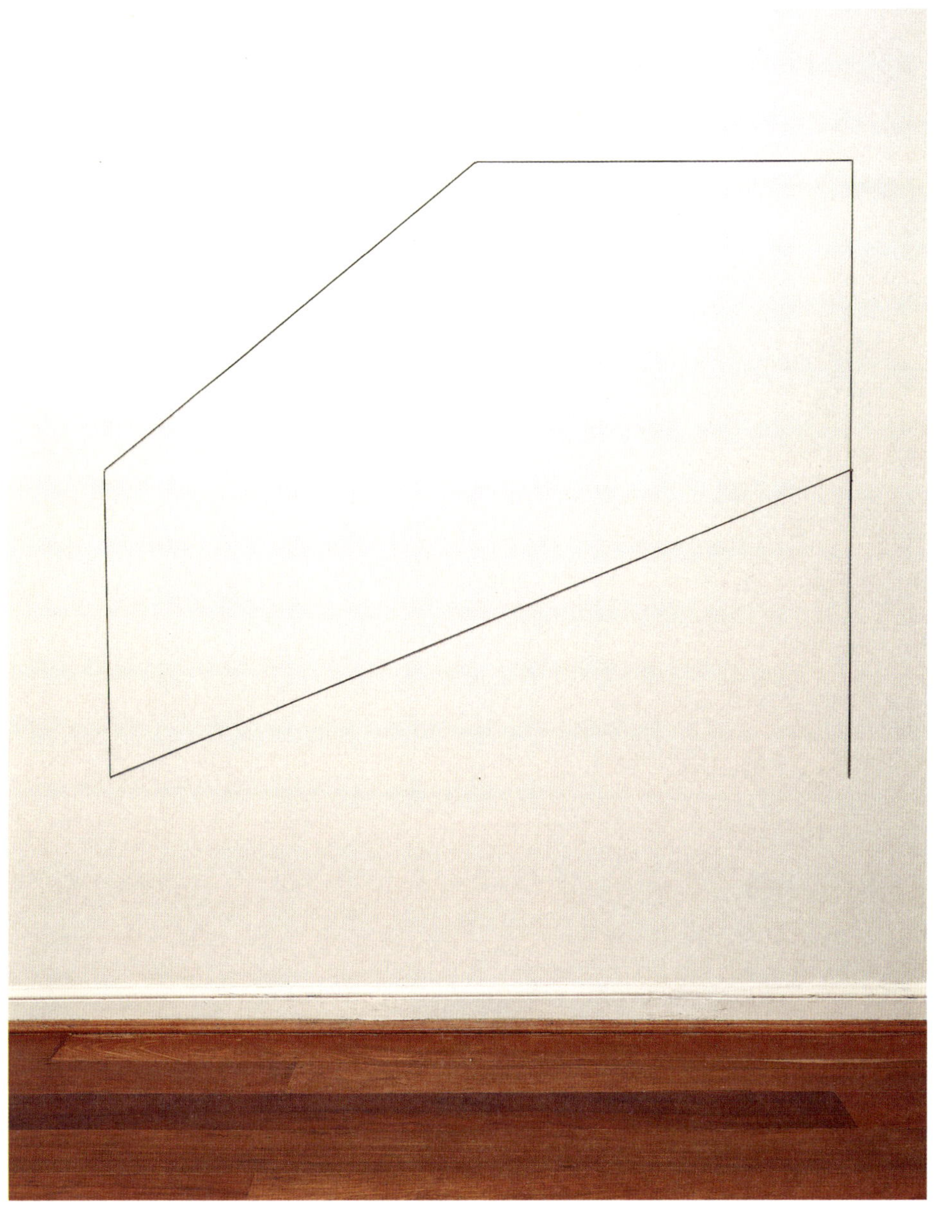
Fig. 1. *Always* [*Siempre*], 1967.

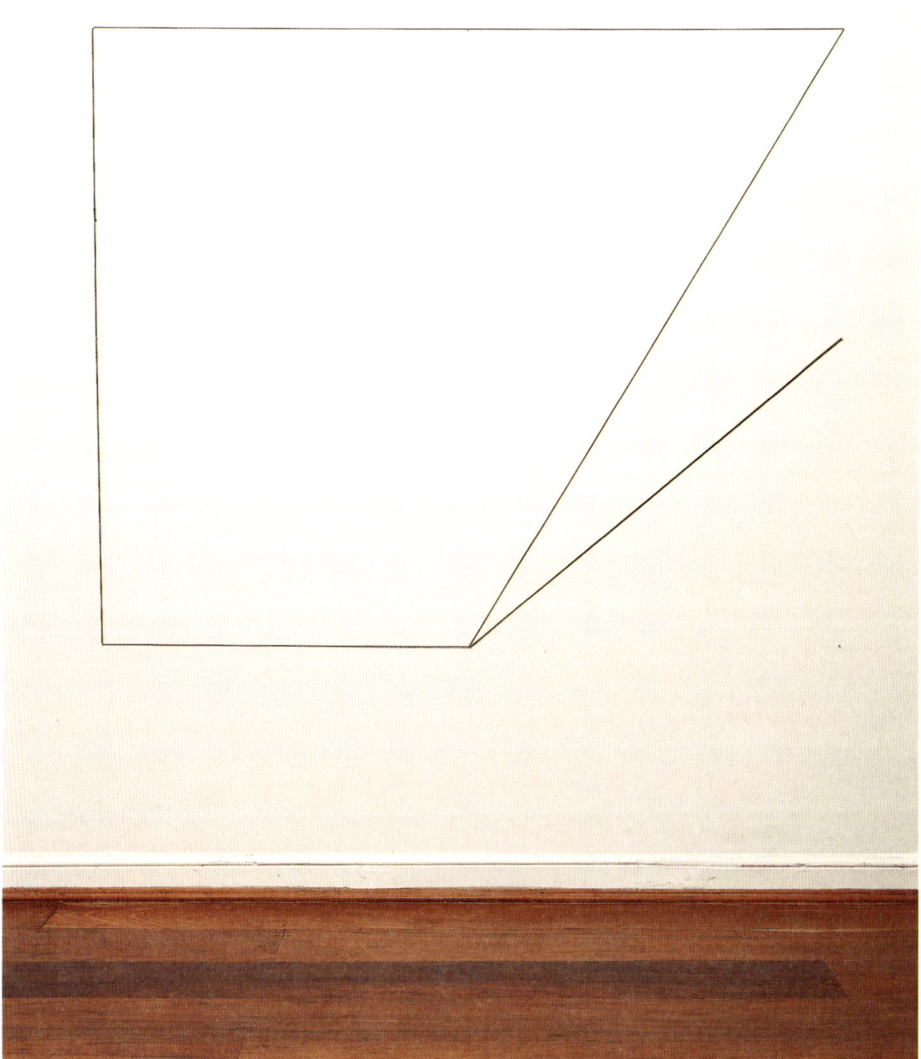

Fig. 1a. *Always* [*Siempre*], 1967.

Balzac, publicado en 1831, un texto admirado por innumerables artistas, entre ellos Cézanne y Picasso.

 Sí, era algo que no tendría fin, y aquello me atrajo profundamente. Es decir, la posibilidad de realizar un objeto finito —porque la operación de hacer un dibujo o producir un objeto es una acción que concluye necesariamente en un momento dado— y que aun así desencadenaba un infinito que le era particular. Encuentro, además, que eso es lo que he estado haciendo desde entonces y hasta hoy. La forma no se agota, y el mundo como representación tampoco.

 Es una experiencia sin duda afín a la de Picasso cuando afirmaba que la línea perfecta no existía, que en realidad había una infinidad de líneas posibles, y que un dibujo no hacía más que materializar una de ellas, la que en ese momento se hacía posible para él.[1]

 Y todas merecen el mismo respeto ¿cierto?

 Cada una enuncia una virtualidad de lo real, una posibilidad por explorar. Siempre me han parecido conmovedoras esas obras —y Picasso lo hizo a menudo— donde una pintura, que es un dibujo pintado en cierto modo, prevalece sobre el fondo, pero un fondo donde todavía se deja ver la huella de otras líneas abandonadas en el proceso de ejecución. Es como si la obra conservara la memoria de las posibilidades que se le ofrecieron al artista mientras trabajaba, virtualidades que luego desechó o dejó de lado en su búsqueda de una expresión más completa, más lograda, o en todo caso de la que mejor expresaba en ese preciso instante su pensamiento [Fig. 2].

 Esa es quizás una de las características que más me llama la atención en Picasso, la total familiaridad que tuvo con el error. Me parece que para él no tenía cabida el error.

 Lo aceptaba como virtualidades de lo real, como posibilidades incompletas o aún no realizadas, como potencialidades.

 No es que él aceptara el error. Es diferente lo que trato de explicar. Es como si él tuviera la certidumbre de que si el error ocurría, podría ser integrado al

---

1. Hélène Parmelin explica cómo Picasso se refería a la línea de los dibujos que le mostraba diciéndole que… "son los únicos que existen, en el fondo, porque ellos dan la única línea posible entre mil [. . .], posible para mí en ese momento". Hélène Parmelin, *Picasso dit. . .*, (París, Ed. Gonthier, 1966), p. 35.

sistema. Podía ser un estímulo; es decir, no le preocupaba el hecho de equivocarse, y como él siempre encontró que podía integrarlos, nunca se inquietó por ellos. Y eso es muy bello, creo, en Picasso.

 Pero también podríamos verlo como si el error, o eso que vemos como tal en un momento dado, fuera una realidad incompleta, que no ha conseguido aún su forma adecuada, o que, sencillamente, responde a parámetros distintos a los que nos guían. Pienso por ejemplo en esa falta de acabado que se les criticaba a los impresionistas (los bordes imprecisos, las líneas sueltas, segmentos de la tela sin pintar, etc.) que para los académicos de entonces era un desatino, o algo en todo caso propio del estudio, no de la obra acabada; pues bien, esos supuestos errores eran indicios de un concepto nuevo de la pintura y del mundo, que se desarrolló luego, a lo largo del siglo XX, y cobró sentido.

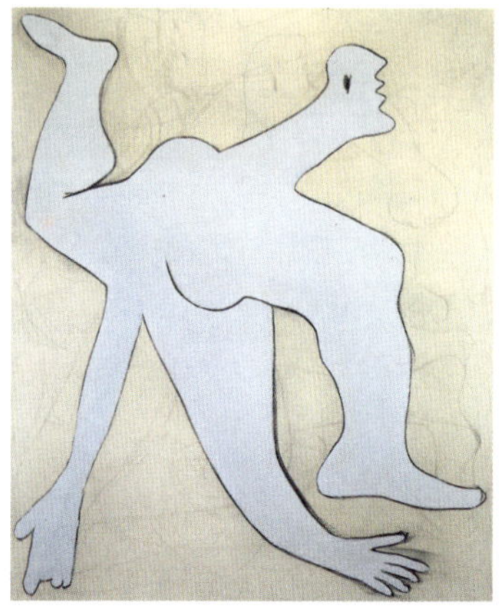

Fig. 2. Pablo Picasso, *The Blue Acrobat* [*El acróbata azul*], 1929.

 En ese caso, me parece, lo que llamamos realidad no es suficiente. No existe la línea perfecta. Es algo por hacer, la obra es una realidad inventada; porque el artista no solo produce una ilusión, genera una ilusión que a partir de allí forma parte de la realidad. Y claro, en su resentimiento, algunos dicen, como intentando poner en duda su utilidad, "que el arte no modifica el mundo". . . ; pero el arte no tiene por qué hacerlo, basta con que modifique al lenguaje, a nuestras expectativas, y a las personas. Así, es ya mucho lo que logra. Es decir, tal vez algunos conservadores se apoyen en un tipo de frustración y, quizás por esperar del arte una función que nunca ha sido la suya (me refiero a la espera de que la obra sea la representación fiel del mundo, como si ella pudiera sustituir la realidad), lo condenan cuando no responde a sus expectativas.

 Lo único real en el arte es el arte, decía Paul Valéry, o sea que el arte antes que imitar lo real, crea realidades.

 Sí, ya ves lo generoso que fue Valéry con su concepto de realidad, y eso es muy sugestivo. Esa generosidad con el concepto de la realidad que, de alguna manera, el arte promulga, construye. Una que se hace y no una que se acepta. No es algo que se incorpora, sino una realidad siempre en proceso de formación y que siempre lo estará. Y por eso, quizás, la realidad es siempre diferente de lo que las personas esperan que sea. La salud del arte consiste justamente en esa capacidad crítica para contraponerse a lo que el público generalmente espera.

<sup>AJ</sup> Y por eso son tan significativas las experiencias juveniles que describías al inicio, las de un dibujo que exigía la confección de otro, y ese otro la de uno nuevo y así, sucesivamente, sin límite asignable. Lo interesante, me parece, es que no era algo que hubieras decidido hacer conscientemente, sino que se te imponía como una necesidad, como una exigencia de la práctica artística en ese momento.

<sup>WC</sup> Cada dibujo era un paso, y se iban acumulando el uno al otro. . . Recuerdo que un día, cuando tenía veintiún años, me sentí aterrado por la cantidad de dibujos que había hecho. Me sentí, digámoslo así, oprimido por el cúmulo de operaciones que había realizado en la búsqueda de algo que no podía definir claramente. Quizás incluso trabajando sin perseguir nada específico, solo experimentando, buscando un camino, lo que es muy diferente. En todo caso, aquella cantidad de dibujos se hizo para mí un poco autoritaria y obsesiva. Lo que sucede, cuando se produce algo, es que esa cosa luego se hace parte de nuestra vida y puede convertirse en un peso, si no se le da el uso adecuado. Yo, creo —tuve la suerte de comprenderlo bastante temprano—, que todo material no tiene necesariamente que convertirse en obra de arte. En ese momento decidí que si yo quería avanzar, tendría que liberarme de todo lo que había acumulado, y que sería suficiente mantener una selección de hechos en la memoria. Entonces recuerdo haber botado unos cuatro mil dibujos de los que había elaborado entre los catorce y los veintiún años. Fue una de las decisiones más importantes que haya tomado en mi vida, porque me llevó a comprender la importancia de recomenzar otra vez desde el principio. Este acto me marcó tanto que incluso hoy está presente en mis decisiones. Es como si una pieza, por ejemplo, comenzara un asunto y lo acabara también por completo. Ahí todo está cerrado, y entonces comienzo de nuevo, a partir de otro material, de otro procedimiento o de otra actitud. Esa idea de recomenzar de cero es fundamental; o sea, la voluntad de no dejarse aprisionar por el hechizo de un estilo formal, incluso por la presencia de las obras anteriores.

<sup>AJ</sup> Cada vez que observo a un artista luchando contra sí mismo, y contra lo que ha producido, recuerdo una bella observación de Roland Barthes cuando afirmaba que si algo nuevo debía surgir en la obra de un artista, solo sería posible tras

una lucha constante contra lo que él llamó esas dos fuerzas ciegas, esos dos horizontes del estilo y de la historia del arte.

<sup>WC</sup> Es muy curioso lo que acabas de decir, porque son de alguna forma dos desafíos que permean constantemente en mi obra. Por eso utilizo la historia del arte como si fuera un material de trabajo. Porque uno puede incorporar ese material sin ser citacionista, cuando hablo de algún artista, inclusive si pudiera hablar de todo lo que sucedió anteriormente. Lo que pasa es que la historia del arte está presente para nosotros como si se tratara de una segunda naturaleza.

<sup>AJ</sup> Ese es estrictamente el término que utiliza Roland Barthes para calificar esa fuerza ciega de la historia del arte. Para él es algo que se nos impone como un horizonte, una segunda naturaleza.

<sup>WC</sup> Es un asunto que me parece fundamental, porque el artista de hoy está inundado de informaciones como quizás nunca lo estuvo en otros momentos de la historia, y eso ha llegado a ser un nuevo paisaje para él. De alguna manera, uno se ve obligado a liberarse de ese pasado de una forma más grave que en otros tiempos. Hoy, si te acercas a una biblioteca, encuentras la historia de la pintura rupestre y del Expresionismo alemán al lado del Cubismo y del Surrealismo, de Dadá y de mil asuntos más. Todo está acumulado en nuestro presente bajo forma editorial. Es imposible negar esa presencia actual de lo pasado, de la historia del arte.

<sup>AJ</sup> Y es algo que los intelectuales y los artistas perciben tan pronto como la industria editorial alcanza un cierto grado de madurez. Pienso por ejemplo en un ensayo de André Malraux, *El museo imaginario*, de 1947. Su tema es justamente el impacto que tuvo y tiene en nuestro mundo la posibilidad de tener presentes, en una especie de museo imaginario, las obras que no existen en nuestros museos, las que se nos imponen de alguna manera, y que comienzan a interactuar en el libro y en nuestra mente. Entre los argumentos más interesantes del ensayo figura precisamente el peso que alcanza la reproducción de esas piezas, imponiéndole una lectura que las descontextualiza y las acerca a la textura cultural de nuestra mirada. Lo que sucede allí es que la publicación integra esas obras a nuestro imaginario, como nunca antes había ocurrido. Es algo muy reciente, de la segunda mitad del siglo XX, no más. ¿Es así como funciona, en tu caso, ese intento por domesticar el peso de la historia, integrándola?

<sup>WC</sup> No, no es integrándola, solo que no puedo evitar considerarla. Es el hecho de

esa presencia del arte como si fuera un flujo constante, que le debe tanto a Duchamp como a Rembrandt, a Braque como Vermeer o al hombre que hace su primer dibujo en las cavernas; es decir, es como si el arte no pudiera ser lo que es sin la contribución de todos, absolutamente todos esos artistas.

<sup>AJ</sup> Como si esa segunda naturaleza del arte estuviera hoy tan presente para nosotros como lo fueron los bosques y los sistemas montañosos para los nómadas de la prehistoria ¿cierto?, algo sencillamente tan presente que no puede eludirse, porque vives dentro, formas parte de eso.

<sup>WC</sup> Es exactamente así como lo veo. Y ese río no tiene una fuente, ni un mar donde llegar.

<sup>AJ</sup> Y tú serías —y seríamos todos— una nueva especie de nómada en medio de esa otra naturaleza. La cultura, y su entorno natural: la enormidad de la urbe contemporánea es hoy nuestra verdadera naturaleza. De ella salimos de vez en cuando para ver los vestigios del mundo natural, lo que queda todavía del universo animal y vegetal de los inicios. La maqueta, como proyección íntima de un espacio posible, imaginable, me parece una de las vías más lógicas para enfrentarse a ese mundo artificial —y tan humano— de la urbe. Ese es en todo caso el camino que tomaste desde tu primera exhibición individual.

<sup>WC</sup> Sin duda. Hice mi primera exposición en 1965, en el centro académico de una universidad de filosofía, en Río de Janeiro. Allí expuse pequeños objetos hechos en cartón y materiales diversos, con los que abordaba un asunto bastante juvenil, porque se trataba de mis primeras experiencias sexuales. Yo había leído algunos textos surrealistas y quedé muy impresionado por la manera como ellos abordaban la sexualidad. Por lo menos en ese momento, yo encontraba que los surrealistas habían inventado una manera revolucionaria de tratar la subjetividad.

<sup>AJ</sup> ¿Y cómo funcionaban esas maquetas?

<sup>WC</sup> Yo estaba interesado en abordar las experiencias sexuales del adolescente, y esa violencia que significa pasar de ser una persona dependiente de la familia a convertirse en un individuo autónomo. Es decir que, en esas primeras maquetas comenzaba a tratar el tema del individuo ante la sociedad. Incluso si hoy en día encuentro que no tienen ninguna trascendencia artística, siento que fueron importantes para el aprendizaje de las posibilidades de construir, a través de

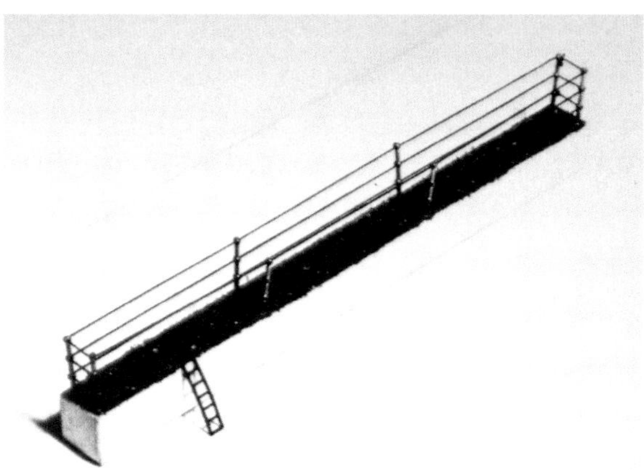

Fig. 3. *Maquette*
[*Maqueta*] *II*, 1967.

pequeños montajes tridimensionales, una realidad fuera de mí. Todas esas construcciones eran, no podían dejar de serlo, manifestaciones subjetivas, y no es un
azar si fui invitado por la facultad de filosofía para exponerlas. Lo único, quizás,
que me desagradó en esa muestra, es que si yo había percibido características
subjetivas en mi obra, no quería que su asunto siguiera siendo mi subjetividad.
Después de esta exposición, hacia 1966–67, empecé con las maquetas de objetos
tridimensionales en el mundo, que son aquellas maquetas de construcciones
arquitectónicas imaginarias.

Y lo hice a partir de algunos temas planteados por Jorge Luis Borges, que
fue el autor que más me interesó en ese período. Borges me aportaba esa idea
de que era factible materializar construcciones imaginarias. Entonces enfrenté
esas maquetas como si yo mismo fuera un arquitecto borgiano, como si ese
tipo de arquitecto pudiera existir. Fue una manera de deslocalizar mi subjetividad y orientarla hacia el mundo [Fig. 3]. También me influenció mucho la
arquitectura utópica de Étienne-Louis Boullée,[2] un arquitecto francés del siglo
XVIII, conocido en particular por esos proyectos —casi metafísicos— de edificios
que era imposible construir con las técnicas de su época, porque desafiaban los
límites de lo posible [Fig. 4].

AJ Esas maquetas de 1966–67, orientadas hacia el mundo, nacen en cierta forma
como una reacción a los primeros objetos de 1965.

2. Étienne-Louis Boullée (1728–1799). Arquitecto visionario francés, miembro de la Academia Real de Arquitectura. Tuvo una considerable influencia en su tiempo, tanto por su actividad docente como por la audacia de
sus proyectos, a menudo utópicos. Inspirado por la antigüedad greco romana, le dio una importancia central a
las formas geométricas como la esfera, el cubo y la pirámide, a partir de las cuales pensó estructuras grandio-
sas y sorprendentes.

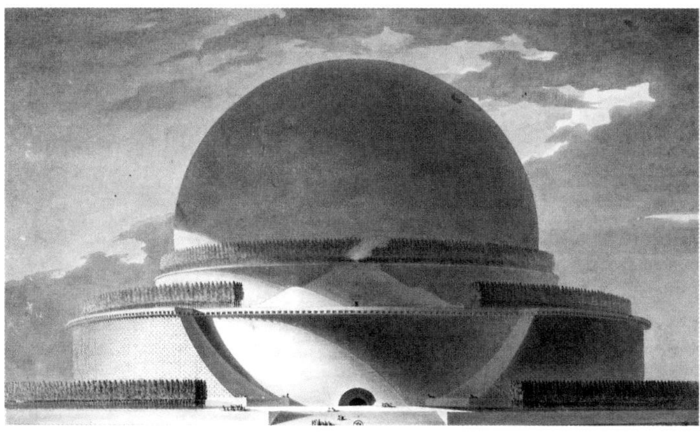

Fig. 4. Étienne-Louis Boullée, *Cénotaphe à Newton* [*Cenotafio para Newton*], 1780–93.

 Reacción es quizás una palabra muy fuerte. Yo preferiría hablar de una corrección de perspectiva. En todo caso, en ese momento entiendo, quizás intuitivamente, algo importante. Y es que tal vez fui demasiado ingenuo al principio, porque me dejaba llevar muy ciegamente por las influencias que recibía. Hay que decir, también, que fui criado en una familia de clase media, en un ambiente y en una casa donde no había una biblioteca. Mi padre tenía libros de arquitectura, ingeniería y algo, muy poco, de literatura. Con ello quiero decir que no recibí ninguna noción sobre esa segunda naturaleza de la cultura. La cultura fue para mí un descubrimiento, porque aunque mi padre me apoyó mucho, y siempre, mi formación fue un esfuerzo personal. Fue la comprensión de que la cultura era algo que debía ser descubierto. Es como si la cultura hubiese realmente llegado a mí como una nueva posibilidad de vida.

 Cuando organizas esa primera exposición de 1965, no habías comenzado todavía los cursos con Ivan Serpa en el Museu de Arte Moderna de Río de Janeiro.

 Sí, las clases de Serpa son anteriores. Es a partir de allí que empiezo a comprender cómo funcionaba el mundo del arte. Llegué a los cursos de Serpa, en 1964, de una manera curiosa. Yo tenía conocimiento, por supuesto, de que en el Museu de Arte Moderna se daban cursos de arte, y con características más interesantes que las que podía ofrecerme la Escola de Belas Artes. Frecuenté dos o tres talleres de pintura en esa escuela; cursos de modelo vivo, por ejemplo, y aquello me pareció extremadamente tedioso, porque la modelo permanecía inmóvil, como si no fuera una mujer, o como si hubiera sido destituida de su sexualidad para ser utilizada. Y los artistas pintaban aquel cuerpo reducido a la condición de modelo. Yo sentía que aquella persona no formaba parte de la realidad, y tampoco por supuesto la representación que los alumnos hacían de ella. Las clases, además, me parecían sin vigor. No sé de donde saqué la idea de que debían ser estimulantes, lo cierto es que había una diferencia entre esa experiencia y lo que yo esperaba del arte.

<sup>AJ</sup> Lo que estabas experimentando, en cierto modo, era justamente la duda moderna sobre las posibilidades de la representación pictórica para acercarse a la verdad del mundo; como cuando Cézanne se preguntaba si era cierto que el color y la forma existían por separado, como se lo habían enseñado en la academia, o si constituían más bien una unidad inseparable, como él creía observarlo en la naturaleza.

<sup>WC</sup> Tal vez entendí allí algo que me hizo dudar de la representación, o de su autonomía. De cualquier manera, como era además una persona que estaba atraída por la posibilidad de conocer el mundo a través de una disponibilidad ante el asombro, era inevitable que llegara a los libros. Era evidente que iba a necesitar las informaciones que, en la época, por otra parte, no eran de tan fácil acceso como hoy en día. Tuve que buscar en los libros lo que no encontraba en ningún otro lugar. Entonces supe que había un profesor en el Museu de Arte Moderna que dictaba clases de arte y me quedé con esa curiosidad. Más adelante, un día de 1964, estaba en una librería que vendía ejemplares de segunda mano, ojeando algunas publicaciones de arte, y me topé con una persona que acababa de comprar un texto de Jean Cocteau titulado *Opium*. Ahí comencé a conversar con esa persona y me quedé muy interesado. Luego me enteré, por el encargado de la librería, que había estado hablando con Ivan Serpa. Así nació el estímulo necesario para que dos o tres meses después, me inscribiera en sus clases; porque pude percatarme de que Serpa era una persona muy informada –lo que luego pude corroborar en sus cursos– y que por eso mismo él podía introducirme a esa segunda naturaleza que sería la cultura, y específicamente la cultura relativa al arte.[3]

<sup>AJ</sup> ¿Y cómo eran sus clases?

<sup>WC</sup> Eran como una especie de entrenamiento donde cada quien hacía en su casa lo que estimaba que debía hacer, para luego someterlo no solo al profesor, sino a los demás alumnos. Aquello era incluso algo cruel, pero yo diría que fue la

---

3. El interés de Waltercio Caldas por el libro y su función va más allá de lo habitual, y lo ha llevado a crear una considerable colección de libros de arte, en primeras ediciones, que mantiene con su obra una relación de familiaridad para nada desestimable.

primera gran lección que recibí de él, porque aquella frontera entre lo que significaba hacer una cosa para sí mismo y hacerla para los demás, quedaba destruida por completo, estallada. Y era así porque, por una parte, uno tenía objetivamente la oportunidad de hacer en su casa lo que quería, pero luego debía someter aquello a otras personas, una de las cuales era extremadamente competente y conocedora del asunto, que era él.

De manera que en sus clases encontré algunas lecciones fundamentales: primero, ese enfrentamiento con el mundo. Enseguida, la información detallada que Serpa nos daba para situar aquello en el mundo del arte, que era algo de lo que nosotros no teníamos ninguna noción, porque no podíamos saber cuánto de lo que habíamos hecho era una novedad. En tercer lugar, encuentro que sus clases eran extremadamente interesantes, porque incluso si indirectamente él terminaba estimulando la expresión personal, no lo conseguía a través de la búsqueda de un estilo, sino estimulando la necesidad de comprender lo que pasaba en las cosas que producíamos. Era una manera mucho más inteligente de abordar la creación plástica. Eso, tal vez, resultaba difícil para un artista que estuviera buscando posibilidades de expresión propias y que, enfrentado en las clases de Serpa a significados tan vastos, pudiera sentirse perdido. Pero para mí fue totalmente lo contrario, quizás porque no estaba obsesionado con la búsqueda de una expresión personal.

Otra de las experiencias que tuve en las clases de Serpa fue el ambiente que lo rodeaba: el hecho de que las clases se dieran en el Museu de Arte Moderna, con la presencia de otros profesores y las exhibiciones que hacían allí. Desde entonces frecuenté las exposiciones del Museo, y de las galerías también, y eso me enseñó lo que significaba ser artista, porque en la época nadie sabía muy bien lo que eso quería decir. O sea que a partir de allí, comienzo a entrever la posibilidad de expresarme, yo también, a través del arte.

# LA NATURALEZA DEL ARTE
## Inventar su propio artista

 En la época yo no sabía con certeza lo que significaba ser artista, y creo que muchos de nosotros apenas lo sospechábamos. La primera noticia que tuve sobre Lygia Clark fue en una revista de moda, donde ella aparece como una señora que hacía objetos, una ama de casa que tenía una actividad inusual e inesperada. Lo cierto es que esa profesión no tenía un perfil muy claro. Eran personas que hacían cosas a las que se les daba el nombre de arte. Es decir, que producían objetos que no eran ni útiles ni funcionales, que no eran reconocibles, de modo que terminaba diciéndose que aquello debía ser arte. Es como si a causa de esa indefinición cada artista brasileño de ese período hubiera inaugurado para sí una manera de ser artista. Yo mismo me vi forzado a inventar el tipo de artista que quería ser, y eso lo observo en todos los artistas brasileños. Veo a Hélio Oiticica inventando el artista que le hubiera gustado ser, veo a Lygia inventando el suyo, veo a Tunga, a José Resende y a Cildo Meireles, todos intentando una manera particular de ser artista.

Con ello quiero señalar que es difícil ver en Brasil toda una generación de artistas, donde no sea posible reconocer un estilo general que pueda relacionar las obras unas con otras. Es el caso de los neoconcretos de los años cinquenta y sesenta, por ejemplo, donde, más allá de las diferencias personales, se puede detectar un cierto grado de parentesco, una determinada afinidad formal entre ellos. Eso no sucedía en mi generación, precisamente por esa necesidad de inventar un artista "otro" para un arte "otro". Ya no bastaba simplemente con suplantar un *ismo* por otro.

 Y no obstante, ¿no es lógico pensar que esa necesidad de inventarse como artista haya sido aun superior entre los neoconcretos, precisamente porque hacían su obra en un medio donde no se sabía muy bien lo que eso quería decir?

 Muy buena tu pregunta, porque es un reto. Yo te respondería, sin embargo, diciéndote que los neoconcretos no se vieron obligados a hacerlo porque el modelo del artista moderno aún les convenía. Y no lo hacen porque el modelo del artista no es cuestionado sino cuando se alcanza una determinada complejidad en el ambiente cultural. Por ejemplo, cuando se llega a contar con una gran diversidad de *ismos* y con ellos muchas maneras de ser artista, de modo que cada uno se vería así ante la dificultad de definir su propia forma de serlo. Es lo que ocurre en el caso de Lygia Clark, cuando a mediados de su carrera llega a creer que se encontraba fuera del arte, e incluso llegó a decir que negaba su propia condición de artista.

AJ El artista y poeta Ferreira Gullar afirma que era cierto, porque en realidad después de sus *Bichos* Clark ya había dejado de hacer arte.

WC Ese es otro asunto bien interesante. . . A mi entender, lo que sucede ahí es algo distinto, porque yo encuentro que él está tomando una afirmación revolucionaria, la de una artista consciente de los límites que debía superar, para deducir de allí una limitación del arte contemporáneo en su conjunto. Desde mi punto de vista, Lygia nunca dudó de la eficacia de la práctica artística de una manera general, apenas la consideró insuficiente, tal y como la percibía, para sus nuevos propósitos. No veo allí una negación del arte, sino una crítica precisa y esclarecedora de las ingenuidades programáticas de su tiempo.

AJ Y ese es justamente el momento en que tu generación inicia su trabajo. Ella habría entendido que sus objetos no podían ya ser pensados desde los conceptos tradicionales del arte, y por eso sintió que, en cierta forma, dejaba de ser artista. Pero ustedes, que comienzan su obra cuando esas nociones tradicionales han perdido ya su pertinencia y su fuerza, comprenden de alguna manera que parte de su esfuerzo consiste justamente en definir las características de ese nuevo ámbito de lo artístico y de lo que significa ser artista en él. A ver, yo lo veía así: una obra de arte, hasta bien avanzado el siglo XX, consistía en producir una imagen que pudiera mantener una relación de cercanía con el mundo; un doble "informado" del mundo, por supuesto pensado desde la cultura y para cumplir con sus fines, ¿cierto? Eso es un paisaje romántico, eso una naturaleza muerta de Van Gogh, e incluso un bodegón cubista. Son una imagen del mundo, o de un pedazo de mundo, informado por la cultura. Pero con artistas como Duchamp, y luego individuos como Clark y Oiticica en Brasil, el arte comienza a funcionar de otra manera. Quizás porque ahora el artista se sitúa de lleno en la esfera de la cultura (porque sabe que no existe un afuera posible para nosotros), y desde allí genera, produce objetos, situaciones, o simplemente tensiones capaces de enriquecer ese ámbito cultural desde el cual observamos el mundo y definimos nuestra interacción con él. Y claro, ni su manera de operar, ni sus productos, son ya exactamente equivalentes. Y por eso se puede comprender que individuos como Joseph Beuys y Lygia Clark se hayan sentido ya fuera del ámbito del arte.

Algodão Negativo    Negative Cotton

<sup>WC</sup> Exactamente. Y por eso te digo que negarse como artista, que era lo que ocurría con Lygia, es diferente de lo que mi generación debió afrontar, que era la necesidad de construir una posibilidad nueva para el arte. Es decir, en su momento ella fue capaz de crear otra posibilidad, quizás sin definirlo con certeza. Lo que tal vez distingue su generación de la mía, es que nosotros nos vimos enfrentados a una complejidad de variables mucho mayor, y ese exceso nos hizo dudar de todas ellas. No se trataba solamente de la dificultad de escoger entre muchas opciones y programas estéticos. Es allí donde radica la novedad. Sucede algo similar a lo que produjeron los artistas Dadá en su tiempo, porque ellos ni siquiera querían ser artistas, al menos en el sentido habitual del término.

<sup>AJ</sup> No quisieron o no pudieron seguir funcionando como el artista tradicional, pero actuaron en el ámbito del lenguaje –y con ello dentro de los parámetros del arte–, y por eso era natural que fueran integrados a su ámbito de sentido.

<sup>WC</sup> Sin duda, pero es ingenuo pensar que esa integración se produzca sin que el medio cobre un precio por ello. Hay algo perverso en esa inserción, en el sentido de que una vez que forma parte de la cultura, ese nuevo objeto de arte comienza de inmediato a erosionarla, y termina transformándola.

<sup>AJ</sup> Es tan ingenuo como creerse ese cuento del anti-arte. Porque habría que establecer una diferencia entre la voluntad de romper con una determinada manera de hacer arte (ese trabajo negativo que estaba por hacerse, según Tristan Tzara), y eso que algunos llaman anti-arte, algo que a mi entender no existe. Una acción en el campo del arte es ya una forma de hacer arte, incluso si lo que se busca es destruir una manera de pensarlo y de hacerlo.

<sup>WC</sup> Por supuesto, cuando yo hablo de anti-arte en realidad me refiero al carácter restringido de lo que entonces se entendía por arte.

<sup>AJ</sup> Es precisamente lo que dice Maurice Merleau-Ponty cuando afirma que el arte moderno no había consistido en escoger entre el dibujo y el color, o incluso entre la figuración y la creación de signos, como en "multiplicar los sistemas de equivalencia".[4] Es decir, que la representación pictórica del tipo "realista" era un sistema de equivalencias, uno más entre muchos otros, solo que hasta finales del siglo XIX se creyó ser el único, o al menos el único que mantenía una relación de correspondencia eficaz con lo real.

4. Merleau-Ponty, Maurice. *L'oeil et l'esprit* (París: Ed. Gallimard, 1964), p. 71.

 Es perfecto, y en ese sentido, todos los artistas que comenzamos a trabajar en los años sesenta, lo hicimos ya en un mundo donde el arte en su acepción restringida había muerto hace ya tiempo. Pero para los Dadá era muy diferente, porque en su época no existía siquiera el Surrealismo, que le permitió al artista sacar sus temas incluso de los sueños y ya no solo del mundo. El Surrealismo amplió considerablemente las fronteras del arte en su momento. Y así, cada generación fue abriendo posibilidades nuevas, que se han acumulado hasta llegar al presente, donde la información te permite un acceso simultáneo a múltiples versiones, además de todas aquellas que una multitud de artistas está explorando en el mundo entero. Y uno, como artista, tiene que tomar una actitud frente a ese caos. Ya no se trata solamente de ser figurativo o abstracto, pop o conceptual, porque todas esas posibilidades existen juntas, se integran y producen nuevas sublecturas.

 Quizás por eso decías que ustedes fueron una alternativa en Brasil, porque no tuvieron alternativa. . .

 No exactamente, con esa frase me refería a dos palabras fetiche utilizadas en los años setenta para designar situaciones que no se entendían, todo lo que fuera hecho de forma no convencional. Cada vez que un artista buscaba encontrar una expresión personal para lo que hacía, era calificado como "experimental". La sala experimental en el Museu de Arte Moderna de Río, había sido creada específicamente para los jóvenes artistas que, por la naturaleza de su obra, no encontraban lugar en el circuito de las galerías. Y los artistas como yo, que trabajaban en eso, que enfrentaban ese riesgo, nos sentíamos un poco ofendidos, porque era como si se tratara de una clasificación frívola, de un rótulo cómodo para englobar todo lo que no se comprendía y que excedía las prácticas del arte. Pero a mí me parecía que la experimentación estaba tan íntimamente unida al aprendizaje y a la práctica artística, que no podía ser empleada contra el arte. Al fin de cuentas, el arte es el proceso de experimentar, lo que enunció muy bien Mário Pedrosa cuando dijo que el arte era un ejercicio experimental de la libertad. Por eso, cuando escuché a Mário Pedrosa hablar tan radicalmente del proceso de experimentación, sentí que había redimido el término experimental. Mário lo colocó en una fórmula perfecta, y ya no como si lo experimental fuera una simple reacción precaria contra el arte. El mundo era, en verdad, experimental, por la urgencia misma de las transformaciones que requería.

Otro concepto simplificador era justamente la noción de lo "alternativo", que escondía el mismo problema. Era como si el medio cultural quisiera disminuir el valor de cualquier actividad que escapara a los parámetros que el sistema quería preservar. Entonces, estas dos palabras adquirieron para mí un tono reaccionario, y es por eso que dije que nosotros preferimos la alternativa, porque no tuvimos alternativa. Era una manera de decir que lo que estaba en juego era mucho más complejo y fundamental que la ingenuidad de querer hacer algo nuevo, en contra de las formas establecidas.

AJ En la Venezuela de los años setenta y ochenta sucedía algo similar, cuando solo parecía admisible aceptar las experiencias renovadoras asimilándolas a un género más: el experimental. Era una manera cómoda de hacerlo porque ampliaba las categorías tradicionales de la pintura, la escultura y el grabado, sin poner en juego el orden establecido. También, y esto era muy gracioso, algunos críticos e incluso artistas, intentaban crear categorías nuevas para propuestas perfectamente convencionales, con lo que esperaban sin duda darles un carácter de vanguardia. Es lo que ocurrió por ejemplo con el llamado dibujo experimental. El dibujo más torpemente representativo se hacía pasar así por una expresión joven, de vanguardia, y gran parte del medio lo aceptaba como tal.

WC Era así, exactamente. En la época, además, la pintura y el grabado eran categorías muy rígidas, y existían grupos de grabadores que eran refractarios a cualquier género que no fuera el grabado, como si solo quisieran trabajar dentro de los límites de una técnica específica. Mucho más tarde [en 1980], experimenté con grabados y quedé atónito, porque descubrí que todo aquel rigor anunciado era en verdad muy relativo. Si existe una práctica artística donde el resultado termina siendo diferente de lo previsto, esa es el grabado. Y recuerdo que me quedé pensando en eso, porque me costaba entender cómo era posible que un proceso con tantas normas, escapara tan radicalmente al control del grabador.

AJ Es interesantísimo, porque te veo creando una visión personal del arte a partir del choque que te producía el encuentro con esa visión conservadora. De manera que tu obra sería casi como el producto de la extrañeza que surge de ese choque.

WC Es clarísimo. Es como si yo hubiera percibido, y estuviera percibiendo hasta hoy, que uno debe estar siempre atento a esos límites, porque ellos se renuevan con cada década, y de alguna manera cercan al creador, en particular a medida que la creación se hace más y más libre. Es como si los medios de representación se hicieran cada vez más sofisticados y necesitaran cada vez más de una visión crítica, porque las posibilidades se estrechan y amplían al mismo tiempo, y los artistas son recuperados cada vez más eficientemente por la cultura del espectáculo.

*Mientras conversábamos y yo intentaba reconstruir el proceso de su producción plástica en el tiempo, nuestra conversación y su modo de argumentar nos traían irremediablemente hasta el presente, como si con cada pregunta que formulaba su respuesta abarcara toda su obra, independientemente del año en el que ella hubiera sido creada: como si los problemas de hoy fueran los mismos del inicio, o como si la manera de abordarlos hoy, a través de experiencias nuevas, fueran las únicas susceptibles de iluminar su obra toda.*

AJ Me cuesta mantener la ilación cronológica de nuestra conversación, porque con cada nueva pregunta, incluso cuando te hablo de un momento muy específico de tu producción, terminamos discutiendo tu obra más reciente.

WC Lo que sucede, en ocasiones como esta, es que cuando comento una pieza en particular, tiendo, no a definirla como un caso único, sino a pensarla dentro del programa general de mi obra. Es como si dijéramos que cada fragmento es el todo, que cada obra es toda la obra.

AJ Es exactamente lo que decía Merleau-Ponty de la pintura,[5] que toda pintura —toda obra densa se entiende— iba siempre hasta el fondo de la pintura, en el sentido de que tocaba su esencia más profunda, fuera cual fuera la época en que se la practicara, del pasado o del presente.

WC Al final, en cierta forma, se acaba produciendo un objeto que cataliza todos los demás, sin ser ninguno de ellos.

AJ En todo caso, nuestra conversación nos trae una y otra vez, irremediablemente, al presente.

WC Me parece un proceso enriquecedor, porque cada vez que se regresa, se comienza de un modo diferente y se añade una luz nueva sobre las ideas.

AJ Volvamos entonces a mediados de los sesenta, cuando inicias tu formación con Ivan Serpa y tu inmersión en el mundo de los museos y las galerías.

5. "Pues, si ni en pintura, ni en otras experiencias incluso, podemos establecer una jerarquía en las civilizaciones ni hablar de progreso, no es porque algún destino nos retenga, es más bien porque en cierto sentido la primera de las pinturas iba hasta el fondo del porvenir". Merleau-Ponty. *L'œil et l'esprit*, p. 92.

WC Allí se da un proceso que hallo fundamental, y es la manera cómo respondo con mi trabajo a las exposiciones y a ese intercambio constante con los artistas y sus obras. De alguna manera, mi trabajo habría comenzado siendo yo espectador de otras obras, dialogando con ellas. Es como si al ver una obra y tratando de comprender lo que un artista quiso decir, me hubiera preguntado: ¿Cómo diría yo eso? o ¿Cómo respondería a lo que este artista está diciendo? Eso me obligó —y fue un gran placer hacerlo— a estar cuidadosamente atento no solo a lo que otros artistas querían expresar, sino también a la manera cómo ellos intentaron decirlo. Siempre estuve muy atento a lo que estaba en la tela y a la manera cómo ella había sido hecha, pensada. Porque me interesaba determinar qué tipo de lenguaje era ese que estaba observando. Me enfrentaba a aquellas obras como un observador que quería aprender; o sea que ni siquiera me planteaba ser artista.

AJ Querías, sencillamente, aprender cómo había sido hecha aquella obra, lo que había logrado, y, supongo, también, determinar sus límites. . .

WC De sus límites todavía continúo aprendiendo. . . De alguna manera, aquellas observaciones me decían que cada artista tenía un modo de enfrentar los desafíos, el modo que prefería en su intento por lograr algo. Ahí me dediqué a buscar las características de este o aquel pintor, de este o aquel escultor. Entonces me di cuenta de que cada uno, más que un repertorio de formas, inventaba un destino. Cada uno respondía, por decirlo así, a una obsesión, y que la tentativa de responder a aquella obsesión se daba en la propia obra. Y eso me pareció sencillamente crucial para construir una expresividad propia. No estoy hablando de la voluntad de ser artista, sino de la voluntad de proponerme una voz, una expresión, y esa expresión la hallé en el arte. Ahí empieza un proceso clave, porque entonces comencé a encontrar en el mundo una variedad inmensa de objetos de arte y, por una razón que no sabría explicar, comencé a fabricar objetos que no encontraba en ninguna parte, solo para verlos surgir. Fueron los que mostré en mi primera exposición individual de 1965.

Es ahí, quizás, donde pude reconocer en mí esa necesidad de expresión, y en esos objetos, una capacidad incluso mayor para hacerse independientes de mí. Y eso me fascinó y me fascina hasta hoy; es decir, la capacidad que tiene un objeto para resistirse a ser la expresión personal de un individuo, y solo suya, para convertirse en uno independiente de su autor.

*Una obra densa trasciende sin duda a su autor, y a las ideas que la hicieron possible. Es una especie de organismo que, una vez agregado al mundo, evolu-*

*ciona con el tiempo y cobra formas nuevas para quien la observa. Se convierte en una fuente de sentido imprevisible, porque la vida cambia, y con ella nuestra mirada; de manera que una obra potente dice incluso más de lo que su artífice creyó poner en ella. Solo le falta un terreno fértil, y una mirada cómplice. Obras mayores permanecen a menudo durante siglos en el olvido (El jardín de las delicias del Bosco, es un ejemplo contundente), hasta que una mirada fresca, desde premisas insospechadas para su autor, la saca de nuevo a la luz y la hace pertinente. ¿Cómo verán nuestras obras los siglos por venir, qué les dirán de nosotros?*

WC Eso es lo que aprendo en ese momento, y en particular con las maquetas que hago justo después, en 1966–67, donde abandono los temas personales para abordar cuestiones espaciales y de arquitectura. Tal vez ya sea conveniente mencionar esa no-autoría estratégica que tienen mis obras; esa decisión casi casual que pertenece a su poética profunda, porque esa des-autoría deliberada me enseña mucho de lo que soy.

La obra por sí sola dice algo, se impone. Sus materiales, su estructura, se imponen como evidencias plásticas. El estado anímico del artista se impone también. Son tantas, en definitiva, las variables que entran en juego en la creación, que encuentro imposible privilegiar una en especial. Cuando un artista dice que solo hace lo que siente, es una mentira, porque él nunca tiene acceso pragmático a su sensibilidad. Su sensibilidad no está allí, simplemente disponible para su uso, sino que está sometida a una serie de presiones incontrolables —o de las cuales solo controla unas cuantas—, otras las modifica, las altera. Lo mejor de un trabajo es que la resultante del esfuerzo que requiere hacerlo, lo que surge de allí, es fundamental para todo el conjunto de la obra, y lo contrario sería perder las nuevas perspectivas que se generan a partir de él. Hoy en día dependo casi completamente del asombro productivo que lo justifica.

AJ En 1967 haces además las escenografías para una pieza de Eugène Ionesco, lo que te ofrece la posibilidad de trabajar al límite de dos prácticas artísticas, entre las artes plásticas y el teatro.

WC Lo que me interesó allí fue la ocasión de trabajar con el espacio literal y no con espacios metafóricos. Esa fue la gran lección de mi experiencia con el teatro, incluso si resulta irónico que ese trabajo comenzara justamente por la elaboración de una maqueta. Esta experiencia me hizo recordar la visita a la Bienal de Sao Paulo, en 1965, donde pude ver por primera vez las maquetas de un gran escenógrafo checo: Josef Svoboda [Fig. 5].[6] Sus escenografías me llamaron mucho la atención porque tenían una familiaridad con las mías, semejanzas que no eran formales, por supuesto, pero que me remitían en cierto modo al tratamiento del espacio tal y como yo lo entendía. Siempre me gustaron las escalas pequeñas que sugieren otras mayores, como si pudieran construirse espacios imaginarios. Ellas muestran el mundo de manera distanciada, el espacio representado, consolidándose metafísicamente, y eso fue lo que me conmovió en sus maquetas.

Ese año de 1967, Ronaldo Tapajós, un amigo que hacía teatro, me pidió que le hiciera la escenografía para *La lección*, de Eugène Ionesco. A él le tocó dirigirla como parte de sus trabajos de fin de curso en la universidad. Ambos éramos admiradores del teatro de lo absurdo y leíamos a Ionesco, Beckett, Sartre y Arrabal, y ya hacíamos algunos montajes en nuestro propio vecindario. Los textos teatrales, además, me atraían particularmente, porque proponen para su lectura una imaginación espacial de las escenas.

AJ Claro, porque están pensados para su materialización en el espacio.

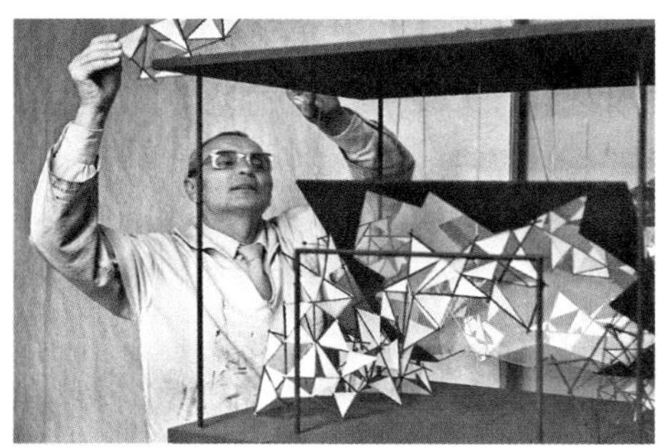

Fig. 5. Josef Svoboda, construyendo la maqueta para el ballet *Juan*, 1959.

WC Aquel montaje fue además la primera oportunidad que tuve para presentar un trabajo público, en un espacio real. Fue muy enriquecedora también porque propuse una escenografía en la que pudiera alterarse el concepto de tiempo. Pensé una iluminación que se modificaba con el desarrollo de la acción central, que terminaba en un asesinato. La iluminación fue pensada para aumentar paulatinamente la tensión del espectador hasta el punto de que la intuición de ese asesinato, que solo ocurre al final, se hace insoportable. Me pareció interesante asociar el espacio escénico a la duración narrativa, ya que la acción se desataba tras la aglomeración progresiva de una tensión en el tiempo.

En realidad es curioso que haya podido ver esas maquetas escenográficas de Svoboda en una exposición de artes plásticas como aquella bienal, que estaba dedicada al arte fantástico, donde se englobaba a Dadá y al Surrealismo. La pre-

6. Josef Svoboda (1920–2002), escenógrafo checo, activo en Praga, una de las figuras sobresalientes del teatro durante la segunda mitad del siglo XX. Fundador, junto a M. Radok, de la Laterna Magika y creador de diversas herramientas para el teatro, como la multipantalla y otros dispositivos de iluminación de influencia planetaria.

O moto perpétuo é um mecanismo imaginado para manter constante um movimento, sem realizar necessariamente uma operação útil. Nunca foi construído, apesar das muitas tentativas. Os insucessos criaram a convicção de que tal máquina é impossível, pois contraria as leis da ciência moderna. Curioso notar que, não obstante os fracassos, as realizações de suas impossibilidades levaram a descobertas as mais variadas.

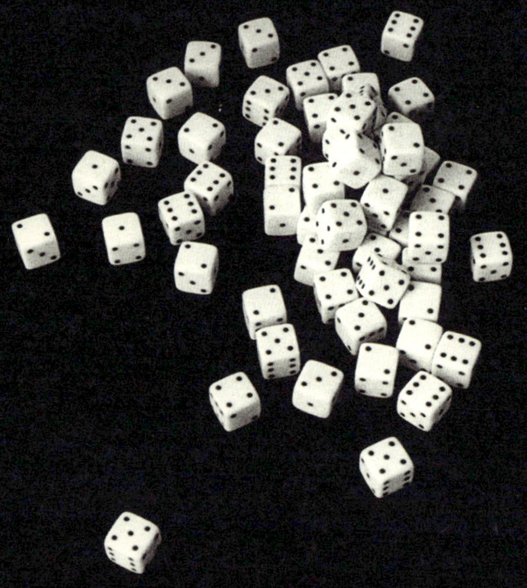

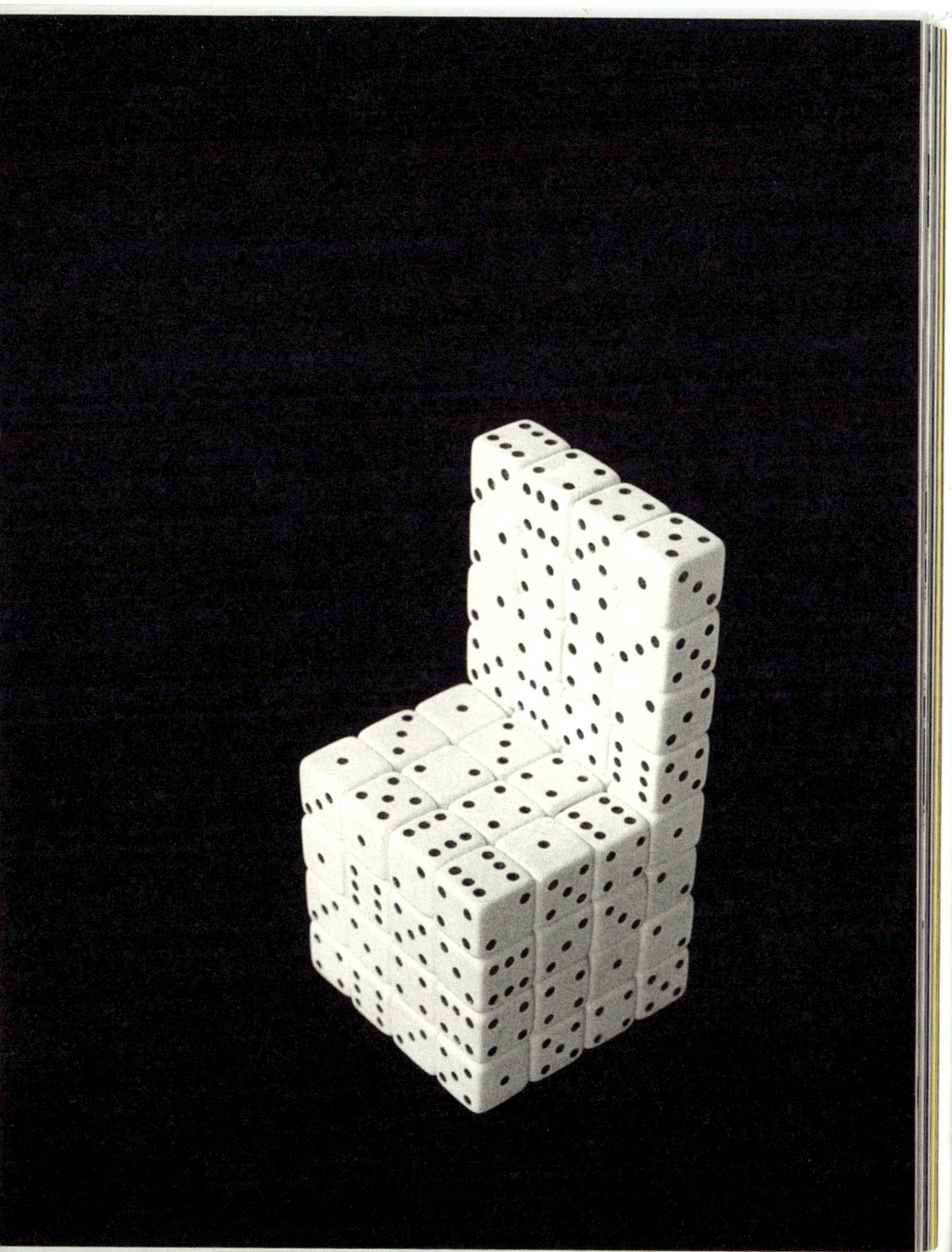

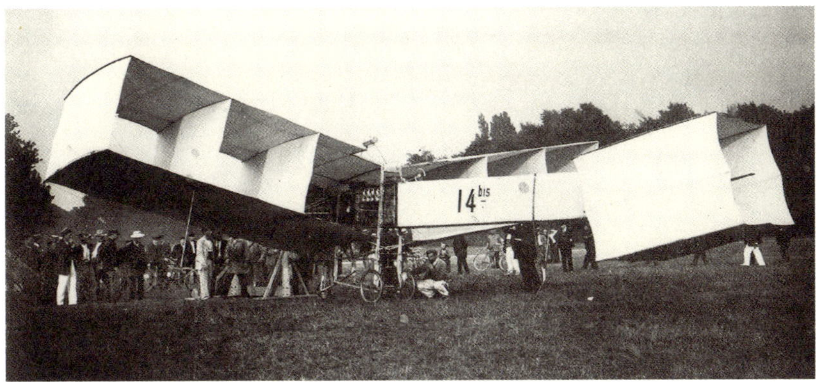

Fig. 6. Avión No 14-Bis del piloto brasileño Santos-Dumont, Bagatelle, Francia, 23 de octubre, 1906.

sencia de esas maquetas causó en mí una disfunción similar a la que había gene-
rado el avión de [Alberto] Santos-Dumont[7] en el aeropuerto de Río, durante mi
infancia. Era la reproducción a escala real de un objeto extraño, un avión, una
estructura que inventaba la posibilidad del vuelo, y encontrarme con él resultó
un impacto tremendo [Fig. 6].

AJ Y sin embargo, si no me equivoco, las de Svoboda eran maquetas en el sentido
estricto de la palabra; es decir, objetos a escala, planeados para ser realizados a
un tamaño mayor y muy preciso, mientras las tuyas no exigían necesariamente
su materialización a una escala diferente.

WC Sí, mis maquetas fueron pensadas para ser construidas a una escala mayor, solo
que dentro de una perspectiva más utópica. En una época en la que los pintores tenían dificultades para conseguir espacios donde colgar sus cuadros, era
absolutamente impensable que un joven artista estuviera coqueteando con la
idea de usar un terreno de 200 m². Sin embargo, ellas expresaban el deseo de
ser mayores, aunque con la certeza de que era y sería imposible realizarlas. No
obstante, tienes razón en un punto, y es que funcionan de la misma manera,
cumplen su función, incluso a esa escala de maqueta. No necesitan ser construidas, les basta ser una hipótesis. Tomemos por ejemplo esta maqueta, *Noche*,
que es de las primeras de 1967 [Fig. 7]. Es como si fuera un sitio olvidado del
mundo. Dos casas pequeñas, una noche inmensa, en una calle cualquiera. Pero
ella está construida de tal suerte que aquí, en este pequeño rincón, hay un cielo
interno, la noche universal. Es un lugar indeterminado, donde no pasa nada ni

7. Alberto Santos-Dumont (1873–1932), fue un aviador brasileño, precursor de la aviación, considerado en Brasil
como el primero en volar cumpliendo un circuito preestablecido. Su hazaña se realiza el día 23 de octubre de
1906 en el campo de Bagatelle, en París. El aeropuerto nacional de Río de Janeiro lleva por ello su nombre.

nadie, pero que, al mismo tiempo, lo contiene todo. Lo grandioso del universo en una situación casi íntima. Recuerdo que en esa época había un camión que circulaba por Río, donde un artista mostraba paisajes pintados en cabezas de alfileres. Uno entraba en el camión y se encontraba con una serie de mesas con microscopios. Entonces uno podía sentarse y ver los paisajes que el artista había pintado en los alfileres. Esa idea, la sospecha de que uno podía pintar algo muy grande en un espacio muy pequeño, me impresionó mucho en la época, sobre todo porque yo mismo buscaba el modo de producir esos juegos de escala.

En otra de esas maquetas, hoy destruida, había una casa que estaba siendo absorbida por un sistema hidráulico que la transformaba en un líquido espeso y negro, como el petróleo, y luego lo vertía en una piscina. . . Eso me recuerda. . . ¡qué curiosos son los mecanismos de asociación mental! . . . que en la época yo era también un lector de ficciones científicas y leí un libro que me impactó muchísimo. Se llamaba *Way Station* [*Estación de tránsito*] de Clifford D. Simak. Es la historia de una casa y de un niño. El niño está paseando por un campo y llega a una casa aislada en medio del paisaje, una casa que, por la descripción del libro, se encuentra allí de manera extraña. Era ligeramente diferente a las casas de la región, y eso llamó su atención, e hizo que se acercara para ver lo que había dentro. Entonces constata que estaba herméticamente cerrada. Mira por las ventanas y cree observar que allí no vive nadie. Por la descripción del libro, en aquella casa parecen suceder cosas que no son de este mundo. Poco a poco se hace evidente que era en realidad una especie de estación intergaláctica; es decir, un lugar en la tierra donde los que viajan por el cosmos pueden detenerse un tiempo, para luego continuar su viaje.

No recuerdo exactamente cómo ocurre, pero lo cierto es que el niño consigue entrar en la casa y se hace amigo del extraño ser que la habitaba. Entonces se dedica a observar los restos dejados por los habitantes de otras galaxias. ¡La capacidad del autor para inventar objetos era sorprendente! Recuerdo uno en particular: era una pirámide hecha de esferas que se movían constantemente las unas con respecto a las otras, sin que la pirámide dejara por ello de tener una configuración precisa. El autor describía cuatro o cinco de los objetos olvidados allí por los viajeros, y esas imágenes me causaron un gran impacto. En ese libro descubrí la posibilidad de imaginar objetos que no comparten necesariamente la temperatura, los materiales y las formas de nuestro mundo. Hoy puedo afirmar que lo más cercano a un objeto de arte son los objetos desconocidos.

Recuerdo otra historia similar, esta vez de Jorge Luis Borges, en uno de esos cuentos donde él describe situaciones inexplicables: un hombre muerto es encontrado en la frontera, nadie sabe de dónde viene y el autor sugiere que aquel hombre es el destino. Al final del cuento, se dice que si bien no se sabía

Fig. 7. *Maquette* [*Maqueta*] *V, A noite* [*La noche*], 1967.

quién era ni de dónde venía, había una cosa cierta, y era la presencia de un pequeño cubo que llevaba consigo en el bolsillo, un cubo de un metal que nadie logró identificar. Medía más o menos cuatro centímetros de lado, pero tenía la peculiaridad de ser tan pesado que ninguno de los presentes logró levantarlo del piso.

Si algo puedo decir con certidumbre es que esas dos referencias están siempre presentes en mi trabajo. Es como si yo persiguiera constantemente la posibilidad de producir objetos que, si no generan la duda de ser cosas reconocibles, sí que sean al menos capaces de provocar tensiones inesperadas en la percepción que tenemos de ellos. Por eso, la reacción del público ante mis objetos me interesa; porque es muy común, y lo fue sobre todo en los años setenta, que la gente encontrara que ellos también podían hacer objetos como los míos. Lo decían, claro, porque no los reconocían como producciones artísticas, y por eso pensaban que ellos también podían fabricarlos. A algunas de esas personas les llegué a preguntar si habían entendido lo que ellos significaban, y siempre respondían que no, que no sabían qué significaban ni para qué podían servir. Y eso me parecía por lo menos curioso; en verdad me costaba comprender cómo podían considerarse capaces de producir objetos que no podían descifrar. ¿Cómo podrían entonces concebirlos y fabricarlos? Porque ahí reside la paradoja, en esa osadía de los artistas para concebir objetos que no existían, pero que ahora están ahí, delante de nosotros, como una realidad inventada.

<sup>AJ</sup> Lo que el público no comprende, a menudo, es que lo complejo de una obra –su importancia y su belleza– no reside en su ejecución material, técnica, sino en el haber imaginado la posibilidad de su existencia. Y eso es lo que hace tan radicalmente difícil explicarles a algunas personas por qué el *Cuadrado negro sobre el fondo blanco* de Malevich, que es tan fácil de producir materialmente, sea quizás una de las obras más improbables que hayan sido realizadas en el siglo XX.

<sup>WC</sup> Sí, y que sigue siendo improbable a pesar de las garantías históricas. . . , porque tal vez esas personas no sepan que eso que reconocen como producciones artísticas de todos los tiempos, es todavía insuficiente para abarcar la dimensión de los asombros.

<sup>AJ</sup> Por eso insistía en la diferencia de naturaleza que se observa entre tus maquetas de 1967 y las de Svoboda, porque las tuyas no responden a una escala precisa, sino a una en todo caso indeterminada. No son una maqueta en el sentido utilitario del término.

<sup>WC</sup> No, por supuesto. ¿Podríamos hablar aquí de una escala hipotética? Es decir, ¿cuál sería el espacio específico sugerido por esas maquetas? ¿Sería, en todo caso, uno engendrado, inventado por ellas mismas? De mis trabajos suele decirse que es como si estuvieran siempre queriendo fundar el espacio que ocupan. Y estamos hablando aquí de un artista, en un momento cultural, que exigía más espacios para la actividad creadora. El artista brasileño de entonces no solo crea su obra, sino que también crea, por necesidad, las condiciones culturales para esa obra. Es decir, todos nosotros, una generación entera, se dedicaba a crear urgentemente nuevos espacios y nuevas condiciones. O sea que la necesidad de un ambiente cultural más abierto es incluso un esfuerzo de sobrevivencia estética.

 Y por eso es bellísimo que esas obras hayan sido pensadas como maquetas para un espacio posible, pero no determinado previamente.

 Es como si ese espacio fuera utópico, pero imaginado y paradójicamente posible. Por eso es que me siento tan a gusto hoy en día al hacer esculturas al aire libre, porque de alguna manera esa posibilidad ya era mi deseo desde el inicio, pues hasta mis esculturas al aire libre poseen un aspecto sorprendentemente intimista. Por eso digo que mi escultura a gran escala no es en realidad pública, sino íntima.

 Me parece muy instructivo comparar este modo de pensar el espacio en tu obra con la que puede observarse en algunas piezas de Jesús Soto. Cuando yo le preguntaba, por ejemplo, las razones de su interés por el cuadrado, se refirió entre otras cosas al hecho de que un cuadrado no tenía un tamaño determinado. Un árbol, decía, tiene una dimensión precisa, puede ser una o varias veces más grande que un hombre, nunca infinito o microscópico, mientras un cuadrado puede ser pensado de cualquier tamaño. No está atado a una escala determinada.

 La imagen del árbol tiene una escala mental ya prescrita, como la de muchos objetos creados por nosotros. Nadie imagina un libro de cuatro metros. Las figuras geométricas, por el contrario, son abstracciones, no tienen escala. Hay un objeto en mi *Manual da ciência popular* de 1982, que se titula *Princípio de realidade* [Fig. 8]. En el texto que lo acompaña digo de esos objetos que no tienen escala, lo que quiere decir que pueden hacerse de cualquier tamaño. Y si los llamo *Princípio de realidade*, es porque resulta graciosa la relación entre la idea de realidad y la falta de escala, y me recuerda una frase de Mondrian: la línea recta es una línea curva en su mayor tensión. Como si él considerara todo el tiempo que las líneas son siempre curvas, incluso la línea recta, que depende de la tensión natural de un horizonte hipotético.

 Es seductora la comparación, porque toda la obra de Soto, y en particular su producción de los años cincuenta, fue concebida de esta manera, como fragmentos de una realidad impensablemente mayor.

 ¿Existe acaso otro modo de pensar el arte que no sea así, es decir, como un hecho imposible, constante e inevitable? El arte estaría destruido si un día pudiéramos definirlo como algo apenas posible. En cierta forma, el arte es exactamente esa búsqueda incesante que altera la propia idea de búsqueda;

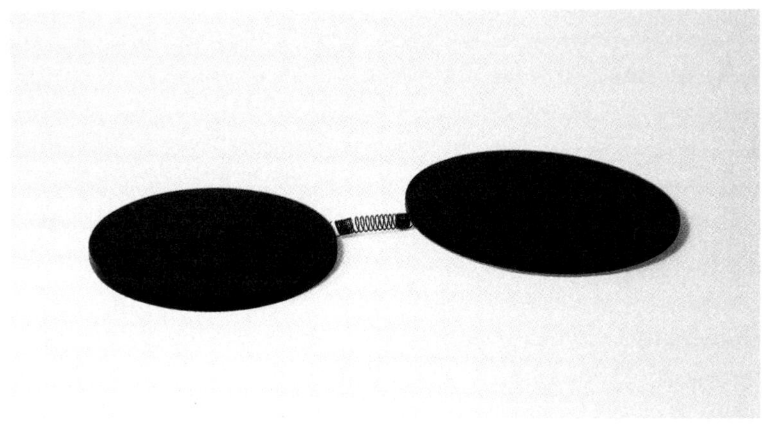

Fig. 8. *Princípio de realidade* [*Principio de realidad*], 1981.

porque no tiene objeto, uno no está buscando nada y es infinita la novedad de los encuentros.

AJ Por eso, lo que me pareció interesante en tus textos, al menos en los textos de un libro como *Notas, (   ) etc*, 2006, es precisamente esa clara voluntad de no cerrar el sentido de lo que se dice [Fig. 9][8]. Es como sí, voluntariamente, te propusieras construir una frase hasta el punto en el que algo parece decirse, justo antes de que se concrete uno cualquiera de los sentidos que se sugieren.

WC Es como mirar el océano. El mar nunca va a darnos el verdadero sentido de sí mismo, pero va a devolvernos la imaginación de nuestras expectativas para que la elaboremos aún más.

*La mejor visión de una cosa sugiere*
*su futuro inacabado*

AJ Frases como esta están construidas de tal manera que parecen querer decirme algo, pero algo que yo no podría descifrar exactamente, o que en todo caso debo completar. Es como enfrentarme a la probabilidad de sentido.

WC Sí, pero hay allí un pequeño detalle: no es que ellas quieran apuntar a algo. Ellas dicen, pero en lo que dicen no está contenido un significado restrictivo. Es como si quisiera colocar a las palabras en su máxima relación con las otras, que cada una mantenga la libertad conquistada por su autonomía. Como si

8. Waltercio Caldas, *Notas, (   ) etc*, (São Paulo: Gabinete de Arte Raquel Arnaud, 2006).

no quisiera cerrar el significado en la conclusión, sino en la posibilidad de la conclusión, como si quisiera liberarme del carácter afirmativo de los aforismos.

AJ Por eso mismo, quizás, las llamabas frases, porque no te parecía conveniente, o preciso, llamarlas versos. . .

WC Las llamé *Notas*. Me tomó tiempo encontrarles un título, porque no era suficiente una palabra. Por eso las llamé *Notas*. Y luego agregué el paréntesis vacío y ese *etc.,* que deja imaginar algo que no se conoce, y añade un tercer precipicio, como si las cosas, todas, fueran otras. Un elemento es conocido, es temporal: *Notas*. El segundo es algo sugerido pero ignorado. Y el tercero, ese *etc.,* es un disparo hacia lo desconocido. Me da mucho trabajo desnudar frases . . . [risas].

AJ Hay un hecho curioso en ellas, como si esas frases se acercaran a los límites del verso sin llegar a serlo, incluso sin querer serlo.

WC Es como si solo quisieran de la poesía su libertad. . .

AJ Y a la vez, parecen un aforismo.

WC Del aforismo solo quiero la forma sintética y circunstancial. . .

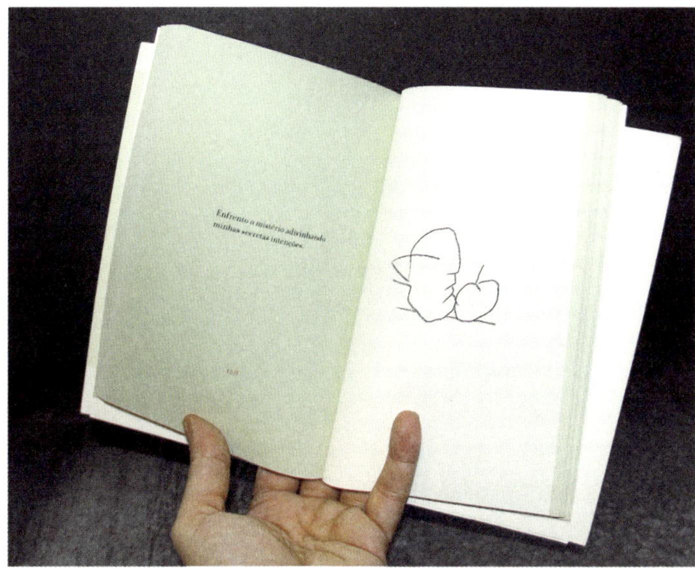


Fig. 9. *Notas, (   ) etc,* 2006.

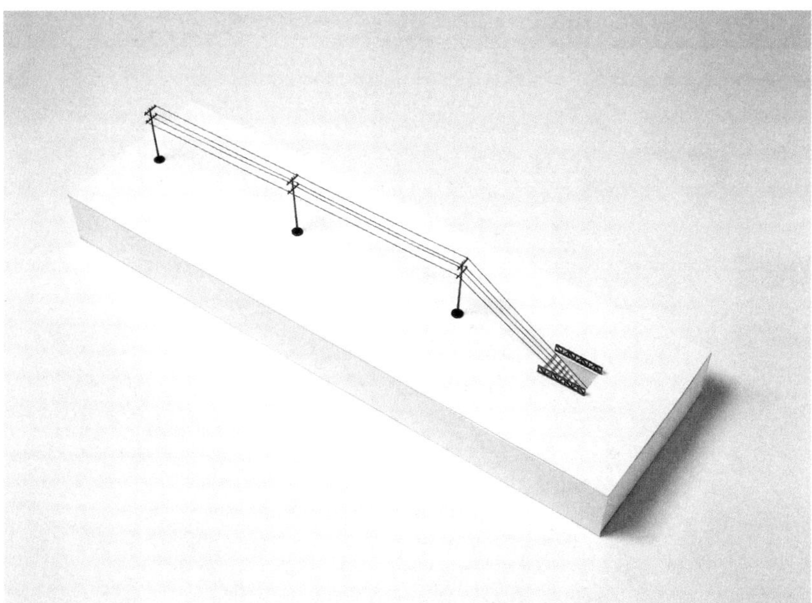

Fig. 10. *Maquette* [*Maqueta*] *I*, 1967.

<sup></sup>AJ Entonces estamos efectivamente, como lo decía el crítico de arte Ronaldo Brito,[9] ante un arte de los límites. Y esa es una característica que encontramos no solo en tus libros, en esas frases, sino también en tus objetos y dibujos.

WC Sí, es como si yo me sintiera cómodo con el arte solamente cuando imagino para él una dimensión mayor de la que yo mismo soy capaz de alcanzar o de imaginar.

AJ Y por eso me pareció tan significativo cuando dijiste que empezaste construyendo objetos (y no esculturas), y tratando de producir lo que no encontrabas en los otros artistas. Era como hacer lo que no veías en ellos, como abrir una brecha entre sus obras, en esa segunda naturaleza de la cultura.

WC Y eso se va haciendo aún más grave con la edad, porque se incorporan cosas que uno mismo no quiere hacer, incluso obras que hizo anteriormente. Entonces uno se encuentra ante la tentación de liberarse de su propia historia, y eso crea una situación nueva. En ese momento aprendes lo importante que es dejar "abiertos" ciertos trabajos, porque sabes que necesitarás de esa apertura en el

9. Ronaldo Brito escribe: "El trabajo está atado a los límites del arte, su exigencia es situarse, desde allí, en los extremos máximos. Más que conciencia, el trabajo tiene la obsesión de los límites. Respira esa tensión y extrae fuerza de esa ambigüedad". En *Aparelhos*, (Río de Janeiro: GBM Editora de Arte, 1979), p. ii.

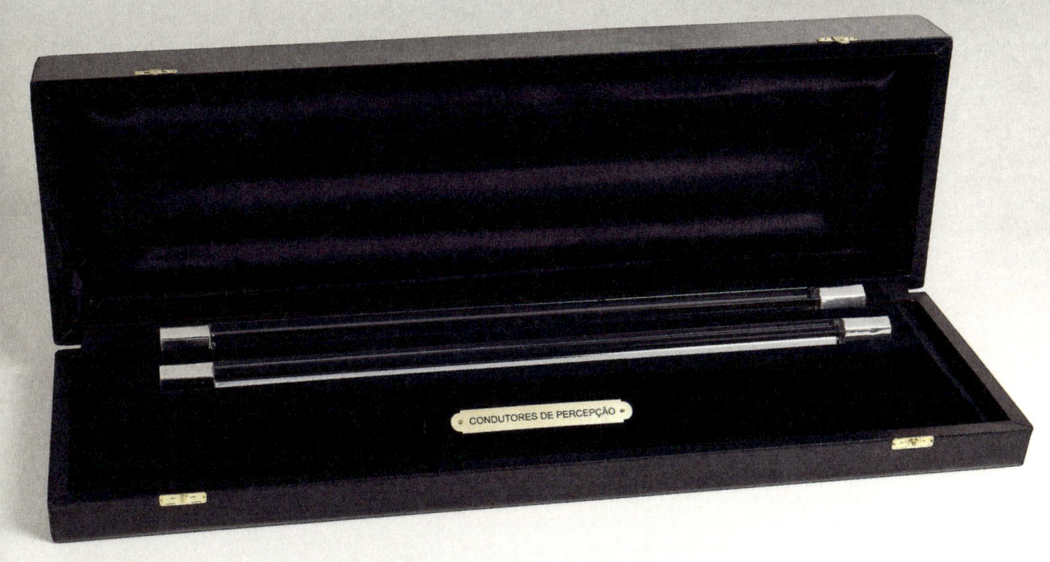

Fig. 11. *Condutores de percepção* [*Conductores de percepción*], 1969.

futuro. Y eso se convierte en una obsesión. Esa libertad se hace materia de las obras.

<sup>AJ</sup> Volvamos, nuevamente, a los años sesenta, para discutir ahora una serie que considero muy significativa, los *Condutores de percepção*, de 1969. Esta serie representa quizás el inicio claro de lo que podríamos llamar tu producción madura. Sin embargo, cuando la comparamos con algunas maquetas de 1967, como la *Maqueta I*, por ejemplo, constatamos que su funcionamiento es bastante similar [Figs. 10 y 11].

<sup>WC</sup> Ambas son conductores de energía.

<sup>AJ</sup> Sin duda, son conductores, pero conductores que están imposibilitados para cumplir su función.

<sup>WC</sup> Yo te diría que el azul no necesita ser verdadero para ser azul. El arte se ocupa de sugestiones, es decir, de proponer in-evidencias. Matisse lo abordó cuando demostró que el azul podía ser absolutamente nuevo utilizando el mismo azul de siempre. El problema reside en la relación entre los colores; esto es, que es en la manera como se organiza una frase que se produce el sentido. El hecho de que yo utilice objetos reconocibles en esas primeras maquetas no indica

necesariamente que ellos deban funcionar como en la realidad. El problema está en otro lugar, y en mi caso un objeto está bien empleado si él simplemente demuestra que todavía podría llegar a ser otro. Un conductor no necesita necesariamente conducir efectivamente algo, basta con sugerir la posibilidad de que pudiera hacerlo. Hay evidentemente alguna libertad plástica en estas sugerencias.

<sup>AJ</sup> Por supuesto, pero en realidad me refería a algo más elemental: el hecho de que al estar interrumpidos, esos cables eléctricos no conducen energía, pero sugieren la posibilidad de que aquello podría continuar indefinidamente en la dirección indicada por ambos extremos, con ese enigma extra que significa el que uno de sus bordes penetre, de manera inhabitual, en la calzada.

<sup>WC</sup> Es una serie que nace del intento por establecer una relación límite, por decirlo así, entre lo que el objeto es y lo que dice de sí mismo. Allí aparece la relación no solo entre el título y el objeto, sino también entre la palabra, lo que ella expresa y lo que ella es. Está claro que esos objetos no son conductores de percepción, en el sentido técnico. Al final, ¿qué podría ser un conductor de percepción? Pero también es innegable que la palabra tiene el poder de transformar ese objeto en un conductor de percepción. Es decir, que utilizo la palabra para definir su función, nombrándolo. Yo diría que son obras donde la percepción del objeto es en realidad el conductor sugerido. Como si fuera posible, por ejemplo, realizar la autonomía de una idea, utilizando cosas y palabras, no necesariamente agregando una a la otra, sino confrontándolas.

Y de la confrontación surge un objeto de un nuevo tipo que ya no es solo palabra o solo objeto, sino una idea justificada por la presencia del objeto. Y tal vez por eso puede considerarse como un objeto de tercer tipo, más complejo de lo que parece ser. La serie completa de estos objetos de los años sesenta consta de unos diez o doce trabajos, todos destacan el límite entre los nombres y las cosas.

<sup>AJ</sup> Del límite que ocupa en nuestro espacio de sentido, y de los que nuestra percepción le impone.

<sup>WC</sup> Sí, de los límites que nuestra percepción intenta imponerle. Para eso, el objeto tendría que ser activo. Un objeto activo no se entrega a la mirada, sino que nos obliga a verlo con una nueva actitud. Porque uno no es pasivo cuando observa una obra de arte. Inmediatamente ella te llama y te invita a un juego, y uno se ve dentro del juego. No es un objeto sobre el cual yo pueda depositar autorita-

riamente mis ideas, porque él perturba la expectativa que me he hecho sobre él. Uno puede incluso cerrar esa caja y negar ese enfrentamiento, pero ya fue abierta y no podemos negar lo que vimos. Esos conductores de percepción pueden decirnos que a partir de este momento ya no somos los mismos.

AJ Lo que haces entre la palabra y el objeto, la relación que instauras entre ellos, es similar a la que los surrealistas buscaban establecer entre una palabra y otra dentro del verso. Esos objetos funcionan un poco como el verso descrito por Pierre Reverdy, cuando decía que la imagen poética era el resultado del choque entre dos palabras distintas y distantes, y que la fuerza de la imagen poética dependía de la potencia del choque, del chisporroteo que pudiera producir el encuentro de dos realidades dispares.

WC Después de Dadá y el Surrealismo nada ha sido hecho sin considerar esa posibilidad inaugural. Lo que encuentro fundamental en ellos es el hecho de que algo más que el mundo conocido pueda motivar a los artistas. Con ellos, por primera vez, el mundo subjetivo también puede ser tratado como materia de arte. Y ahí reside, a mi entender, la gran libertad introducida por los surrealistas. Ahora, hay otro aspecto en estos objetos que quiero señalar. En esa época, parte del arte nos hacía creer que era posible, e incluso indispensable, manipular la obra de arte para comprenderla mejor. Pero a mí nunca me pareció que aquello fuera una regla. Aun cuando admiro la obra de Lygia Clark, encuentro que su intención de que la obra sea manipulada es una propiedad más del objeto, como el color o la materia.

De manera que en esos objetos-caja, yo estaba buscando uno que no necesitara ser manipulado, y donde el secreto, o quizás el hermetismo, fuera también capital para su aparición. Para mí, que he sido un artista siempre preocupado por los procesos de desciframiento en la obra de arte, esa dificultad era aún más importante. Incluso, cuando entro en una exposición y percibo que el artista está tratando de facilitarme esa confrontación a la que nos invita toda obra de arte, me siento casi ofendido, porque entiendo que soy yo quien debe hacer el esfuerzo necesario para desentrañar lo que aquello significa, si lo quiero, si estoy disponible para intentarlo. Por eso mismo, nunca me ofende si algunas personas me dicen que mi trabajo es difícil de comprender, porque encuentro que esa es una característica del arte, como lo es del cielo, del mar, de la naturaleza misma. Es decir, ¿cómo puede comprenderse un árbol?, ¿hay un modo adecuado de hacerlo?

AJ Me interesa muchísimo lo que estás diciendo, porque cuando uno lee lo que han escrito artistas como Lygia Clark y algunos críticos, particularmente en los años sesenta, parece que quisieran oponer la densidad psíquica de esos objetos manipulables —que es real— a la relación puramente óptica que, según ellos, se daba entre el espectador y la pintura, olvidando que eso nunca fue así, que la pintura fue y ha sido siempre una experiencia mental, cultural, más que óptica.

WC Ella ha dicho (aunque yo nunca la escuché) que el cerebro también es una víscera. Y es que quizás Lygia encontró, como cualquier artista que asuma ese riesgo, que la relación del espectador con la pintura era insuficiente. Entonces se comprende mejor su actitud. Tatlin halló que la experiencia del arte tenía límites en su tiempo, y entonces intentó construir un avión. Cada artista, en su momento, siente que el arte realizado es insuficiente, que la experimentación no tiene ya vuelta atrás, que debe ir hacia delante, porque a partir de cierto punto solo existe salvación por el movimiento que amplía el horizonte. Un punto sin retorno posible.

Es un momento crucial para el artista, en el que la obra se aniquila y se hace al mismo tiempo, en la que uno se siente impedido para cerrarla pues ella solo se cerrará con la muerte. En ese sentido, les doy un crédito muy grande a los artistas Dadá por haber puesto la moralidad cultural bajo sospecha, y por haber colocado el cadáver sonámbulo del conformismo ante el abismo. Duchamp es quien llega y le da un soplo preciso, tan preciso, que le impide a ese cadáver volver a la vida. Lo importante es la calidad de ese soplo de Duchamp, la calidad espontánea del acto, como la de todas sus manifestaciones, que surgen como si fueran hechas por casualidad, y con cierta indiferencia. Así garantiza que ese cadáver no volverá insepulto. No hablo de "la muerte del arte", pero sí de lo inapropiado de creer en la garantía que representa una historia definitiva del arte.

AJ La mayoría de los artistas pasa por etapas o períodos de su producción que pueden ser ubicados cronológicamente con bastante exactitud, de manera que con solo observar la paleta empleada, o el tema tratado, podríamos determinar a qué momento corresponde. En ti, por el contrario, se hace a veces considerablemente difícil situar una obra por sus particularidades materiales o formales, salvo quizás en los objetos construidos por ti. Casi me atrevería a afirmar que, en tu caso, son las exposiciones y los libros los que marcan con mayor precisión un ciclo o una faceta crucial en tu carrera. Es lo que sucede, por ejemplo, con la exhibición que organizas en 1973 para el Museu de Arte Moderna de Río de Janeiro (MAM).

WC Es curioso que esa exposición tan temprana haya sido planeada como una retrospectiva. Yo venía trabajando en solitario desde 1965, y algunos de mis objetos circulaban por dos o tres colecciones privadas, pero nada más. Cuando la directora del museo me invita a exponer, hice una selección de lo que había venido produciendo en los últimos cinco años. No tuve muchos inconvenientes al presentarlos, porque se trataba de objetos que tenían ya una cierta conexión entre sí. En todo caso, organicé la muestra en torno a dos vectores. Uno era el de los objetos-caja dentro de pequeñas urnas de vidrio, y que incluía también los *Condutores de percepção*. Allí expuse, entre otras, una obra titulada *O louco* [*El loco*], de 1971, una caja larga que debía abrirse esperando que contuviera algo, y resulta que el público se encontraba con ese hombrecillo que camina en una calle, un espacio inmenso dentro de la caja [Fig. 12].

El segundo vector era el de los dibujos, instalados en una sala aparte. Con esos dibujos intenté hacer una especie de enciclopedia visual, como si se tratara de definiciones visuales para objetos registrados en esa analogía imaginaria. Había un dibujo para el astronauta, uno para la locomotora, el cohete, etc., etc. El objetivo era que cada uno representara la imagen de un objeto: eran pequeñas viñetas de un almanaque inconcluso. Para darte una idea, imagínate una esfera dibujada en el papel, una esfera en sí pequeña, de donde salía una multitud de pájaros, lo que hacía que fuera percibida como algo enorme. Lo titulé *Ciência* [*Ciencia*]. Recuerdo otro donde se veían los rieles de un tren, y sobre ellos solo humo saliendo encima de los rieles, pero sin el tren. Luego, entre ambos –el humo y los rieles– había una cuenta, una serie de números adicionados, como una matemática fuera de lugar. Ahí expuse también *O coleccionador* [*El coleccionista*], de 1973, como si se tratara de alguien que coleccionara la palabra "Fim" [fin], como los Fin que aparecen al final de las películas [Fig. 13].

AJ Y claro, se trataba de una colección, en principio, infinita, o al menos de duración y extensión indeterminadas.

WC Y esa fue, además, la obra que coloqué al final la exposición.

AJ Son sin duda objetos borgianos. Las descripciones que haces me llevan a recordar ese cuento de Borges donde se describen las ruinas, a escala 1:1, de un mundo perdido, que habría cubierto el planeta entero. Lo recuerdo como un cuento donde ruinas reales se convertían en fragmentos dispersos de un mundo imaginario que habría desaparecido por completo.

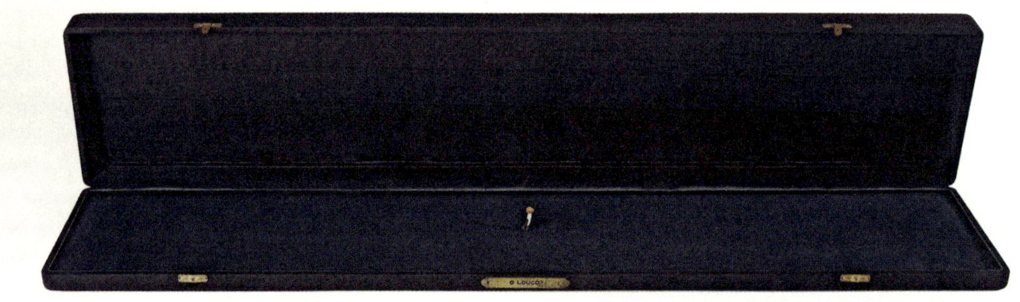

Fig. 12. *O louco* [*El loco*], 1971.

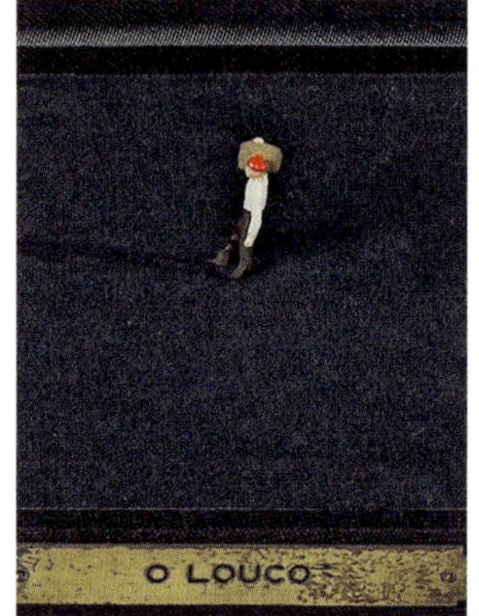


WC Sí, es como si fuera posible hacer una especie de arqueología del imaginario humano o algo así, ¿cierto?

AJ Exacto, pero de un imaginario cuyos fragmentos quedan esparcidos por el mundo, son reales.

WC Eso es lo interesante, que el arte permita la realización de una escala que no es ni humana ni inhumana. En ese sentido, el arte sería una tercera escala, una escala específica. . . Llegué incluso a elaborar objetos que llamé "objetos de tercer tipo", de los que ya hablamos antes, los hice hacia 1997. Es algo, además, que tiene que ver con la manera cómo trato, por ejemplo, el funcionamiento de los espejos.

AJ Que es un tema típicamente borgiano y una de las grandes preocupaciones de la pintura representativa. Antes, sin embargo, de tratar el tema de los espejos, me gustaría abordar la exposición que hiciste con ese sugestivo título de *A natureza dos jogos* [*La naturaleza de los juegos*], de 1975, en el Museu de Arte de São Paulo. ¿Por qué te interesaste por los juegos?

WC Porque yo estaba realizando mis primeras exposiciones, y la relación entre las obras y el medio ambiente cultural tomaba para mí, a veces, la forma de un

166

juego. Entre 1973 y 1975 se dan los primeros acercamientos a ese asunto de las exhibiciones, que para mí nunca fueron una simple colección de objetos dispuestos en el ambiente. Desde mi primera exposición en el Museu de Arte Moderna do Rio de Janeiro, reconocí en el montaje la posibilidad de realizar otro trabajo, una nueva condición poética para las obras. Es decir que la solución no vendría dada solamente por la ubicación de los objetos en el espacio, sino que sería conceptual, que dependería también de cuestiones de escala, de arquitectura y de espacios narrativos en las instituciones, museos y galerías.

<sup>AJ</sup> Pienso que para ti, como lo es para mí, la exposición es una especie de gesto cultural que uno introduce en un espacio mayor, que es el medio cultural en el que se actúa.

<sup>WC</sup> Sí, solo que una cosa es confrontar un objeto conocido a otro, para ir creando paso a paso nuevas asociaciones, y otra tener que enfrentarse a un objeto desconocido, y relacionarlo a otro que tampoco conocemos. En ese momento se desarticula el juego y uno se encuentra de nuevo perdido en el espacio [Fig. 14]. Y esa situación obliga al visitante a repensar las relaciones entre todos los elementos considerados anteriormente. Y en cierto modo las obras van a exigir ese tipo de reconsideración todo el tiempo, porque si ellas son realmente nue-

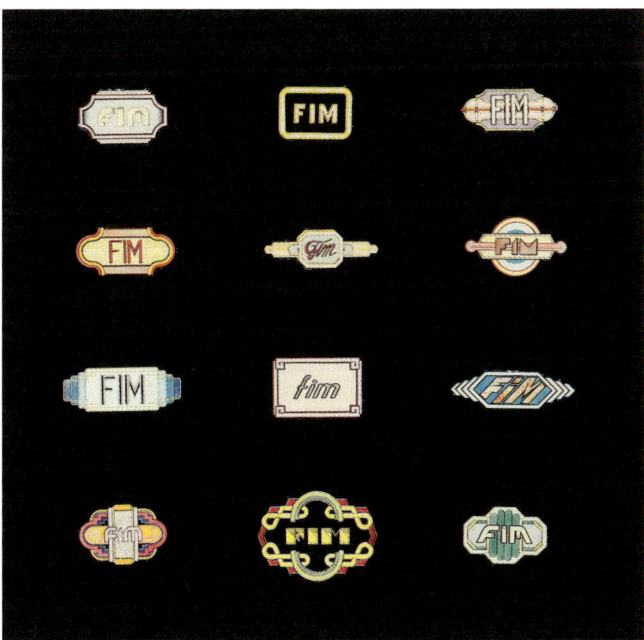

Fig. 13. *O colecionador [El coleccionista]*, 1973.

vas, si aportan algo nunca visto, eso quiere decir que durante un tiempo van a permanecer como algo inclasificable, extraño. Y luego, poco a poco, un texto informativo y los rótulos de las obras van a reducir esa extrañeza, y la obra comienza a ser ubicable dentro de una historia. Pero ese instante inaugural de perplejidad y desconocimiento es muy importante, y me parece que es el momento privilegiado de las obras de arte. Mi ambición secreta sería conseguir que ese momento dure el mayor tiempo posible. Eso porque cuando uno identifica o clasifica una obra, nunca más podrá verla por primera vez, y solo podrá reconocerla. Y eso me suena como una pérdida.

AJ Es así como yo veía la tarea del curador; como una persona cuya función ideal consistiría en potenciar los sentidos de una obra o de un conjunto de obras. Un curador es un individuo que produce sentido a partir de su reflexión sobre el arte. Desde ese punto de vista, podría proceder de diversas maneras, dependiendo de la o las obras con las que trabaje. Es decir que, cuando estamos en presencia de una obra nueva, por ejemplo, su labor podría consistir en hacerla legible para el público de la época, ubicándola como tú dices, o al menos

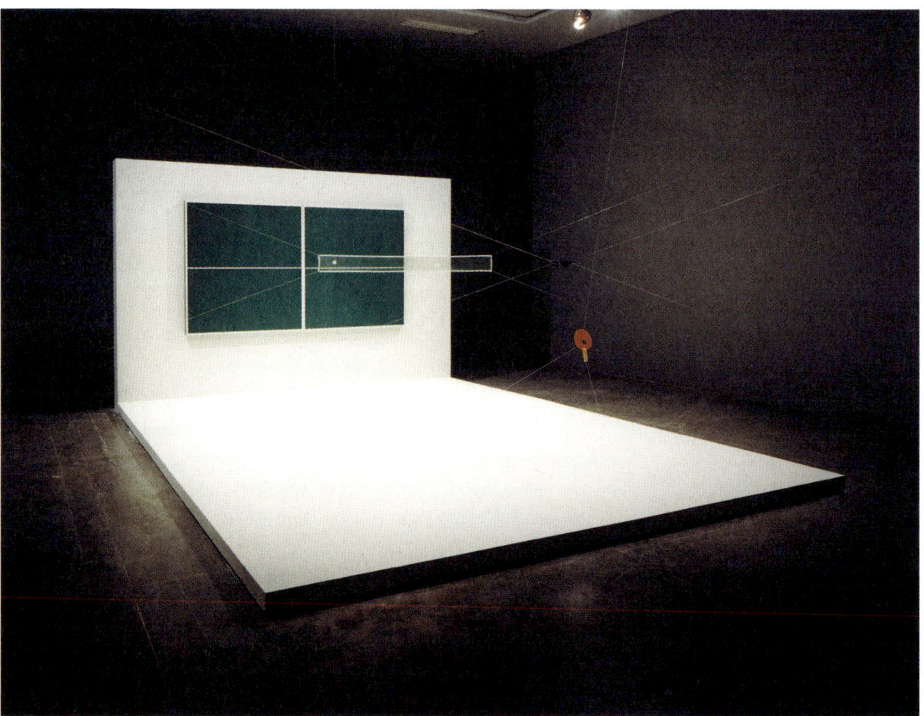

Fig. 14. *Ping-Ping, A construção de abismo no piscar dos cegos* [*Ping-Ping, La construcción de abismo en un parpadeo de los ciegos*], 1980.

dándole al público algunas pistas de lectura. Mientras que en el caso de una obra perfectamente inscrita en la historia del arte, su función sería más compleja, porque consistiría, por una parte, en hacerla legible para el espectador, inscribiéndola en su contexto histórico, pero también, de algún modo, buscando los medios para que esa obra despliegue su potencial de contemporaneidad. Y eso no se consigue sino restituyendo en parte su opacidad primera, su capacidad de asombro. Un curador sería pues un individuo que, interrogando las obras desde perspectivas diferentes (las que se hacen posible en su tiempo), estaría en capacidad de develar en ella zonas de opacidad o de sentido desconocidas.

WC  Yo diría que sí, siempre y cuando el curador sea sensible a la propuesta poética de la obra, porque se supone que ella tiene esa prerrogativa antes que el curador.

AJ  Yo te diría también que sí, mientras no se confunda esa propuesta poética con un supuesto sentido que estaría inscrito en la obra de manera definitiva y unívoca, como si no fuera posible ver en ella otra cosa que eso que el artista habría inscrito, porque entonces toda obra, una vez conocida la versión de su autor, quedaría condenada irremediablemente a esa versión. Jamás podría hablarnos de nuevo.

WC  Por eso es que todo artista fue y sigue siendo contemporáneo de algún modo. Es decir que la de Velázquez puede ser vista como una obra todavía actual, e incluso con mayor placer, precisamente por ese cúmulo de información que no tuvieron sus contemporáneos.

AJ  Y en ese sentido, la mejor y más importante tarea de un curador sería esa: la de revelar su particular forma de ser contemporánea.

WC  Quizás, aunque lo que sucede hoy en día es lo contrario, ¿cierto? A menudo el curador intenta imponerle a una obra contemporánea características que la limitan, en el sentido de que procura hacer que una historia rápida, actual, la justifique. Tanto, que a mi entender una exposición bien concebida, al suponer que el curador haya sido competente en su tarea, sería una que hubiera superado las expectativas del curador. Porque si una obra no resiste a la versión del curador y no es capaz de decir otra cosa, siempre otra cosa más, será insignificante.

AJ  Es así, estrictamente. Una obra densa es aquella que supera las expectativas de su autor y las de su espectador. . . ¿No te parece? Solo que no se puede esperar que eso ocurra en una sola exposición, en un único texto. No se puede decir todo en una muestra, ni puedes pretender agotar las virtualidades de una obra en un simple ensayo. De lo contrario, te arriesgas a la imposibilidad de comunicar, de decir algo legible.

<sup>WC</sup> En ese sentido, una de las virtudes mayores de toda obra de arte sería su capacidad de resistencia, su capacidad para resistir a cualquier versión, incluso a la del artista.

<sup>AJ</sup> Es así como entiendo las preocupaciones que tuviste desde tu primera exposición, cuando intuiste que debías pensar sobre la recepción de tu obra.

<sup>WC</sup> Sí, salvo que la exhibición debe ser pensada como arquitectura. Es como si yo me dijera, al reunir las obras: "tengo ya la materia prima, pero no es suficiente ubicarlas". Es imperativo construir con ellas una poética otra, la poética de la espacialidad, de su presencia pública. En ese momento entendí algo crucial para mí, y es que contrariamente a lo que buscaban Hélio Oiticica y Lygia Clark, mis objetos necesitaban una cierta distancia silenciosa ante el público. En ese sentido, nunca he realizado un objeto o una escultura que pretenda crear una empatía fácil con el observador. Nunca los pensé como manipulables. Mis objetos debían estar físicamente concluidos, pero preservando un silencio incompleto.

En general los visitantes de bienales y grandes exposiciones no pasan más de quince segundos delante de una obra, entonces es necesario dedicarle una atención crítica a esos instantes de contacto. Hay que establecer entre el espectador y las obras, entre ambos y el espacio, una tensión que produzca sentido. Hay que pensar la evidencia plástica de los ambientes, un poco como lo hace Gastón Bachelard en su libro *La poética del espacio*. De manera que pienso el recinto museal como una prolongación de mi trabajo, de mi relación con el espacio.

<sup>AJ</sup> Como uno más de los componentes de ese juego de sentido que emerge en y de la exposición. . .

<sup>WC</sup> Ahí está. Con *A natureza dos jogos* entendí que podía tratar la exposición como un juego entre los objetos y los espectadores.

<sup>AJ</sup> ¿Y las obras se referían a juegos conocidos o partían de una noción más general o conceptual del juego?

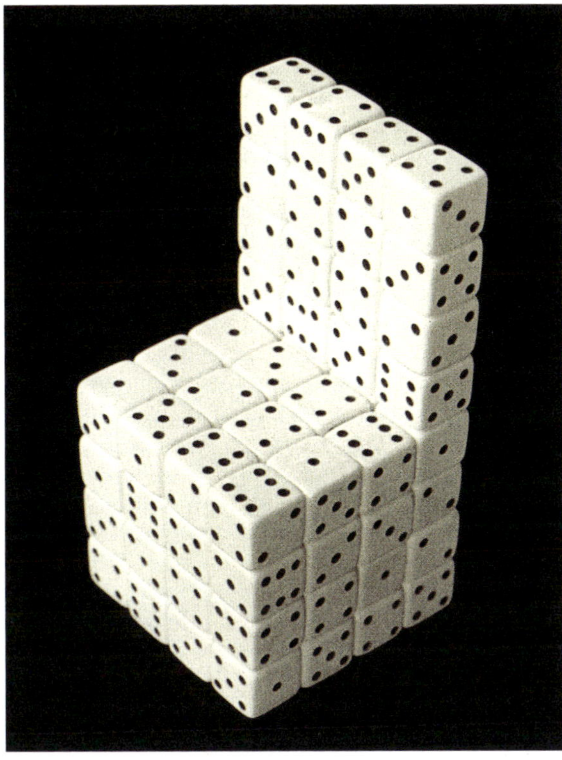

Fig. 15. *Moto perpétuo*
[*Movimiento perpetuo*],
1973.

 Yo diría que se trataba de una noción general del juego, del azar, del árbitro. Usaba los dados como una materia prima [Fig. 15]. Allí mostré *Leitura silenciosa* [*Lectura silenciosa*], de 1975, que se refería al método de enseñanza que consiste en pedirle a un alumno que lea en silencio un texto, para que luego nos lo explique. El objetivo es determinar cuánto ha comprendido del texto. Pero en mi caso se trataba de objetos dibujados, y era paradójico sugerirle al público que hiciera de ellos una lectura en silencio [Fig. 16]. La muestra tenía también conductores de percepción e incluso el primer espejo de luz, como ese que está en la Colección Patricia Phelps de Cisneros.

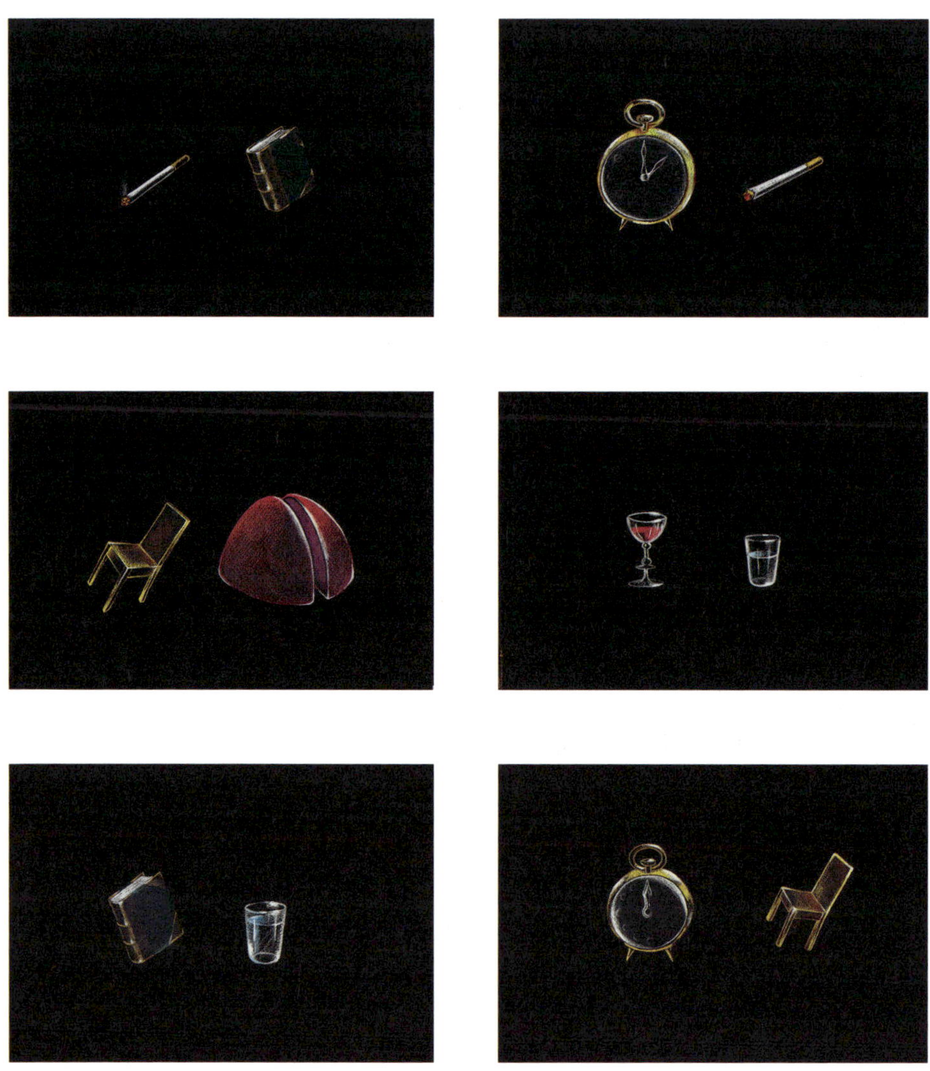

Fig. 16. *Leitura* [*Lectura*] *silenciosa*, 1975.

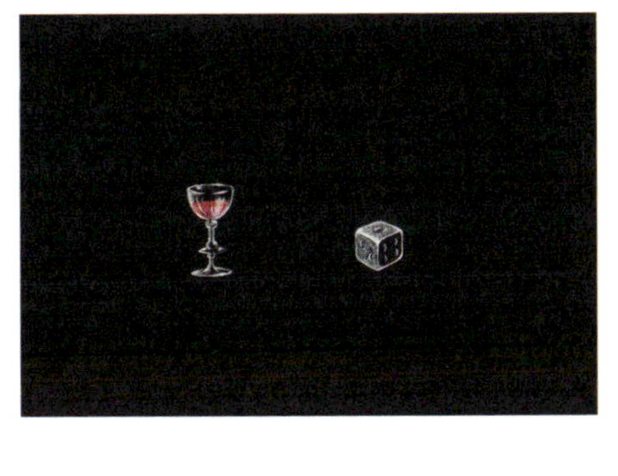

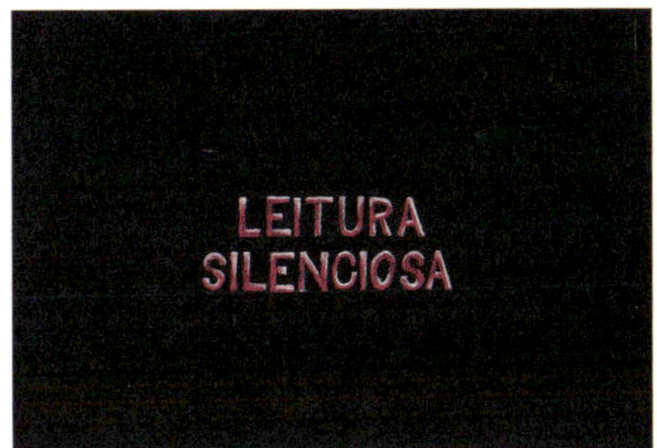
LEITURA
SILENCIOSA

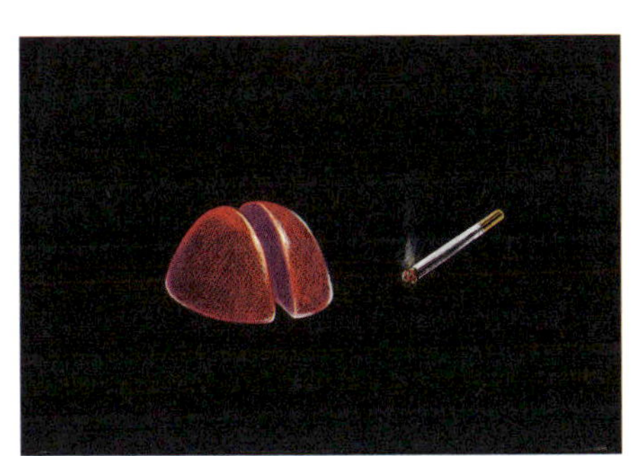

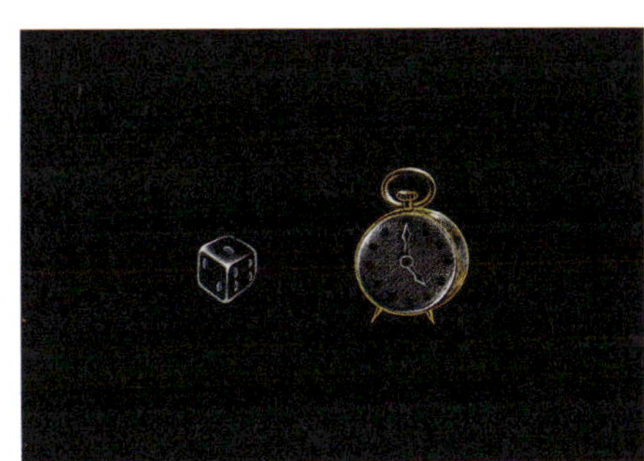

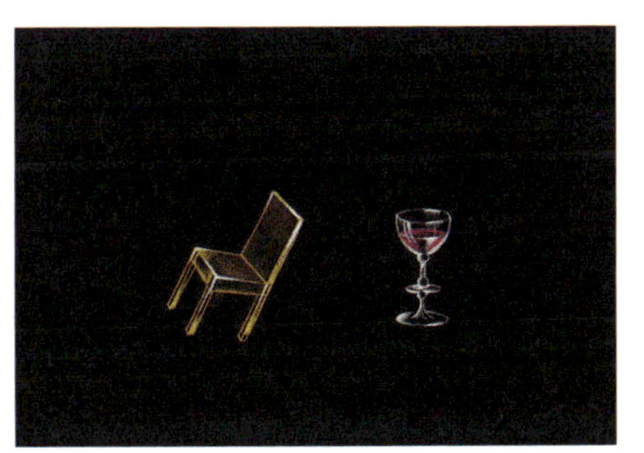

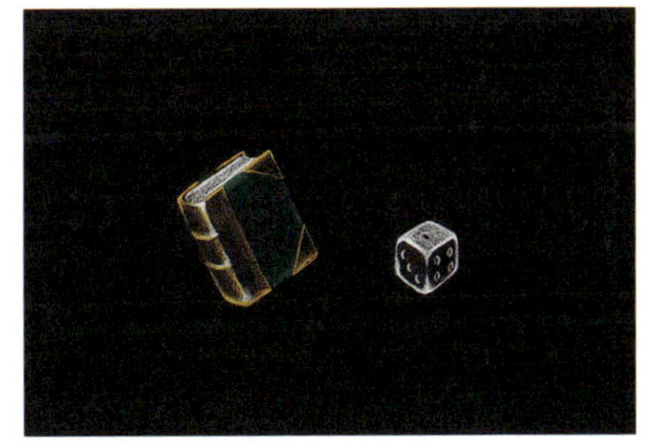

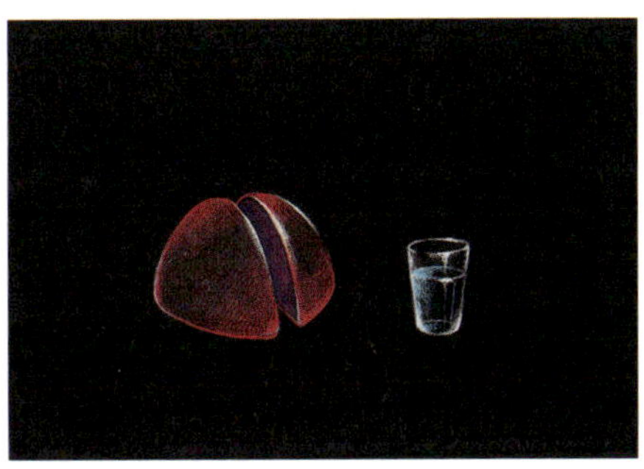

# LA INFINITA POSIBILIDAD DEL ENCUENTRO
## *The point of no return.*

*En varios puntos de nuestra conversación, Waltercio Caldas insistió en el peso
que tienen para un artista, y para él en particular, no solo esa segunda naturaleza del arte y su historia, sino además el conjunto de los objetos realizados por
él. Lo recordaba cuando era todavía un adolescente, destruyendo la multitud de
dibujos que había hecho entre los catorce y los veintiún años, para "liberarse"
de su presencia opresiva. Lo señalaba, también, al hablar de sus primeras
maquetas. A partir de un determinado momento lo que hacemos comienza a
pesar sobre nosotros, a oponernos su resistencia. El estilo nos acecha y con él la
costumbre. "¿Es que Dios tiene un estilo? (le preguntaba Picasso a Malraux)*
[. . .] Él hizo la guitarra, el arlequín, el basset, el gato, la lechuza, la
paloma. Como yo. El elefante y la ballena, bien, ¿pero el elefante y la
ardilla? Un desorden!!! Él hizo lo que no existía. Yo también!!".[10] *Y esa
exigencia lo lleva en su caso hasta a decir que un artista no debía dibujar a su
manera (Ingres dibujaba como Ingres, cuando en realidad habría que dibujar
como la cosa que se dibuja). . .* "Si tomas por ejemplo un árbol. Debajo de
ese árbol hay una cabra, y al lado de la cabra una niña que cuida a la
cabra. Pues bien! hace falta un dibujo diferente para cada uno. La cabra
es redonda, la niña cuadrada, el árbol es un árbol [. . .] Y sin embargo,
nos servimos del mismo dibujo para los tres".[11]

WC Uno intenta crear lo que no existe, agregar al mundo conocido algo nuevo para
que la visión y los sentidos se sorprendan. En mi caso, ya te lo dije, comencé
fabricando objetos que no encontraba en ningún sitio. Esa es en todo caso la
tarea del artista tal y como yo la entiendo: mejorar la calidad de lo desconocido.
Pero los objetos que creamos se adicionan a lo real y pasan a existir para nosotros como el resto de los objetos, y entonces es necesario enfrentar un hecho
distinto, y es que la realidad de las cosas que hicimos viene a modificar la de las
que estamos por imaginar. Cuando un joven está empezando a producir objetos
que lo sorprenden, después de cierto tiempo comienza a percibir lo que ha realizado. Entonces, poco a poco, esos objetos le imponen su presencia y cambian
su propio universo. En ese momento hay que desarrollar una postura diferente

10. Citado por André Malraux en *Picasso's Mask*, trad. June Guicharnaud con Jacques Guicharnaud (Nueva
York: Da Capo, 1994), p. 18.

11. Citado por Hélène Parmelin en *Picasso dit. . .*, op. cit., p. 40.

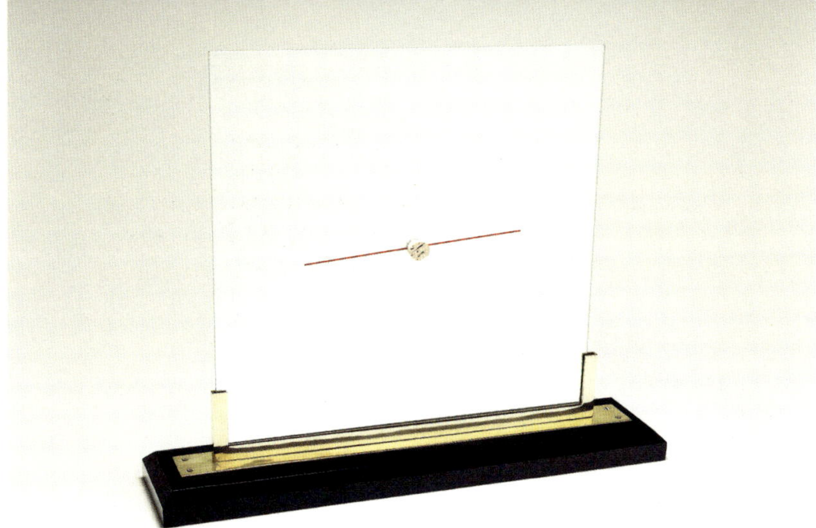

Fig. 17. *O [El] limitógrafo*, 1975.

para seguir produciendo a pesar de uno mismo, nuestro pasado ya no es virgen. Hoy, por ejemplo, si quisiera tratar el tema de los espejos, ya no me interesaría retomar lo que hice. Puedo partir de los espejos que concebí anteriormente, o contra ellos, pero no quiero repetirme. A los espejos no hay que duplicarlos aún más. A partir de cierto punto, debemos luchar contra nuestra propia obra. Otra vez *The point of no return*.

<sup>AJ</sup> ¿Y cuándo se manifiesta, en tu caso, ese punto de no retorno?

<sup>WC</sup> A partir de 1975, y desde entonces, constantemente. Si comparas las exposiciones de 1973 y la de 1976, observarás un cambio significativo. Ahí paso de los *Condutores de percepção* al *Limitógrafo*, de 1975, que sería como una máquina medidora de límites. En ella, un corcho cierra o detiene una línea en el espacio [Fig. 17]. Es una obra de pasaje, que nace en una coyuntura muy importante, porque aparece el *Convite ao raciocínio* [Invitación al razonamiento], de 1978, y con ella piezas muy diversas [Fig. 18]. Es decir, es un periodo en el que amplié mucho mis posibilidades, abrí mis fronteras, y no quise ser un artista con un estilo característico. La movilidad sería mi libertad, mi programa, y comencé a expandir mi trabajo en diversas áreas y con materiales muy variados.

<sup>AJ</sup> ¿El *Espelho com luz* es representativo de una de esas áreas?

<sup>WC</sup> En ese momento era muy difícil privilegiar un objeto específico. Cada uno de ellos fue hecho en un contexto en el que hacía cuatro, cinco, diez objetos

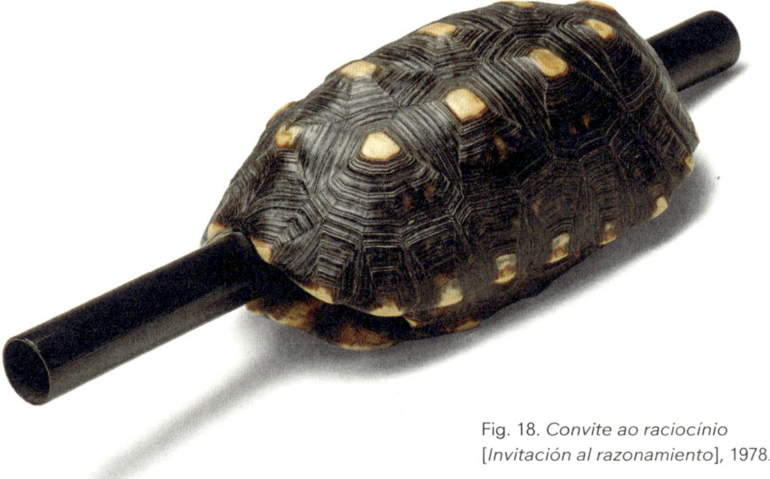

Fig. 18. *Convite ao raciocínio*
[*Invitación al razonamiento*], 1978.

al mismo tiempo, y esa diversidad era lo que me importaba. Pero algo nuevo estaba pasando y las obras se unifican ahora a través de algo invisible. Un hilo interno, ausente y presente al mismo tiempo.

AJ ¿Y sería posible definir ese hilo invisible?

WC Lo que quiero resaltar es que todos esos trabajos, aparentemente muy diversos, tenían un rasgo en común que les pertenecía, y llegué a la conclusión de que yo no necesitaba, como lo sospechaba, de una formalidad identificadora. Que lo importante era hacer exactamente el objeto que estaba imaginando, el más estimulante para añadirle nuevas formas a esa diversidad. Una vez escribí que me basta con saber cuáles son mis intenciones secretas. Termino, sí, mirando hacia ciertos puntos recurrentes en mi obra, y puedo decir que en realidad estamos condenados a ser quienes somos. Y eso que quiere cambiar en nosotros es nuestra voluntad de concretar lo siguiente.

AJ Entiendo, pero ese problema del estilo está siempre allí, acechando al artista, e incluso en los materiales que se emplean comienza a manifestarse una identidad que se reconoce de inmediato, especialmente cuando construyes objetos inventados por ti.

WC Me parece que la palabra estilo se presta a confusiones. Yo preferiría hablar de un procedimiento formal que puede llegar a aprisionarnos, y en ese sentido es un asunto que viene desde siempre, y que puede tener soluciones diversas. Una es la que percibo en Morandi, cuando escoge un solo asunto y descubre en él una infinidad de posibilidades, de la misma manera que Cézanne se concentra en la montaña Sainte-Victoire para hacer a partir de allí una cantidad de telas.

La otra es la de Picasso, que cambia constantemente sus temas y procesos, pero mantiene una identidad formal que puede distinguirse en cualquiera de sus etapas.

Cuando un artista, como Morandi o como Cézanne, se decide por un solo tema, es porque el protagonismo no está allí, sino en la pintura, en todos los sentidos plásticos que se desarrollan en el acto de pintar. Entonces, transponiéndolo a una situación más modesta, como la mía, me parece que esa variedad de posibilidades formales, como la utilización de un sinfín de materiales, es una conquista que no puede ser despreciada, no después del Dadaísmo. Entonces procuro una libertad formal que sea lo suficientemente dinámica como para aceptar los más diversos materiales y actitudes, y eso me parece fundamental. Está claro que tengo una predilección por ciertos materiales, y es indudable que en determinadas épocas esa preferencia acaba siendo significativa, pero sé que cuento con la libertad de cambiarlos y de emplear aquellos que convengan más al tipo de situación que estoy trabajando. Por lo demás, tengo un caudal muy grande de temas.

AJ Por supuesto, pero esa libertad se aplica más específicamente a las obras donde contrapones objetos diferentes, objetos que no han sido producidos por ti. Tan pronto como eres tú el que los construye, las escaleras por ejemplo, o algunos espejos, es inevitable que surja una identidad en tu modo de trabajar, y que eso termine convirtiéndose en un estilo; es decir, en una identidad formal que te es propia.

WC Sí, pero eso puede ocurrir de otras maneras, como en aquellos primeros dibujos que yo hacía y donde me interesaba más el pasaje de uno a otro que cada uno de ellos. Era esa dinámica de pasaje de uno a otro lo que me atraía, y la identidad formal que pudiera haber entre ellos me importaba mucho menos. Es lo que sucede también con mis objetos, el hecho de que entre ellos exista en común una determinada manera de hacerlos, que los une de alguna manera, y que tal vez ese sea el hilo del que estamos hablando. Eso es fundamental, porque tengo que preservarle su libertad a cada obra, y eso no se consigue de una vez y para siempre. Es como si te dijera que cada obra nueva tiene que liberarse del pasado, de una relación formal posible, y además crear condiciones para la próxima. Y ese esfuerzo las justifica, por generar nuevas posibilidades que se van materializando en un hilo conductor invisible entre ellas.

AJ Pero incluso esa movilidad tiene momentos que podrían ser identificados como característicos.

WC Sí, podrían ser característicos de preferencias que van ocurriendo. Pero cada vez que sobreviene, hago lo posible para que no sea un formalismo. Incluso, pienso que soy un artista de una sola fase, solo intento que esa fase esté siempre al inicio. No busco estructurar un programa que pueda luego seguir y desarrollar. Lo que me motiva exactamente son las nuevas situaciones por descubrir. Y algunos artistas pueden encontrar ese infinito incluso dentro de un procedimiento muy restringido. Morandi es un ejemplo de lo que trato de explicarte. Quizás tenga que ver con la manera como los artistas producían sus obras hasta, digamos, los años cuarenta. Pero a partir de ahí me parece que los *ismos* se hacen sospechosos, insuficientes y limitados. Ya no importa si se es abstracto o figurativo, esa opción simplista ya no corresponde al interés de los artistas, ya no está ligada a problemas de estilo. Un artista puede ser conceptual o figurativo, pop surrealista o neofigurativo. Es decir, que a partir de un cierto instante coexisten múltiples tendencias y estilos. Y esa es quizás una marca de la época en la que yo comencé a trabajar. Los *ismos* anteriores pasan a ser vistos como históricos. Y en esa complejidad máxima de tendencias diversas, los artistas enfrentaban, y todavía enfrentan, el desafío de conseguir una expresividad propia.

Vale la pena recordar que fui alumno de Ivan Serpa, es decir, de un artista que tenía una gran curiosidad por los procesos artísticos, y que experimentaba varias técnicas a la vez: la abstracción, la figuración, e incluso dentro de la abstracción, a veces era geométrico, otras no. Y yo encuentro que mi trabajo se desarrolla en un momento más complejo, en el que comienzan incluso a producirse cruces con otras disciplinas. Hay artistas conceptuales que se preocupan por los problemas científicos, otros que se concentran en el lenguaje y comienzan a reflexionar sobre las obras de arte desde la escritura. . . Yo encuentro que mi proceso de búsqueda responde a una real necesidad de entender el mundo, porque la inserción de las obras de arte en la cultura llegó a convertirse también en un problema artístico.

Por lo tanto no me importa saber qué tipo de arte voy a hacer dentro de un año. Lo que me interesa es caminar con mis propios pies, lo que me mueve es el camino mismo produciendo sentidos, generando situaciones que pueden convertirse en cosas. Y por eso es que cada pieza acaba siendo nuclear, casi autónoma, como si solo ella iniciara y concluyera lo planteado. No me preocupa darle una coherencia formal o conceptual a esa variedad de objetos, el modo de pensarlos y de producirlos va configurando ya un lazo entre ellos y la realidad.

AJ Y sin embargo, es a partir de esos objetos autónomos que irán configurándose los núcleos que caracterizan tu trabajo.

WC Por supuesto, solo que es algo que surge naturalmente, porque hacia 1975–78, cuando prefiero ser un artista sin estilo formal determinado, y con una movilidad crítica como meta, todavía no tengo un conjunto suficientemente denso de obras como para que esos núcleos de interés se hagan evidentes.

AJ Podríamos decir, utilizando una metáfora astronómica, que esos cuerpos aislados irían paulatinamente aglomerándose en conjuntos cada vez más densos, siguiendo de alguna manera las leyes de la gravedad. Es decir, que ellos irían aglutinándose en conjuntos mayores en función de sus afinidades íntimas, como si esas cercanías constituyeran una fuerza de gravedad que los atrae, independientemente de su fecha de producción, para conformar núcleos completos como el de los espejos, por ejemplo. Al principio, podríamos considerarlos como objetos borgianos, pero luego se hace evidente que el núcleo de los espejos comienza a individualizarse, e incluso se siente, como en escaleras, que ellos podrían convertirse en un núcleo aparte.

WC Sí, es seguro, no serían objetos lanzados hacia el futuro, como quizás lo pensaron los artistas de las vanguardias históricas, sino cuerpos que orbitarían en torno a inquietudes actuales. No responden a esa especie de utopía que generó las vanguardias. Pienso que las vanguardias pierden su pertinencia cuando dejamos de ver en ellas un programa de acción, y las convertimos en un sustantivo, un eslogan. Ese pasaje de un deseo de acción concreta sobre lo real que las caracterizó, a ser solo objetos, estilos, movimientos, es lo que algunos llaman el fracaso de las vanguardias. Me niego a pensar que el hecho de que la transformación de la realidad haya quedado por debajo de las aspiraciones de la gente, y de los artistas, pueda ser considerado como un fracaso que desautorice a esos artistas como simples productores de utopías.

AJ Por supuesto, porque aun por debajo de las expectativas que generaron, esas obras modificaron nuestro mundo.

WC Lo modificaron, sí, y alcanzaron buena parte de sus objetivos. Pero es cierto, también, que esa utopía productiva se pierde hacia los años ochenta, y que los artistas se hacen por así decir más pragmáticos, cuando se ocupan por ejemplo de su inserción en el mercado. Me parece que a partir de cierto momento, digámoslo así, ese estar en el mundo real que los artistas tanto reivindicaron, se encuentra al final con una cierta tiranía de lo real (las exigencias del mercado, por ejemplo), y me parece que ahora es urgente discutir los conflictos entre arte, el mercado y la cultura del espectáculo.

*RRRRRRR*

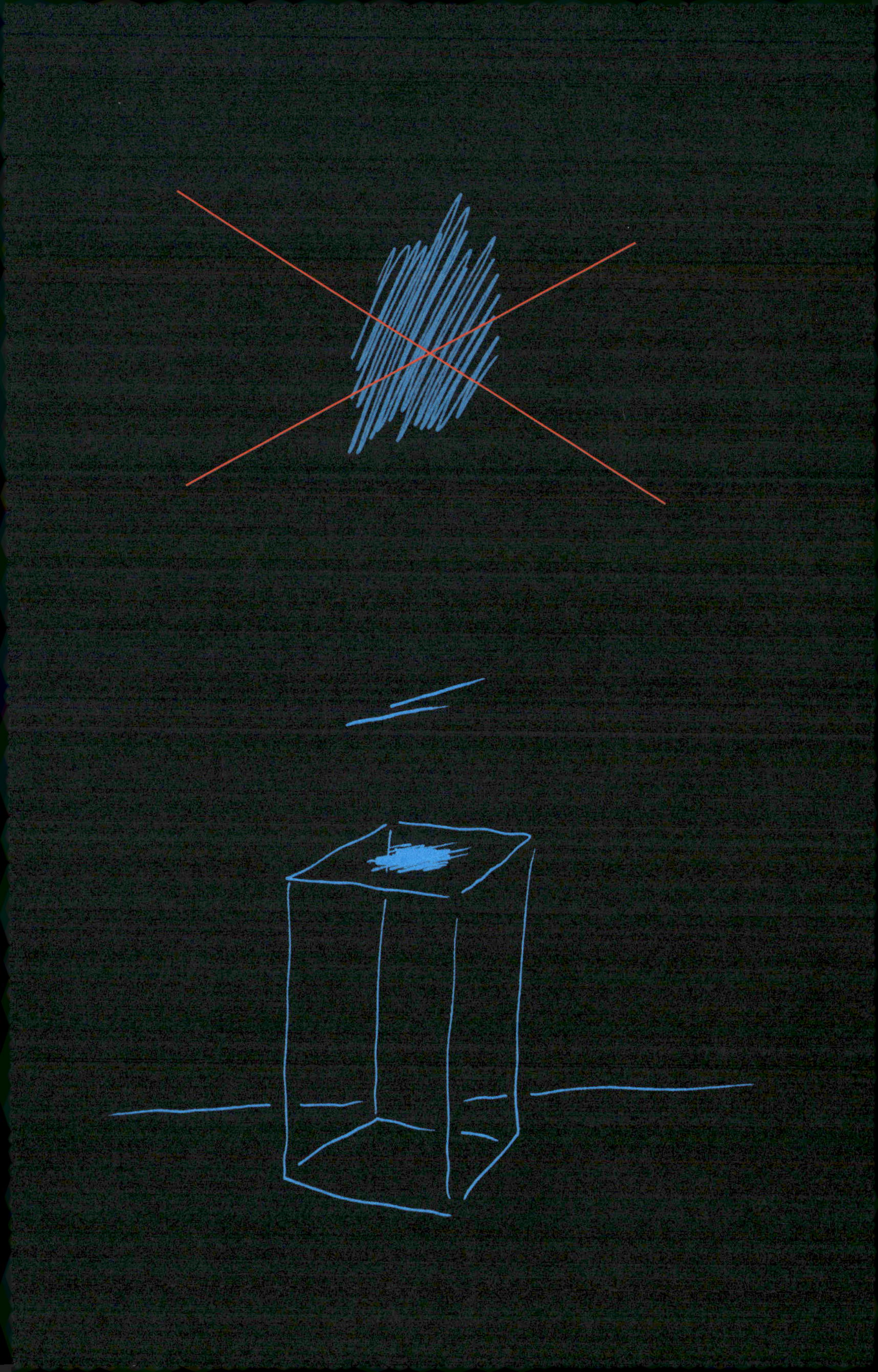

# LOS ESPEJOS
## Una máquina mimética

Hoy, al cabo de tantos y perplejos
Años de errar bajo la varia luna
Me pregunto qué azar de la fortuna
Hizo que yo temiera los espejos
[. . .]
Infinitos los veo, elementales
Ejecutores de un antiguo pacto,
Multiplicar el mundo como el acto
Generativo, insomnes y fatales.

Jorge Luis Borges, "Los espejos"

*Hacia 1975, los diferentes objetos que Waltercio Caldas produce, y que en general pudiéramos calificar como objetos borgianos, responden a la voluntad de escapar a esa historia biológica del individuo que lo lleva a actuar de cierta forma, a preferir determinadas configuraciones materiales y cromáticas; en una palabra, a escapar del estilo. Al principio parecen objetos aislados, ideas puntuales: unos son producto de una construcción formal, como sus Escadas [Escaleras], y algunos dibujos. Otros son la simple reorganización de elementos extraídos del entorno –O coleccionador, 1973–, sin ninguna manipulación del autor. Otros son por el contrario objetos intervenidos –como su Espelho com luz [Espejo con luz], de 1975–, o simplemente organizados de manera inesperada –O pequeño príncipe [El principito], de 1978. En ocasiones, también, la obra no es más que un texto o un conjunto de palabras ensambladas de manera enigmática. En ciertas piezas se vale de la fotografía, en otras del collage, del dibujo o de la escultura. Con ello, es evidente, nos encontramos ante una variedad considerable de maneras, técnicas y modos de funcionar, sin que sea posible organizarlos en núcleos realmente autónomos, aun cuando la repetición de algunas obsesiones, de problemas más que temas, comienza a sugerir la posibilidad de conjuntos independientes. Los espejos representan solo una de esas obsesiones, pero una que intriga a los artistas desde los tiempos más remotos.* [Fig. 19]

 Los espejos aparecen en tu obra como un tema recurrente, casi obsesivo. Me parece que ya no podemos eludirlo.

 Es un tema que me gustaría discutir muy cuidadosamente, porque es complejo e inagotable. Aun cuando haya hecho algunos, siento que es un tema que estoy apenas arañando en la superficie. El primer espejo que hice tenía inscrita la palabra Fin, y el espectador se veía a través de la palabra. El segundo es el *Espelho com luz* de la Colección Patricia Phelps de Cisneros [Fig. 20].

 Ahora, colocar la palabra *fim* sobre el espejo me remite a dos posibilidades de lectura, y una de ellas tiene que ver con el tema de las *vanitas*. Es como decirnos: "Ve tu propio fin". . .

 No sé. . . , porque mi espejo no tiene ese carácter mórbido de las *vanitas*. Es más bien un objeto satírico y con buen humor. Para explicártelo mejor, me remito al espejo que hice en 1976. Está hecho en metal pintado, y es un objeto donde un elemento se proyecta hacia el espectador y otro se mantiene en el plano de la pared, como si una parte fuera el reflejo del otro [Fig. 21]. Así se crea una situación especular sin utilizar necesariamente las superficies pulidas de vidrio. Eso fue para mí una novedad, pues ya no necesitaba emplear el objeto espejo

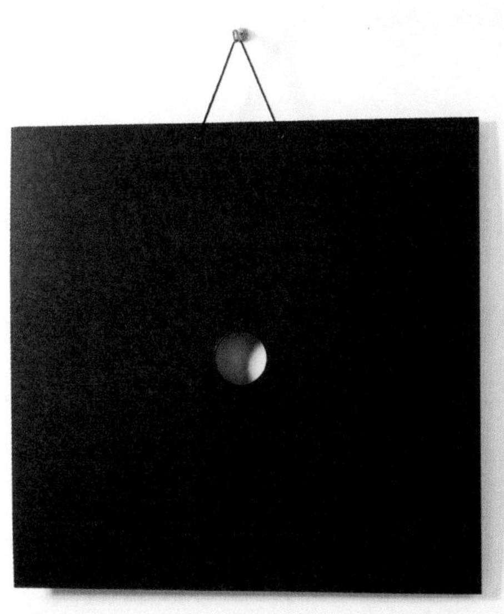

Fig. 19. *Espelho* [*Espejo*], 1975.

Fig. 20. *Espelho com luz* [*Espejo con luz*], 1975.

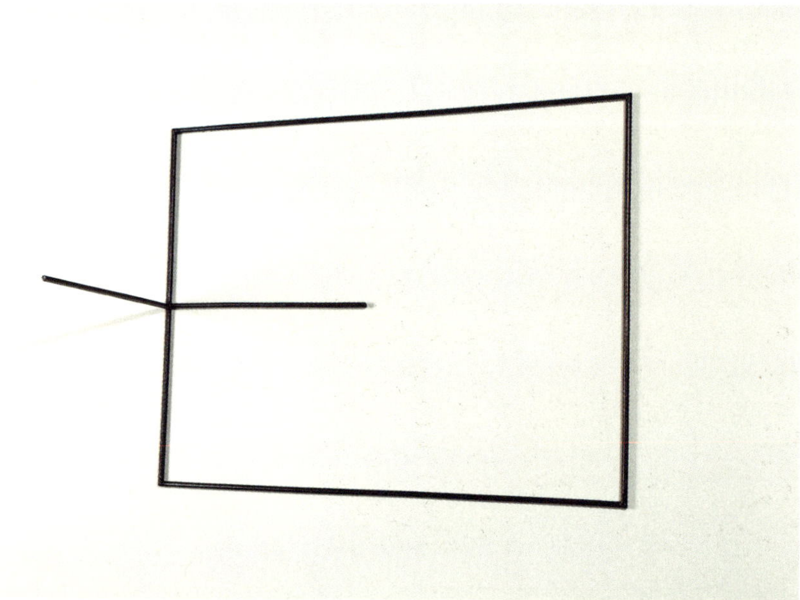

Fig. 21. *Espelho* [*Espejo*], 1976.

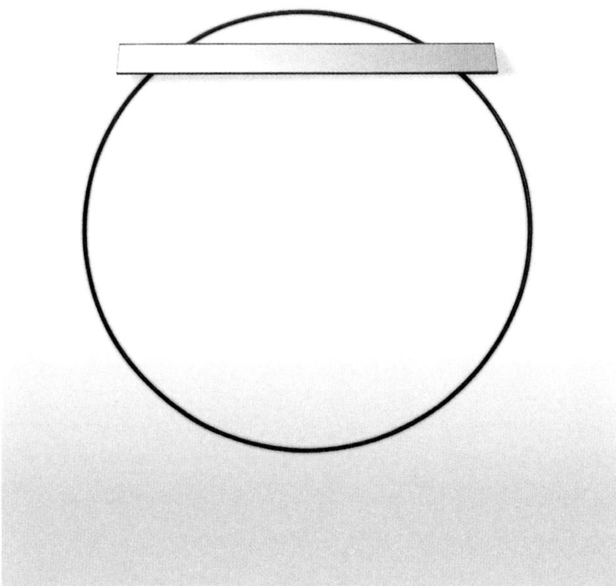

Fig. 22. *Circunferência com espelho a 30°* [*Circunferencia con espejo a 30°*], 1976.

como lo conocemos, sino apenas aislar su funcionamiento mimético. Luego vino *Circunferência com espelho a 30°* [*Circunferencia con espejo a 30°*], de 1976, que muestra paradójicamente lo que uno no ve, y en el cual, además, uno no puede verse. El espectador se encuentra ante una totalidad vacía, que es ese círculo, con su deseo de ver alguna imagen, y el espejo refleja otra dimensión, le ofrece una respuesta inesperada [Fig. 22].

AJ Los espejos, sin duda, plantean una infinidad de problemas. ¿Crees que podrías definir lo que te atrae en ellos?

WC La verdad es que no tengo exactamente claro por qué me interesan. Yo podría decirte que ellos se aproximan a lo que quizás sería una metáfora de la representación, que poseen en su funcionamiento una especie de secreto mimético que intento develar. Pero debo decir que el objeto espejo me seduce menos que la voluntad de construirlo, menos incluso que la posibilidad de producir un artefacto que ejemplarice su manera de funcionar, que ponga en duda eso que los espejos hacen de modo tan banal.

<sup>AJ</sup> Y claro, terminas produciendo un objeto que pone en juego la idea del reflejo, pero que lo hace una sola vez. Es decir, lo que me atrae en esos espejos no reflectantes, es que ellos parecen materializar una especie de idea, en el sentido platónico del término. Esto es, que producen la idea de lo especular sin reflejar ningún objeto particular.

<sup>WC</sup> Me parece importante lo que acabas de mencionar, "como si fuera solo una vez". Quizás mi trabajo pueda ser resumido en esa frase, porque el hecho plástico se da en función de una aparición inicial. Es decir que si pudiéramos caracterizar un momento preciso, sería uno en el que la operación contuviera ya, en sí, la naturaleza misma del instante, es decir, la certeza de que algo acaba de producirse. Así, en cierta forma, funcionan esos espejos, son objetos que incluyen en acto lo que acontece delante de nosotros. Una cosa, por ejemplo, que me impresionó muchísimo en el Museo de Historia Natural de Nueva York, fue ver los primeros espejos aztecas. Resulta que no son relucientes, no están hechos de material reflectante, sino de piedra negra pulida. Esa cualidad seudotransparente de sus espejos confirmó mis intuiciones sobre el lado interior de los espejos. Yo nunca he creído en su reflexibilidad aparente. Los espejos son crueles, nos llevan a creer que son la verdad de lo que vemos, cuando en realidad son una trampa que aceptamos. . . ¿Cómo podría decirlo? . . .

<sup>AJ</sup> ¿Una trampa sutil? . . .

<sup>WC</sup> No, serían más bien arrogantes. Es como si ellos poseyeran una verdad ficticia, que en realidad no es producida por ellos, sino por nuestra expectativa de lo que esperamos ver. En cierto modo, el arte sería una metáfora de esa desilusión, en la medida en que nunca es exactamente lo que conocemos del mundo. A veces, incluso, es insoportable que el arte nos muestre más de lo que esperamos ver. Por eso algunas de mis obras pretenden abordar el desmontaje funcional de los espejos. Siempre tuve el deseo de mostrar eso construyendo un espejo inaugural, uno que reaccionara de forma inexplicable, como si pudiera tener una idea divergente de sí mismo.

Hay otro aspecto interesante en lo que dijiste, y es como si Platón tuviera la idea de que las cosas están definitivamente en su debido lugar. Es decir que nosotros, para él, aprehendemos los lugares correctos de las cosas por nuestra percepción. Mientras que ese tipo de espejos de los que estamos hablando sacan al mundo de su lugar. Hacen que dudemos de la idea de lugar. En *Espelho com luz*, por ejemplo, la imagen no es simplemente un reflejo, es una membrana transparente que funciona ¿cierto? Él nos sugiere que su actividad es más importante que eso que refleja. Como si ese espejo nos diera una información básica a propósito del arte, o nos dijera que el objeto de arte es otra cosa, que habita en un espacio que no es exactamente el nuestro. Sería lo que podemos llamar un objeto de tercer tipo, que no cumple con nuestras expectativas, no es de una especie conocida. Si existen objetos que no son naturales, esos son los espejos . . . y las obras de arte.

Lo que me intrigó en los espejos aztecas, es que cuando uno se ve en ellos, solo percibe las luces más altas. No puede ver las bajas ni los medios tonos. Solo se ven las partes iluminadas del rostro, mientras las zonas de sombra se pierden en la oscuridad de la piedra. El espejo que conocemos nos ofrece todas las luces, porque las refleja de la mejor manera posible, pero el espejo azteca niega la luz. Entonces comprendí por qué las esculturas aztecas poseían exactamente esa característica: cuando un azteca esculpe un rostro de piedra, enfatiza las partes iluminadas, mientras hunde las áreas en sombra o menos iluminadas del rostro en un bajo relieve.

Tengo otro trabajo en el libro *Aparelhos* que es también un espejo, pero que no refleja nada. No fue hecho de metal, sino de papel, y es como si solo estuviera allí para ser atravesado por la mirada. En fin, hay un número considerable de espejos que casi me permitirían hacer una exposición sobre ellos. Si la hiciera, incluiría ese espejo de metal, y el de cartón. Incorporaría también el *Espelho com luz*, la *Circunferência com espelho a 30°*, el *Miroir b* [*Espejo b*] [Fig. 23] –él que hice para Borges–, y uno que estaba en la muestra de la Fundación Gulbenkian, el *Espelho C* [Fig. 24].

AJ ¿Qué diferencia los espejos A de los B y los C? ¿Son series distintas?

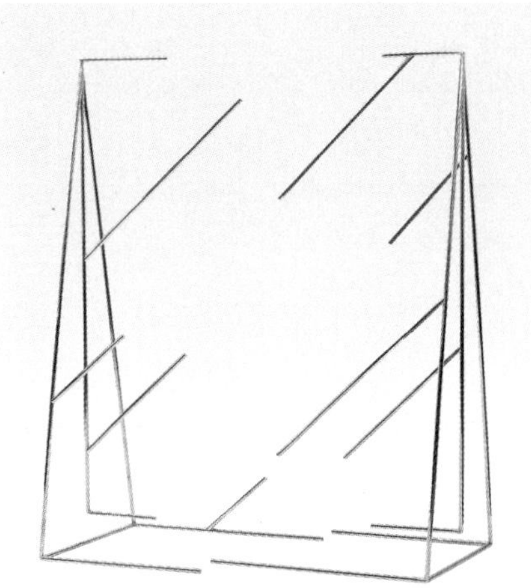

Fig. 23. *Miroir b* [*Espejo b*], 2005.

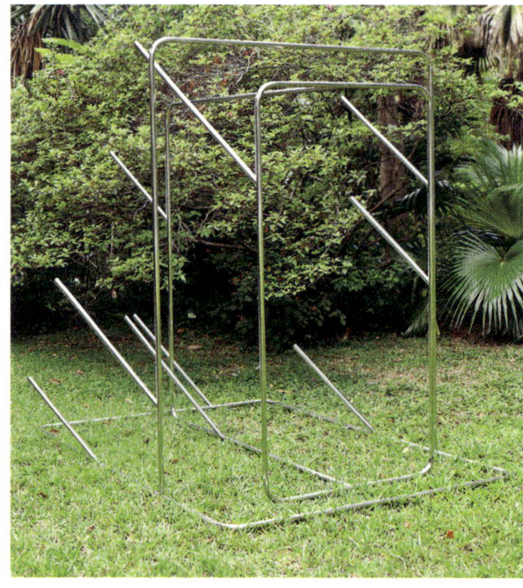

Fig. 24. *Espelho C* [*Espejo C*], 2005.

<sup>WC</sup> No, primero hice varios espejos, todos planos, hasta que un día hice el *Miroir b*, el espejo para Borges, que sale completamente del plano. El *Espelho C* sería ya un espejo de tercer tipo, tridimensional. Es uno donde trato de aislar el problema de su espesor interno. Es como una puerta, un umbral donde uno puede entrar porque la escala lo permite.

<sup>AJ</sup> Y en ese espejo tridimensional existe una particularidad que me interesa mucho, porque parece abrirse al espacio por capas, como si fuera un objeto estratificado, exactamente como ocurrió en los *Contrarelieves* de Lygia Clark y en los *Relieves* espaciales de Hélio Oiticica. ¿Podría haber allí algún tipo de conexión con sus procesos?

<sup>WC</sup> No creo. Mis obras se han abierto al espacio desde el inicio. Es solo una coincidencia temática en este caso.

<sup>AJ</sup> Sí, pero, ¿por qué piensas el espejo en capas o estratos diferentes?

<sup>WC</sup> Buena pregunta. . . No sé, tal vez el reflejo tenga para mí su origen en la transparencia de los volúmenes. Piensa en Narciso y su lago.

<sup>AJ</sup> Siempre he pensado que si muchos artistas (es el caso de Soto, de Oiticica y Clark) abren su obra al espacio por medio de estratos superpuestos, es porque de algún modo consideran el espacio a través de una tradición pictórica. La pintura, justamente, lo ha concebido como una sucesión y superposición de capas transparentes.

 Pero ese es otro problema. Sería más interesante si hubiera capas o estratos diferentes en la imagen, lo que no es exactamente imposible, porque los estratos de una imagen son imaginarios, mientras en la pintura sí puede pensarse en una imagen estratificada.

 Los de la pintura también son imaginarios. . .

 No, en las pinturas son reales. Por ejemplo, cuando tomas un binóculo y observas el paisaje, se ve claramente que el binóculo recorta los planos de la imagen. Su característica principal es la de transformarla en capas, como si fuera un objeto digital que corta la imagen en estratos. Siempre me ha parecido que el binóculo morandiniza las imágenes, porque Morandi tiene la particularidad de darle el mismo valor pictórico al primer plano, al segundo y a los demás, de manera que transforma la imagen en una película densa y opaca. Y es por eso que sus objetos parecen más verdaderos, porque no se someten a la ilusión de la perspectiva. Cuando señalas que algunos artistas se abren al espacio por medio de obras estratificadas, es como si todos salieran de una información pictórica hacia una escultórica.

 Y a través de estrategias pictóricas. . .

 No sé, no estoy seguro, porque las estrategias pictóricas me parecen muy específicas, y sigue siendo posible hacer una escultura en estratos o planos [Fig. 23]. No es necesariamente un asunto pictórico. Además, me parece que la herencia escultórica es más antigua que la pictórica. Creo que el hombre trabajó la piedra antes que los tintes. Cuando el hombre de las cavernas se acerca a las imágenes, las hunde en los muros de una caverna, quizás para explotar la tridimensionalidad de la pared en la oscuridad.

 Y sin embargo, yo siento que tus esculturas, si podemos llamarlas así, están atravesadas por problemas pictóricos e incluso dibujísticos; porque parten de ellos, o sencillamente porque les están aparentados. Muchos de tus espejos B y C, por ejemplo, parecen dibujos en el espacio.

*Circunferência com espelho a 30°* me parece además curiosa por otra circunstancia que no hemos mencionado aún, y es que tiene evidentes cercanías con el uso que se ha hecho de él en la iconografía católica. No soy religioso, pero encuentro que la pintura religiosa se ha visto en la obligación de inventar todo tipo de mecanismos para hablar precisamente de aquello que no puede ser visto, que trasciende el espacio y el tiempo, es decir lo divino.

 Sin duda, alguien alguna vez dijo que la teología era la rama más fantástica del conocimiento, el realismo fantástico del saber. De ahí la astucia y también la crueldad de la religión para transformar problemáticas metafísicas en soluciones demasiado pragmáticas.

 Quizás, pero lo que me interpela es que este espejo a 30° funciona como el espejo de la virgen en la iconografía católica. El suyo es un espejo sin reflejo. Y por eso, cuando se le coloca en las iglesias, se tiene el cuidado de ubicarlo con una inclinación tal que el visitante no pueda ver lo que él refleja, o al menos que refleje la cúpula de la iglesia, como metáfora del infinito, de la bóveda celeste.

 Yo intenté algo similar en el *Espelho com luz*, aunque por otras razones. Cuando te pones frente al espejo, es como si sintieras una cierta distancia crítica ante la imagen, como si él estuviera en cierta forma develando tu intimidad en un espacio público. Tuve ahora la oportunidad de constatarlo, porque mi espejo estuvo expuesto durante algunos meses en MoMA en Nueva York. Las personas que me conocen enviaban imágenes de cosas variadas, menos de ellos mismos en el espejo. Entonces lo que hacían era que me mandaban fotos de un Calder reflejado en mi espejo, que estaba algo distante, o cosas así, como si hubieran sentido la necesidad de evitar la relación habitual con los espejos.

 Por eso me pareció curioso que tú, reflexionando sobre el espejo, recurrieras también a ese artificio para obtener uno que no puede reflejarnos.

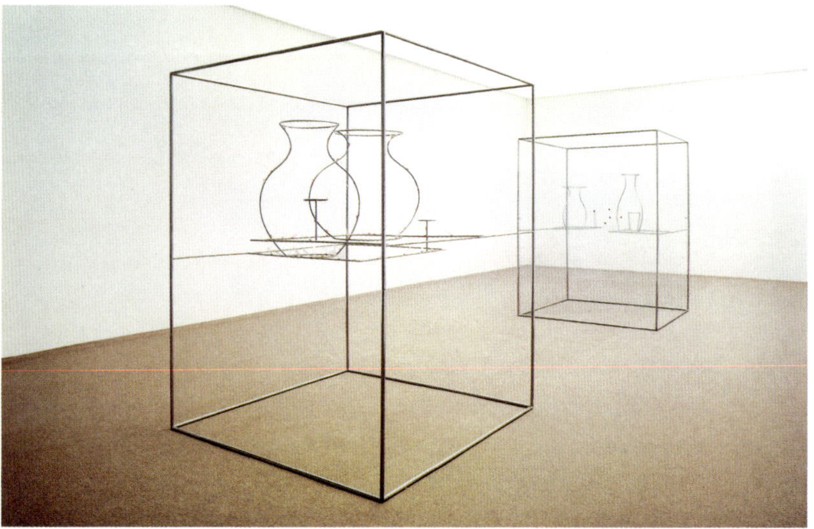

Fig. 25. *A distância entre. . . [La distancia entre. . .], Série Venecia III*, 1997.

 Es como una tentativa por hacer que los espejos puedan partir desde el inicio, como si fuera posible construirlos desde cero, que es un poco mi obsesión con ellos. Es lo que me lleva a pensar en ellos como máquinas, porque si tratas de pensarlos de cero. . . ¿qué sería un cero mimético?, surge una cantidad de cuestionamientos que en el fondo tienen mucho que ver con el arte.

 ¿Ahora, sería posible concebir un objeto que sea solo potencialmente reflectante?

 Perfectamente. El *Espelho C* es un objeto de ese tipo, igual que el *Miroir b*. Son objetos que quieren ser espejos antes que reflejar algo. Es decir, es como si el ajuste final que lo transformaría en espejo, estuviera deliberadamente ausente.

 ¿Entonces ese botón del *Espelho com luz* tendría como función activarlo?

 No, en ese caso el botón sirve exactamente para conseguir su anulación, o al menos para anular en parte su certeza representativa. Ese botón estaría allí, al contrario, para criticar la arrogancia de las apariencias.

> *Hablar del espejo nos remite irremediablemente a la pintura, aun cuando en el caso de Waltercio Caldas estemos lejos de ella desde el punto de vista técnico. En Occidente, al menos, y en particular desde el Renacimiento italiano, es imposible hablar de la pintura sin remitirse a la fascinación que esa curiosa máquina mimética ha ejercido y ejerce sobre los artistas. La perspectiva surge en parte, es el caso de Brunelleschi, apoyándose en él, incorporándolo de alguna manera a la pintura, y cada vez que un artista quería poner a prueba la veracidad de su obra, recurría a él. Eso al menos recomendaba Leonardo da Vinci. El espejo fue juez y reto para la pintura, y no es un azar que una de las mayores cúspides de esa pintura representativa,* Las Meninas *de Velázquez, haya nacido también como una especie de reto lanzado por el pintor al espejo.*

 Supongo que tu interés personal por el espejo es lo que te llevó a interesarte por esta obra mayor de la pintura española y occidental, ¿cierto?

 Ese cuadro, *Las Meninas,* examina muy de cerca al espejo, y Velázquez, en particular, lo asumió con la conciencia absoluta de que su función mimética debía ser desnudada. Yo veo en esta pieza una intención clara del artista por hacer trabajar el reflejo. Y no solo aquí, también aparece en una que hizo unos treinta años antes: *Cristo en la casa de Marta y María,* c. 1618 [Fig. 26]. Es una obra donde Velázquez anticipa lo que va a pasar en *Las Meninas.* En ella, María está mirando al frente del cuadro, y Jesús está reflejado en el espejo del fondo, a la derecha. Esa estratagema sirve para hacernos entender que ella está mirando un espacio que está detrás de nosotros.

<sup>AJ</sup> Como si nosotros estuviéramos ante la posibilidad, con solo voltearnos, de ver a Cristo.

<sup>WC</sup> Más que eso, incluso, es como si estuviéramos dentro de la representación. Que yo sepa, esta es la primera vez que la mirada del espectador es trabajada internamente por la obra; pero es una pieza aún más ingeniosa que eso, y en cierta forma nos anula físicamente. Fíjate que María no nos está viendo a nosotros, sino que mira ligeramente a la izquierda; es decir, hacia Cristo, que se encuentra detrás de nosotros. Verla nos hace transparentes.

<sup>AJ</sup> Pero al mismo tiempo nos integra a la escena.

<sup>WC</sup> Apenas con la mirada. Quizás sea por estas razones que Velázquez es considerado un pintor para pintores, porque habla de problemas ante los cuales la mayoría de los pintores aparecen como víctimas, mientras él elucida la operación fundamental implícita en el acto de pintar un cuadro. Hay además un detalle interesante que, en un artista como Velázquez, no puede considerarse un azar. Es que los límites del espejo coinciden con el límite mismo de la pintura, como si quisiera resaltar la relación entre la pintura y el espejo.

<sup>AJ</sup> Eso nos remite de inmediato a tu libro sobre *Las Meninas*, de 1994, y a las piezas que has hecho basándote en Velázquez. De hecho, una de tus construcciones en metal parece reproducir el esquema básico de esa pintura [Fig. 27].

<sup>WC</sup> Esa serie se llama *Los Velázquez*. Yo transferí el título de *Las Meninas* a *Los Velázquez*, como si existieran varios Velázquez, uno de los cuales sería el que pintaba los fondos y los acontecimientos en las pinturas, y otro el que retrataba a los personajes reales.

<sup>AJ</sup> Es, a la vez, como si hubieras concebido ese cuadro como un espejo vacío; es decir, antes de reflejar a los personajes pintados por Velázquez.

<sup>WC</sup> También, solo que en *Las Meninas* la superficie pictórica está pensada como una piel, o sea como si el objeto espejo hubiera sido pintado. Velázquez pinta el funcionamiento del espejo. Lo hace, por ejemplo, creando situaciones dobles,

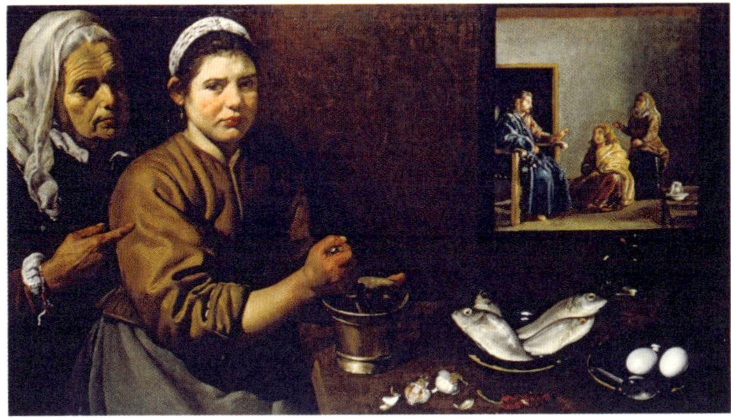

Fig. 26. Diego Velázquez (1599–1660), *Cristo en la casa de Marta y Maria*, c. 1618.

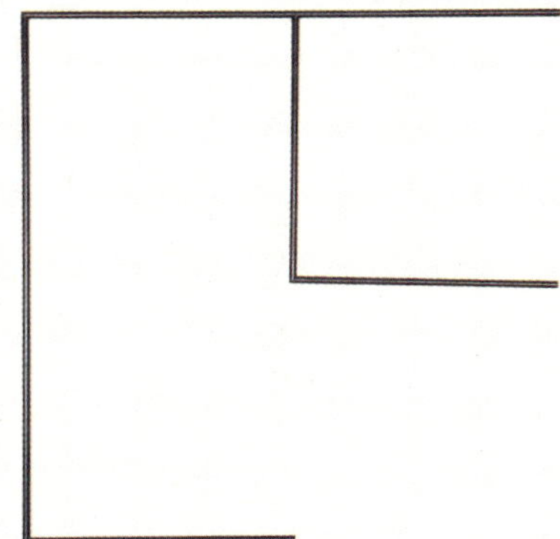

Fig. 27. *Ferro pintado* [*Hierro pintado*], 1978.

como cuando pinta el espejo del fondo y al lado una puerta, del mismo tamaño, que es un hueco hacia el fondo. O sea que coloca un espejo que refleja el espacio hacia delante, y una puerta que abre un hueco hacia atrás. De alguna manera, esos dos rectángulos paralelos se potencian el uno al otro. Ese recurso de la puerta le agrega una capa más a la espacialidad de la obra, que la tridimensionaliza. Todo eso sin hablar de esa solución fantástica que fue mostrar la entrada de las luces por las ventanas de la derecha, con esa última ventana que es la que permite que los reyes reciban la luz necesaria para ser vistos. En mi libro, ese es el único cuadro que pinté al óleo. Los demás son reproducciones hechas por computador [Fig. 28].

<sup>AJ</sup> Pero tiene un vidrio adelante, como si quisieras, en cierta forma, darle cuerpo

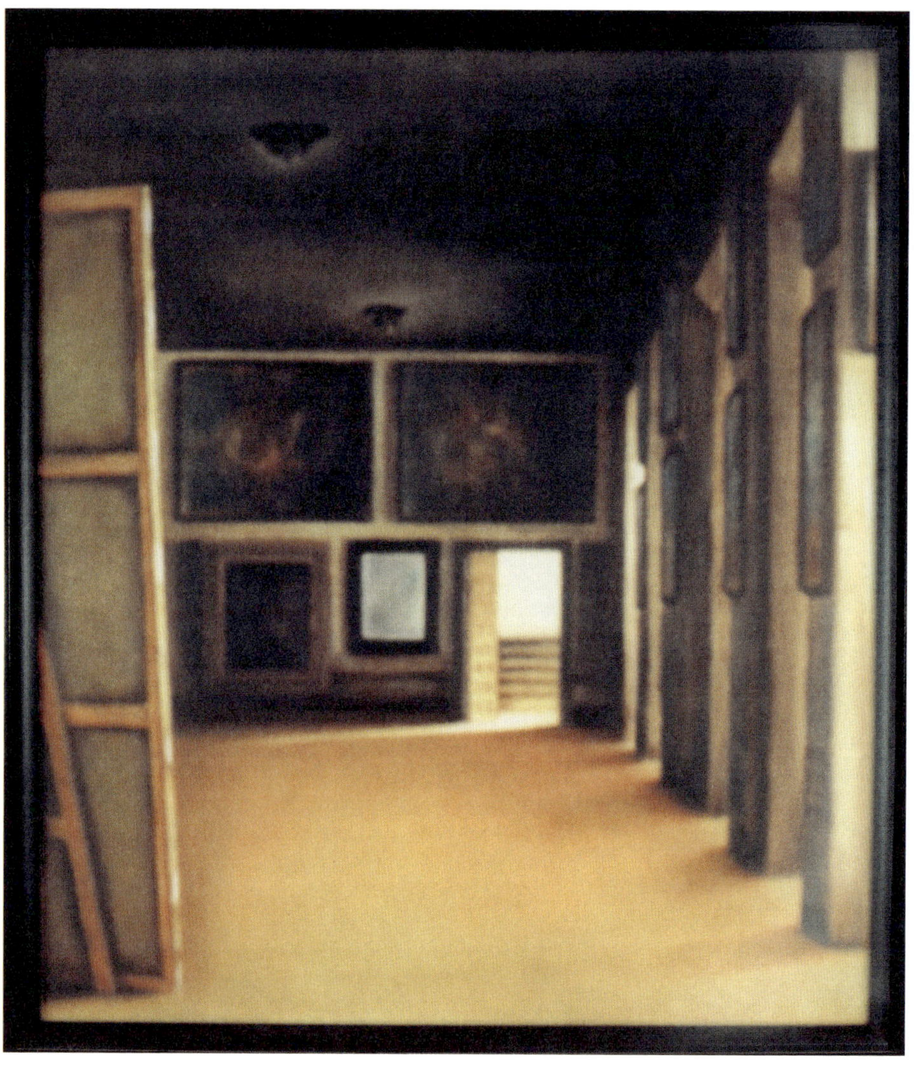

Fig. 28. *Los Velázquez*, 1994.

a la teoría pictórica que, desde el Renacimiento, equipara la tela a un vidrio transparente. . .

 Pero aquí el vidrio no es transparente, no está ausente. En el cuadro del que hablamos, y que hice tres años antes del libro, puse un vidrio lechoso, semitransparente, para desenfocarlo y sacar la imagen de la pintura. Con ese vidrio la imagen parece flotar, ya no está sometida a una superficie plana. En mi proyecto esa pintura se transforma en un objeto con marco, vidrio y volumen. Después tomé la fotografía de ese objeto, y de allí saqué las versiones más grandes, ya reproducidas mecánicamente. En otras imágenes del libro no empleé el vidrio porque me pareció que la reproducción misma creaba una capa suplementaria. Lo que hice fue enfatizar un detalle de la puerta y del espejo para mostrar la importancia de ese paralelismo en el cuadro.

 Ahora, explícame, ¿esta publicación es la réplica intervenida de un libro existente o uno completamente producido por ti?

 Es un libro creado a partir de las reproducciones de Velázquez, como si se tratara precisamente de una publicación sobre la obra del artista. Pero creo, por la duda que señalas, que piensas en otro asunto: la desautoría deliberada de este libro. Si pudiéramos devolverle el foco al texto, se leería: *Libros y espejos en Velázquez*. Recurrí al desenfoque solo para los títulos de los capítulos. Para el texto que acompaña las imágenes lo hice de otra manera, pues cuando tomé un bloque de texto y traté de reproducirlo fuera de foco, surgió una imagen que no me pareció conveniente. Parecía la única figura extraña al libro, como una colonia de microbios. Eso me obligó a crear una mancha específica que pareciera, al final, un texto desenfocado.

 Muchos pintores han dicho justamente eso, que a menudo el artista debe deformar lo que observa para lograr una imagen más plausible de lo real.

 Sí, pero esto de los textos no es un capricho mío, sino un problema velazquiano. Me explico: quizás él haya sido el primero en pintar los libros tal y como los veía. Los pintores de su época los pintaban tan falsos que uno podía leerlos en la tela. Velázquez comprende que aquello no podía ser verdad, que nadie podría leer un libro a la distancia que hay entre el artista y su modelo. Y él los pintó tal y como los veía; es decir, con las manchas grises del texto que podía percibir a la distancia [Fig. 29]. En mi libro, los textos son fieles a esa decisión de Velázquez [Fig. 30].

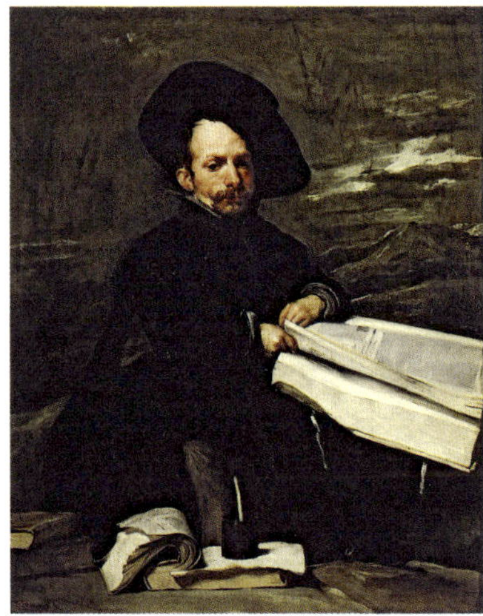

Fig. 29. Diego Velázquez, *El bufón don Diego de Acedo "El primo,"* 1644.

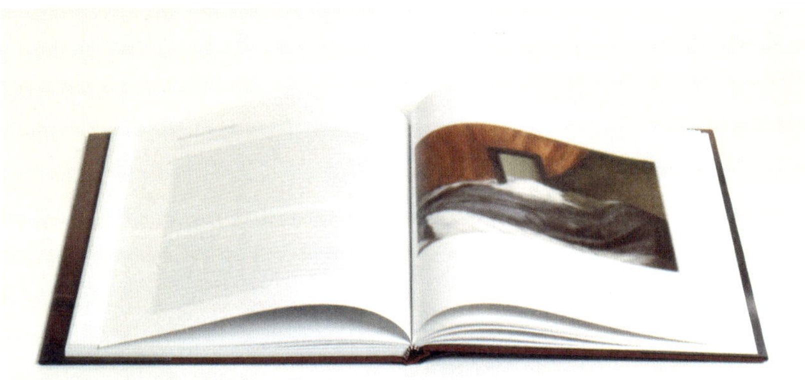

Fig. 30. *Velázquez*, 1996.

AJ Lo fantástico es que con ello se adelanta al problema central de los impresionistas franceses, en el sentido de que lo que ellos buscaban era estrictamente eso: pintar el mundo en su apariencia, en la manera como aparece ante nosotros, no a partir de lo que sabemos o creemos saber sobre él.

WC Pero Velázquez escucha de su maestro [Francisco] Pacheco, una frase que expresa ya ese problema. Él decía: "Yo no pinto una rosa, pinto una mancha que se parece a una rosa". Y eso es parte de lo que Velázquez aprende con Pacheco; es decir, que el pintor pinta borrones que se parecen a las cosas.

# ESCENARIOS ÍNTIMOS
## Libros y exposiciones

*Si Los Velázquez son una reflexión sobre el espejo, no es menos cierto que se trata de un libro, y no de uno dedicado al arte, sino de un libro de artista; esto es, de un particular modo de trabajar, de hacer obra. Eso que llamamos la cultura es, ante todo —así la definía Malraux—, la presencia viva del pasado en cada uno de nosotros, la vida constantemente renovada de ese universo de sentido en el que vivimos inmersos como el pez en el agua. De manera que toda obra de arte, como cada gesto humano, saca de allí su sentido; de la manera cómo, inscribiéndose en ese pasado, lo continúa o lo renueva. Siempre ha sido así, y, no obstante, nunca como hoy ese pasado ha estado tan presente para quienes pretenden agregar su obra a la ya larga historia de las invenciones humanas. Es sin duda por eso que desde el inicio mismo de sus estudios con Ivan Serpa, Waltercio Caldas se sintió llamado a pensar su inscripción en el tiempo, y a hacerlo a través de esas invenciones culturales que, como el libro y las exposiciones, son una puesta en escena de sí mismo y de sus ideas. Progresivamente, estos dos mecanismos de representación se convirtieron para él en mucho más que un registro de lo producido, hasta llegar a ser parte importante de su problemática como artista, como si ambos fueran una forma particular de espejo donde se hace posible reflejarse, pensándose.*

WC Los libros y la biblioteca han llegado a ser para mí una especie de máquina de sentido, que funciona como el órgano para el Capitán Nemo, en su *Nautilius*: un sitio privilegiado donde yo puedo establecer nuevos vínculos entre las cosas. Relacionar sucesos, seguir determinadas pistas y, en definitiva, escoger el tipo de trama que me interesa. ¿Cómo podría orientarme dentro de ese bosque de significados sin su ayuda? Yo soy lector de poesía, de libros técnicos, de literatura, de historia y de arte, de filosofía, y de esa diversidad surgen a menudo conexiones que de otra manera no podría conseguir. Paralelismos entre los autores y sus temas, los textos y las ilustraciones. . .

Por eso, desde muy temprano, el libro forma parte de mi vida, y aparece incluso como tema de varias obras, por ejemplo en *Matisse, talco*, de 1978 [Fig. 31]. Nunca he querido publicar un libro convencional sobre mis trabajos. Recuerdo cuando GBM Editora me invitó a hacer *Aparelhos*, de 1978 [Fig. 32]. Para ese entonces, en Brasil, publicar un libro era como ensamblar una especie de documento histórico que terminaba por enyesar la carrera de los artistas.

Ese tipo de publicación dificultaba incluso su tarea, en la medida en que lo trataba prematuramente desde una perspectiva histórica. Y por eso creo que *Aparelhos* representó para nosotros, me refiero a Ronaldo Brito como crítico, y a mí como artista, un verdadero reto [Fig. 32]. A ninguno de los dos nos motivaba hacer un libro más sobre arte, sino uno que fuera una experiencia dinámica, donde pudiéramos tratar los problemas del arte, y no necesariamente reseñar la carrera de un artista. Nuestro objetivo no era mostrar lo que yo había hecho, sino convertir ese libro en una experiencia que más bien le hiciera preguntarse al lector qué es lo que ocurría en aquel momento, y qué podía suceder en adelante con el arte.

AJ Es lo que se concreta en el *Manual da ciência popular*, que es más una obra editorial que un libro sobre ti [Fig. 33].

WC El *Manual da ciência popular* fue para mí fundamental, porque en él logré resumir una serie de cuestiones específicas e inherentes a mi proceso. Eso sucede dos años después, cuando Fundación Nacional de Arte [Funarte] me invita a hacer un libro. Funarte estaba publicando una serie de libros sobre artistas brasileños; pero como ya yo tenía *Aparelhos*, les dije que no quería otro libro general sobre mis obras. Prefería uno temático, donde pudiera abordar lo que me interesaba en ese momento. De ahí surgió el Manual, de 1982.

El libro propone, con mucho humor, una serie de obras de arte que el lector

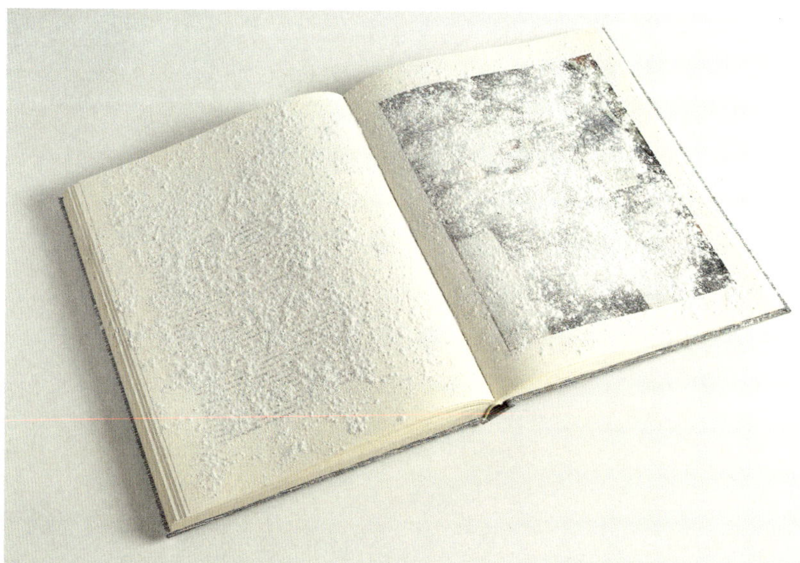

Fig. 31. *Matisse, talco*, 1978.

# Waltercio Caldas Jr.
## "Aparelhos"

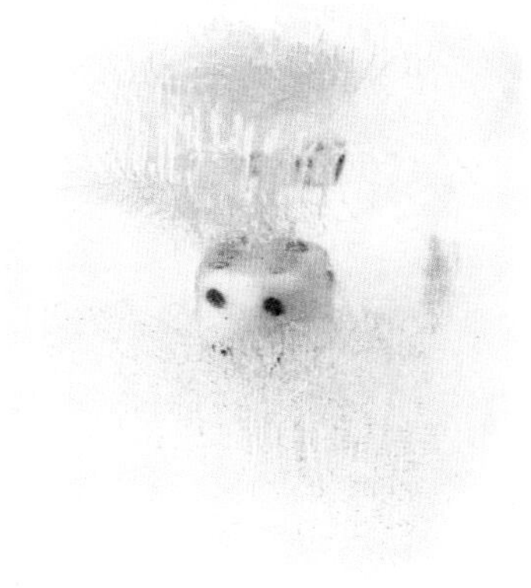

GBM



Fig. 32. Portada de *Aparelhos*
[*Aparatos*], 1979.

puede hacer en su casa, con materiales y herramientas que encuentra en su propio entorno. Para eso utilicé algunas imágenes de *Aparelhos,* a las que uní trabajos recién hechos, sugeridos por la nueva situación, algunos pensados especialmente para el libro, ordenados en torno al tema de "hágalo usted mismo", como en los manuales técnicos. Entre mis objetivos estaba el de introducir la reproducción de las obras como parte de las prerrogativas del artista. La experiencia con *Aparelhos* me permitió detectar que las obras de arte sufren una alteración en sus características al ser reproducidas. A partir de allí, me di cuenta de que la reproducción debía ser también uno de los componentes del lenguaje plástico, y no una simple noticia posterior a su realización. Lo que busqué fue conseguir que la reproducción se integrara como un nuevo interés del trabajo, lo que ya estaba implícito en *Aparelhos*. Esa deliberación está ya presente en la portada del Manual, que es la imagen misma del libro.

A la vez, así como abordaba la inserción de las reproducciones como parte de las obras, también pretendía reflexionar sobre la eventual inclusión de objetos cotidianos y efímeros como obras de arte. La introducción que redacté trataba justamente de eso, decía algo así: ". . . no se engañe el lector con estos objetos, porque después de utilizados como arte, regresarán nuevamente a su estado habitual. . .".

---

AJ Lo que resulta evidente en tu caso es que en la ausencia —si no total, sí bastante

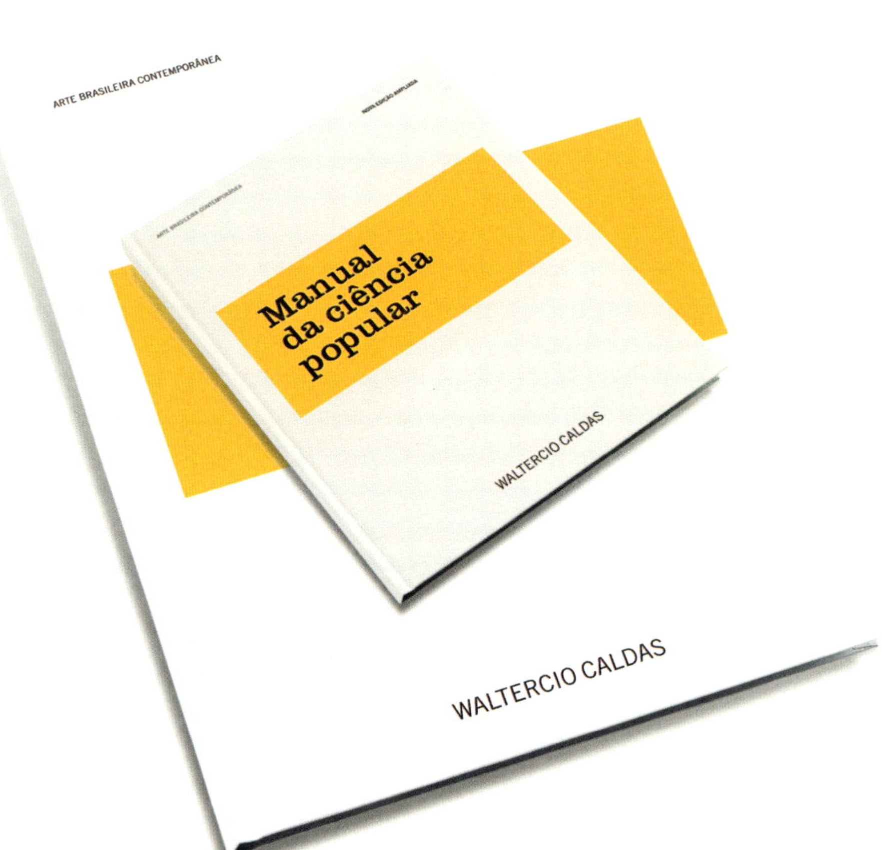


Fig. 33. Portada de *Manual da ciência popular* [*Manual de ciencia popular*], 1982.

pronunciada— de una característica formal reconocible, de un estilo y una paleta inconfundibles, que ayuden a seguir tu desarrollo en el tiempo (o al menos en tu deseo de evitar la emergencia de ese estilo), el libro comienza a funcionar no solo como parte integrante de tu trabajo, sino como una obra que tiene la peculiaridad de construir una mirada sobre los procesos que la hacen posible.

WC  Al escucharte, pienso que mi paleta es la relación entre las cosas, todas las cosas. Esa sería mi paleta, y que cada libro, cada dibujo, como cada muestra, representa una manera distinta de manejar esas conexiones. Cada una de ellas se incorpora a la producción no como registro o reportaje de lo sucedido, sino como producción, una obra más, como si en ese momento los materiales que

Talco pulverizado sobre livro ilustrado de H. Matisse (ver figura 1).

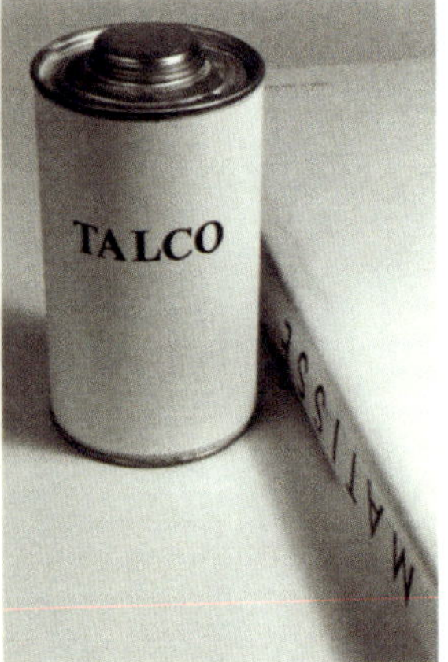

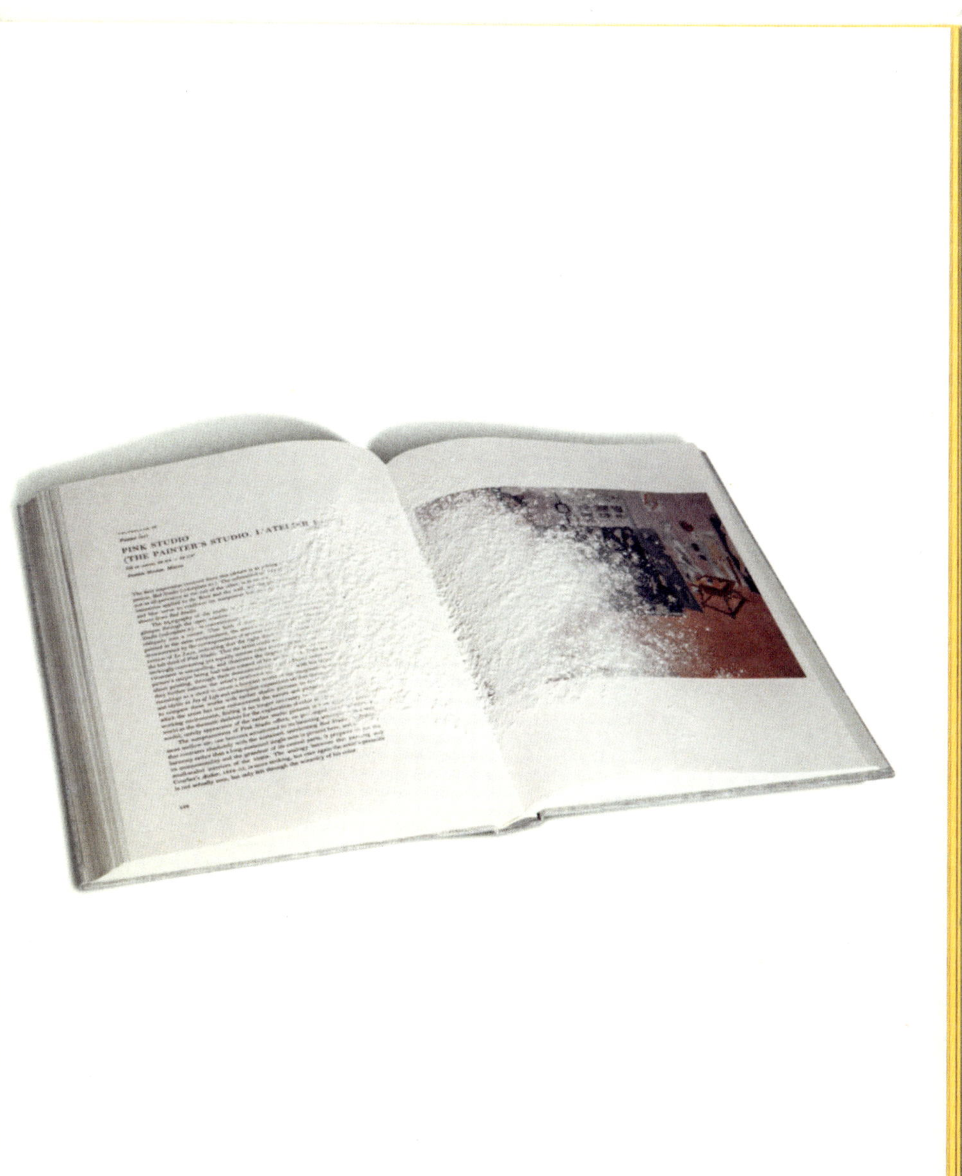

PINK STUDIO
(THE PAINTER'S STUDIO, L'ATELIER

estuviera empleando fueran el material gráfico y la reproducción misma de un objeto. En ese sentido, es como si yo pudiera hacer de mi propio intento la materia prima de mi actividad artística. Cuando hago una exhibición sucede exactamente lo mismo. Cada una es una declaración, un *statement*, y la relación entre los diferentes objetos y esculturas seleccionados para una exposición me interesa tanto como la articulación de esa exposición con las otras. Yo diría, además, que eso sucede con cada pieza en particular, porque cada una está conectada con las demás. Cada una es un pasaje entre la que fue y la que será, e introducirá una modificación significativa en el conjunto, y ese movimiento constante es la poética de mi obra.

AJ Todo esto me interesa, porque siento que la dificultad misma que he venido experimentando cada vez que intento pensar la estructura de estas conversaciones, forma parte integrante de tu trabajo, de tu manera de funcionar y, hasta cierto punto, de una conciencia aguda del contexto de sentido en el que te inscribes. Lo que quiero decir es que cuando un individuo integra las exposiciones y los libros como parte de un dispositivo de sentido, e incluso un aparato temporal de lectura, por decirlo de algún modo (tu negativa a leerla cronológicamente), es porque ha cobrado conciencia de que eso que llamamos la verdad de una obra es simplemente una construcción, que la génesis de sentido no acaba nunca.

WC Sí, eso porque es la única manera de liberarse de una imposición programática que la destruiría. Esa libertad de relacionar las partes entre sí, independientemente de su compromiso cronológico, me parece vital. Un objeto plástico no está restringido solamente a lo que ves, es también lo que no puedes ver. Es como si yo tuviera dos posibilidades: una visible, que sería demostrada mediante los objetos, y una invisible, presente en el vínculo que se establece entre ellos. Luego, es como si la tensión entre esos dos aspectos constituyera también parte de la obra, y creo que ahí se abren siempre horizontes nuevos.

Por ejemplo, estoy sintiendo ahora la necesidad de otro núcleo, uno que nunca percibí como tal, y que estaría presente en la diversidad de actitudes que tengo al dibujar. Yo mismo he privilegiado la presencia de los objetos más que la de los dibujos, y ahora me doy cuenta de que, a través de ellos y su desarrollo en el tiempo, puedo encontrar sorpresas. Tengo que corregir esa distracción.

AJ Sí, pero eso solo se hace viable cuando el conjunto de los dibujos ha alcanzado una densidad suficiente como para originar su propia fuerza de gravedad.

 Como si solo ahora fueran capaces de generar la complejidad necesaria para justificar un interés independiente, con lo cual puedan tener un efecto gravitacional (para continuar con tu metáfora) sobre los conjuntos anteriores. Lo importante, además, para mí, es la garantía de que esos núcleos siempre serán posibles en el futuro, porque son creados por el movimiento mismo de mi trabajo.

*La posibilidad de aprehender la obra producida por un artista desde sus conexiones internas, sin la tiranía de lo cronológico, es sin duda seductora y estimulante. Aun así, negarse programáticamente a la eventualidad de una lectura –también– cronológica, podría convertirse en un velo que esconda parte de la obra, o de sus procesos. A fin de cuentas, es imposible negar que ellas nacieron en momentos específicos y que, por solo dar un ejemplo, Miroir b y Espelho C son impensables antes del primer espejo de metal, de 1975, porque son consecuencia del ámbito de sentido abierto por el primero. Su aparición y su desarrollo en el tiempo forman, pues, parte de la obra. De nada serviría reemplazar una tiranía por otra. Lo importante sería reconocer, e integrar a nuestra experiencia artística, que no existe un acercamiento privilegiado, que la génesis de sentido no acaba nunca, que cada nueva interpretación enriquecerá la pieza que retiene nuestra mirada, y con ella nuestra vida.*

# LA PALABRA Y LAS COSAS
## Hacer, nombrar

*"En el principio era el verbo, y el verbo era Dios". Así comienza el Evangelio de San Juan, y no hay duda de que para nosotros nada existe que no haya sido previamente verbalizado, descrito, nombrado, por la palabra. Y claro, nuestra visión del universo está marcada por la creencia de que existe un mundo real allá afuera, en el que vivimos inmersos y del que formamos parte, ese mismo que el arte ha querido atrapar en su apariencia, y que intentamos describir con el lenguaje. Pero no es menos cierto que esa palabra y esa imagen con la que pretendemos atraparlo, no son el mundo, sino una creación humana, un hecho paralelo que añadimos a lo real. Si algo me sedujo en la poesía de Ferreira Gullar, con quien he tenido la suerte de publicar una de estas conversaciones,[12] es la lucha constante que se entabla en ella entre la palabra y la opacidad ineludible del mundo. La conciencia casi dolorosa de que ella es un objeto más, nunca una huella analógica de lo real. De allí que el artista moderno, y más aún el contemporáneo, no pueda sencillamente ignorar su presencia, su poder. Es al menos lo que ha ocurrido en buena parte del siglo XX, en particular para aquellos artistas que, en la estela dejada por la obra de Marcel Duchamp, han querido agregar la materia gris como un color más en su paleta.*

AJ ¿Cuándo y cómo aparece la palabra en tu producción?

WC La palabra aparece en mi trabajo desde el comienzo y por varias razones. Primero, porque yo tenía como referencia inmediata a movimientos que veían en la palabra un elemento importante. Sin hablar del Cubismo y de Dadá, que ya la habían empleado, me refiero al Pop, el Arte povera y el Arte conceptual. Segundo, cada vez que asignaba un título, aquello se convertía en una decisión compleja, pues veía una relación significativa entre los nombres y los objetos. El primer momento donde esto sucede es en los *Condutores de percepção*, donde el título forma físicamente parte de la obra.

AJ Es prácticamente lo que hace funcionar ese objeto.

WC Lo que lo hace funcionar es exactamente la conexión inesperada entre lo que

12. *Ferreira Gullar in conversation with/en conversación con Ariel Jiménez* (Nueva York: Fundación Cisneros/Colección Patricia Phelps de Cisneros, 2012).

se lee y lo que se ve. Y en esos trabajos encuentro que de alguna manera las palabras proponen una nueva dimensión del objeto, lo hacen depender de la lectura. Y por otro lado, la extrañeza de esas conexiones también le quita a las palabras su poder explicativo, porque a la vez el objeto desmiente al lenguaje. Es como si se creara un espacio vacante entre lo que vemos y lo que sabemos.

AJ A pesar de que visualmente su presencia física es predominante.

WC Sí, y yo diría que hasta la operación de abrir una caja cerrada es fundamental para la situación que se crea. Abrirla es develar el contenido sugerido por las palabras, lo que de inmediato transfigura el objeto. Es como añadirle tiempo a la obra. En *Centro de razão primitiva* [*Centro de razón primitiva*], de 1970, el título se hace tan presente como las agujas que contiene, sin él no se dispara la sugestión necesaria para activarlo. Y no es porque el título sea una explicación del objeto, al contrario [Fig. 34].

AJ El lenguaje es un material, un ingrediente más.

WC Exacto, y es tan curiosa esa situación de un título que activa el objeto, que cuando hago una obra donde el título es una tautología, como en *Talco sobre libro ilustrado de H. Matisse*, el público se pierde aún más.

AJ Por supuesto. Esa redundancia entre el título y lo que se ve no hace más que oscurecer el objeto. Esa es de algún modo la función de la tautología en el arte conceptual: devolverle a lo real su opacidad.

WC Sí, porque la descripción de un objeto no es su título, y ni siquiera lo explica, ni podría existir una versión verbal de aquel objeto. Y yo percibí esa disfunción cuando me encontré ante la incomodidad de tener que hablar de mis trabajos, de explicárselos al público. Lo que yo había planteado con los *Condutores de percepção*, esa articulación ambigua entre el objeto y su título, se aplicaba ahora a mí mismo, o a la relación que se establecía entre las obras, el público y yo mismo. Hablar acerca de mi propio trabajo es ahora un desafío de lenguaje que confronta la autonomía de las obras.

AJ En cierta forma, cuando te pedían explicar una obra, te encontrabas en la obligación de traducirla al lenguaje hablado.

WC Y yo comencé a preguntarme si el artista podía ser un traductor de su propio trabajo. El ejercicio debía consistir más bien en generar una situación nueva para ese otro que ahora hablaba. Y eso me impuso un problema distinto, porque cuando se crea una obra, uno no es sino el autor de un acontecimiento deliberado, y al hablar sobre ese acontecimiento, es casi como si tuviéramos que convertirnos en una persona diferente y distante de la que la hizo.

<sup>AJ</sup> Lo que el público no entiende a veces, es que la lectura que un artista puede hacer de su trabajo no es sino una entre otras tantas posibles, una que está por supuesto muy cerca de sus condiciones de producción, y que por lo tanto es indispensable conocer, pero que de ninguna manera determina lo que ella pueda despertar en los demás. La del artista es una visión que habla de las circunstancias de producción, no de lo que ella es capaz de despertar en sus interlocutores.

<sup>WC</sup> Es solo una lectura, y no siempre la más autorizada, porque yo encuentro que una obra está mejor lograda en la medida en que se resista incluso a la versión del artista. Y es simplemente en ese momento que la obra se transforma en problema, en objeto de estudio para el propio artista. Por consiguiente, se debe pensar el lenguaje adecuado para hablar de esa obra, para establecer una conexión entre él y ella, porque se pasa a trabajar ya no solo con lo que se dice, sino también con el modo de decirlo.

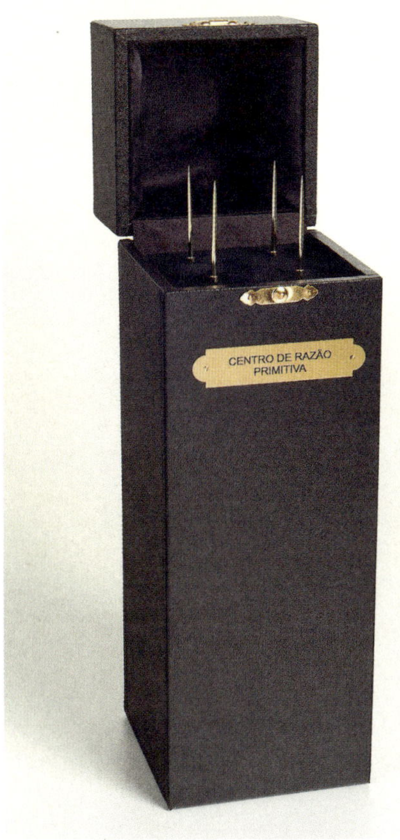


Fig. 34. *Centro de razão primitiva* [*Centro de razón primitiva*], 1970.

<sup>AJ</sup> Hace del discurso sobre la obra una ocasión para producir obra.

<sup>WC</sup> Exacto, y con palabras. Es decir, produciendo tensiones entre la palabra y el objeto. Después me doy cuenta de que el objeto de mi lenguaje es mi propio objeto. En ese momento comienzo a considerar una forma específica para

abordar ese asunto: paso a ser un autor y no un simple traductor de la obra por medio del lenguaje.

<sup>AJ</sup> Lo más terrible, entonces, debe darse cuando te piden explicar una obra que es ya el producto de ese choque con el lenguaje.

<sup>WC</sup> Ese es en realidad un asunto que los artistas enfrentan constantemente, porque de lo que se trata allí es de la autosuficiencia de las obras. Y por eso me parece tan curioso que se requiera del artista una explicación para lo que hace. Nunca fueron los artistas tan solicitados para descifrar su obra y, peor aún, nunca antes se aceptaron tan pasivamente sus explicaciones.

<sup>AJ</sup> Como si la opinión del artista fuera su traducción exacta e irrevocable.

<sup>WC</sup> Y esa necesidad de una traducción se vuelve tan problemática como la obra misma que intenta explicar.

<sup>AJ</sup> Estoy absolutamente de acuerdo en este punto. Lo discutía hace poco con Ferreira Gullar, cuando él me decía que su poesía de los años cincuenta pretendía vencer la opacidad del mundo, y lo hacía buscando un lenguaje que pareciera nacer en el mismo instante de la escritura. En mi opinión, lo que allí sucedía no era que esa opacidad primera del mundo fuera vencida, sino que el arte terminaba creando una nueva, oponiéndole a la opacidad del mundo esa otra opacidad del arte, de la creación humana. Y por eso tú, cuando intentas explicar tu obra, no haces más que producir otro objeto, un objeto verbal distinto al que buscas describir, con lo cual agregas además otra capa de sentido.

<sup>WC</sup> Terminas en una justificativa que es una trampa, y que pasa a ser parte de una vulgata de versiones. A veces el público se conforma con una simple descripción del objeto de arte, como si aquello pudiera ser una explicación. Fue pensando en esa solicitación del público y su deseo de ver las obras traducidas en palabras, que hice el libro *Cronometrias* [2012]. El libro repite una imagen que cambia cada vez que aparece, y esas imágenes están acompañadas por una prosa poética con sugestiones relativas al tiempo y al espacio. El esfuerzo de escribir sobre temas tan abstractos me demostró que las descripciones tienen ventajas insospechadas.

Existen puntos de contacto entre las artes plásticas y el lenguaje escrito u oral, como entre ellos y la música. Los tres pueden generar imágenes, ¿cierto?

Uno puede crear imágenes mentales escuchando música, leyendo un libro o viendo una obra de arte, solo que esas imágenes van a producirse de manera diferente. En *Cronometrias* me hice preguntas ambiciosas, como por ejemplo, si era posible que existiera un reloj que en vez de medir el tiempo midiera el espacio. En esos casos, la relación entre el texto y la imagen no es de contenido e ilustración, sino más bien complementaria.

AJ Escuchándote hablar me vienen a la memoria algunas piezas de la *Série Veneza* [*Venecia*] [1997] donde me parece encontrar una ilustración incluso material de la dificultad que se enfrenta cuando se quiere hacer coincidir el objeto y la palabra. En esas piezas tienes esculturas construidas con partes metálicas, de acabados perfectos, industriales, mientras la manera de pegar los textos es bastante torpe, como si la operación de encolar una palabra a un objeto no pudiera conseguirse con la misma perfección que se alcanza al unir dos piezas metálicas entre sí, sencillamente porque forman parte de realidades distintas [Fig. 35].

WC Y esas palabras son nombres de artistas, y, si lo vemos con cuidado, casi parece que el nombre de los artistas tuviera una historia aparte a la de sus obras. Es como si los nombres se despegaran a veces de sus contenidos originales. Muchas personas los conocen, sin saber nada de sus obras. El otro día leí una entrevista de Luciano Fabro, donde decía que ellos se sorprendieron mucho cuando vieron que el público comenzaba a llamar pobre un arte que ellos en verdad veían como un arte desnudo, sin ningún aderezo, pero nunca pobre. Otras veces ves a un diseñador utilizando el término mínimal para justificar una moda con las características que él cree son la de ese arte, cuando en verdad lo que hace es completamente alegórico y falso. Es como si algunos términos empezaran a tener una vida independiente de sus significados. En el caso que señalas, la *Série Veneza*, ocurre algo decisivo: hablo de varios artistas, y ninguno de sus nombres es utilizado como si se tratara de una cita.

AJ Por supuesto que no, porque es imposible encontrar una relación entre esos nombres y la obra a la que están asociados.

WC Exacto, y por eso me encantó lo que escribió [el curador] Paulo Sérgio Duarte en su texto "La duda feliz", de 2001, donde dice que en esa obra los nombres de los artistas están más a gusto que en los libros. Y eso me pareció fundamental, el hecho de que los nombres encontraran allí, en una escultura, un espacio más acogedor y libre que en las publicaciones sobre ellos y su obra.

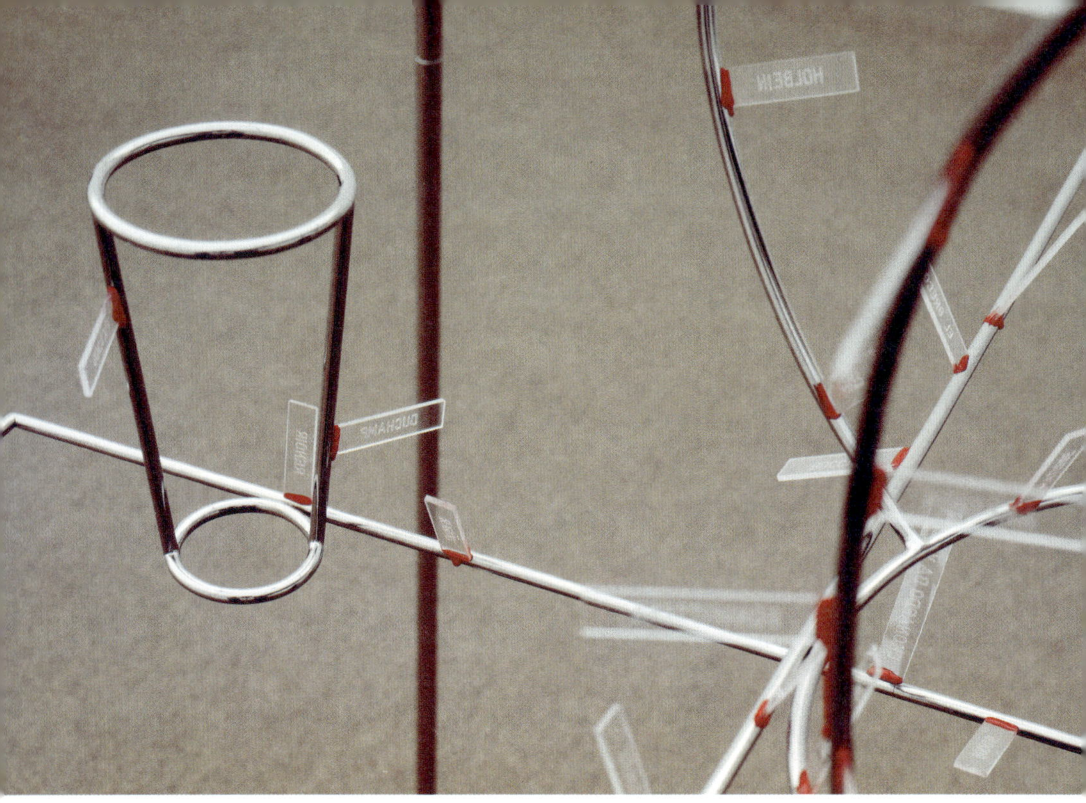

Fig. 35. *A distância entre. . .*, *Série Veneza III*, 1997 (detalle).

AJ A mí, por el contrario, lo que me sorprendió fue la dificultad de esos nombres para encontrar su lugar en las esculturas a las que intentabas asociarlos. . .

WC Es que en realidad suceden ambas cosas, la adecuación y la confrontación hablan de la misma situación.

AJ Sí . . . , es decir, por ejemplo: yo leía el nombre de Matisse, y entonces procuraba conseguir alguna relación entre su nombre y la obra a la que lo asociabas. Luego leía el nombre de Giorgione sobre esa misma escultura, y las relaciones que podía construir eran realmente contradictorias. . . Entonces me pareció que la forma incluso como esos nombres se pegaban a la escultura, de una manera abiertamente artificial, no era del todo insignificante.

WC Es que el objetivo no es relacionar el estilo de esos artistas entre ellos y mi escultura. El vínculo se produce únicamente entre las cosas-nombres. Me interesa apuntar a la distancia entre el arte y la historia del arte, porque es como si la historia constituyera una versión del arte completamente alejada de la práctica del arte. Una cosa es cada objeto en su realidad concreta, otra la explicación que

208

la historia del arte hace de él. Y eso es lo que me lleva a darle a las palabras una existencia física. Por eso, cuando hago un libro sobre Matisse o sobre Velázquez, solo quien crea ver una mujer real en su imagen podría pensar que yo me refiero a Velázquez. En realidad, estoy hablando de ilusiones impresas. De cómo una imagen se transforma en libro, de cómo un libro se transforma en arte y, además, de lo que hace posible que una página con figuras pueda ser vista por el lector como un testimonio confiable.

En ese caso, el artista Velázquez me interesa en la medida en que él mismo abordó problemas similares en su pintura. Mi libro, entonces, intenta tratar los problemas de la representación que él se planteó, pero en mi caso se adicionan también otras capas. La capa de la historia, la de las múltiples versiones velazquianas, de las reproducciones de su obra en publicaciones de épocas distintas y de otros desarrollos históricos. Y hoy, una de esas capas es la dificultad para ver pinturas reproducidas, incluso en libros de gran calidad.

AJ En cierto modo, lo que estás pensando es la función del libro en sí. Por ejemplo, cuando echas talco sobre un libro de Matisse, le devuelves a esa obra la opacidad que el libro busca eliminar explicándola. ¿Cierto?

WC Y Matisse, de alguna manera, hace lo mismo con su *Atelier rouge* [*Taller rojo*; 1911]. Cuando él pinta todo el espacio de su taller y los objetos que contiene en un color dominante, lo que persigue es devolverle su opacidad cromática a la pintura. Porque él está consciente de que no está pintando una silla, sino la imaginación de una silla.

> *Matisse funcionaba de acuerdo a esa estética moderna de la invención. Su tarea no consistía en ofrecernos un simulacro eficaz del mundo, su doble pictórico, sino de agregarle al mundo una realidad distinta: la realidad de la pintura. Waltercio Caldas, por el contrario, como muchos artistas contemporáneos, funciona dentro de una problemática borgiana: un modo de materializar, de darle cuerpo tangible al intrincado mundo de sentido en el que vivimos inmersos; capas y capas de sentido que se superponen a otras, y luego a otras, y así sucesivamente en un movimiento sin fin, como en esa biblioteca de Babel imaginada por Borges, infinita realidad de la cultura, imagen especular de nuestro universo intelectual y nuestra única verdad.*

# TRABAJAR EN LA URBE
## Un horizonte íntimo

*Desde sus primeras maquetas de 1965, su obra aspiraba a lo arquitectónico, intentaba darle cuerpo a espacios imaginarios, como si él mismo fuera una especie de arquitecto borgiano. Para entonces, no obstante, era ingenuo pensar que un joven de poco más de veinte años pretendiera construir estructuras de 200 m² en plena ciudad. Aquello era del orden de la utopía. Hoy, aquella utopía juvenil se ha hecho realidad.*

AJ En un momento de nuestra conversación me decías que te sentías cómodo trabajando a escala urbana, porque desde el inicio tu obra aspiraba ya a esa dimensión, y porque de algún modo todas ellas, incluso en proporciones arqui-tectónicas, conservaban un cierto horizonte íntimo. Y esa aparente contradic-ción me interesa, porque no siempre es fácil pasar del objeto producido en el taller a la envergadura que reclama la ciudad.

WC Yo creo que en este caso podríamos recordar la frase de Charles Chaplin: "Si estás haciendo algo divertido, no necesitas ser divertido para hacerlo". Lo importante no es hacer un objeto grande o pequeño, sino hacerlo del tamaño exacto. En mi caso, incluir una obra en un espacio urbano me pareció siem-pre un asunto de diálogo con la escala de ese lugar. No veo necesariamente la escultura como un aderezo. Nunca la vi como una cosa que viene de afuera, del mundo de la cultura, para imponérsele a lo urbano. En el caso de la escultura que hice en Río de Janeiro, en 1996, la localicé en un espacio al que las personas no le daban ninguna importancia. Era una isla de pasaje en medio del tráfico [Fig. 36].

AJ Pero eso es posible también porque pudiste seleccionar el espacio de tu intervención.

WC Yo lo seleccioné, sí, porque la intención no era hacer una escultura, sino cons-truir un lugar. Era como darle una solución imaginaria a un rincón poco visto, casi invisible para la gente, y por eso encuentro que la palabra "uso" se queda corta ante una situación como esa. Y cuando hablo de una solución imaginaria, estoy refiriéndome al hecho de que la principal desventaja de una obra pública, es que ella es excesivamente visible, y todo el tiempo. El público no escoge

verla o no verla, ella está ahí, siempre presente. Eso me permite decir que ella
no podría hablar en voz alta, sino tan solo susurrarle al individuo, porque todos
los acontecimientos urbanos –como un edificio, por ejemplo–, tienen ya una
elocuencia por su tamaño, por la variedad de su fachada, por la presencia misma
de arquitectura, por la manera como refleja el sol, etc., sin mencionar el valor
simbólico de muchos de ellos, que hoy en día son verdaderos iconos. Mi obra,
por el contrario, llega de una forma más blanda, llega hablando en voz baja. Su
elocuencia está en la evidencia de su presencia.

<sup>AJ</sup> Es lo que me gusta en esta pieza de Río. Cada vez que la veo siento como si ella
fuera la materialización en el espacio real de dos puntos sobre el plano, ¿me
entiendes? Como si tu acción hubiera consistido
únicamente en eso, en señalar desde el plano un
lugar en la ciudad.

<sup>WC</sup> Y en cierto modo es eso lo que he hecho. Una cosa
sería poner allí un objeto, y otra establecer una
relación, una tensión entre dos elementos de la
misma obra, como sucede aquí. La consecuencia
de esa tensión es que el espacio entre esas dos formas se convierte en un tercer elemento.

<sup>AJ</sup> Desde el inicio surge ya la necesidad de
compararlos.

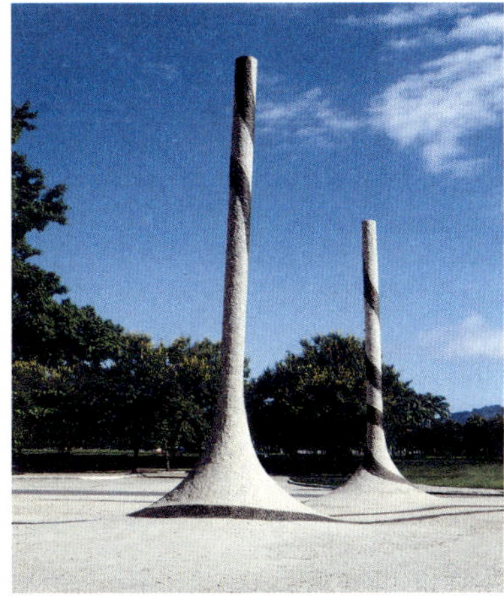
Fig. 36. *Escultura para o Río,* 1996. Ubicada
en Av. Beira Mar, Río de Janeiro, Brasil.

<sup>WC</sup> Y entonces uno se halla con una misma línea que
los envuelve a ambos, y que lo hace como si estu-
viera despegándose del suelo, de esa calzada de piedras que es como la piel de
la ciudad. Mi intención fue crear una escultura que a pesar de su tamaño diera
la sensación de ligereza, y que le otorgara a ese lugar una autonomía plástica.

<sup>AJ</sup> Porque, efectivamente, no se percibe como un objeto colocado en ese punto de
la ciudad, sino como una anomalía que habría tenido lugar allí. Y en ese sentido,
estimo que es una de tus obras públicas mejor resueltas.

<sup>WC</sup> Hay otras que también buscan crear un lugar, como *A passagem* [*El pasaje*; 2009],
en Santiago de Compostela [Fig. 37]. El parque de Belvis donde la imaginé está
en medio de la ciudad, y es al mismo tiempo un sitio neutro. En Santiago de
Compostela el misticismo y lo religioso están presentes en cada esquina. Por

eso, cuando pensé la obra, la imaginé como en una capilla para los que no tienen dioses. Una donde las personas pudieran sencillamente reflexionar sobre todo, esto porque siempre recuerdo una frase de Paul Valéry en la que él decía que era un místico sin Dios. Lo que hice entonces fue deconstruir una capilla, pero haciéndolo sin ningún simbolismo específico. En ese caso, el lugar que se crea está relacionado con la naturaleza de la ciudad donde se encuentra.

La construcción consta de un piso de piedra y una pared, los elementos básicos de una arquitectura, y hay una puerta que está siempre abierta, y un espacio donde se ve un piso más alto, pero todo desposeído del carácter místico. Y eso sucede en parte porque se trata de una casa abierta en medio del paisaje. Hay además una particularidad constructiva, y es que parte de esa obra está hecha en un mármol oscuro, que refleja al visitante como un espejo. Esa pared reflectora está atravesada por otra, más rebelde, que pasa por ahí, lo que recuerda una característica esencial de Santiago: la de ser una ciudad de pasaje. Al mismo tiempo, creo que no hay duda de que estamos ante una obra que ocupa aquel sitio temporalmente, como si fuera, me atrevería a decirlo, una habitación-de-lugar.

Para mí es siempre importante la relación que se establece entre la estructura que construyo y el paisaje que ocupa. Cuando me invitaron a hacer una escultura en Noruega, en 1994, tuve la posibilidad de intervenir en varias ciudades. Visité algunas de ellas, y pude darme cuenta de un rasgo nuevo que justificó mi intervención: observé que, al contrario de Brasil, que es un país inmenso donde pueden encontrarse ciudades enormes lejos unas de otras, Noruega tiene muchas ciudades pequeñas y muy próximas entre sí. A veces, la

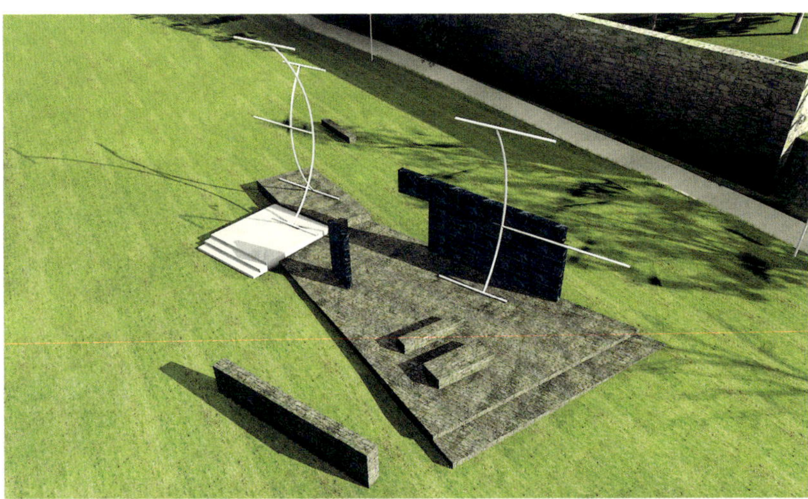

Fig. 37. *A passagem* [*El pasaje*], 2009 (maqueta digital).

distancia entre ellas es de quince kilómetros, de manera que desde el avión, por la noche, puede verse luz por todas partes. Y sin embargo, me pareció también que las casas, en esas ciudades, distaban unas de otras en una proporción que me sorprendió. En realidad, las personas vivían más distantes entre sí de lo que ocurría en Brasil.

Al principio me pregunté cómo era posible que, con ciudades tan cercanas, residieran tan lejos unos de otros, pero después de convivir con ellos algunos días, percibí que en realidad vivían lo más cerca posible. Esa diferencia entre habitar lejos unos de otros en ciudades contiguas, me dio una noción de escala completamente nueva. Era una escala afectiva, que me hizo comprender que ellos habían encontrado un equilibrio entre la proximidad de las ciudades y la intimidad de sus casas. Lo que hice entonces fue considerar esa escala que estaba descubriendo y no la que yo traía conmigo.

AJ Por eso decides hacerla entre una ciudad y otra. . .

WC Exactamente, y además *Omkring* [*Alrededor*], 1994, está instalada en un precipicio donde la escultura se proyecta hacia el espacio [Fig. 38]. Es como si hubiera incorporado el abismo donde se encuentra como un atributo más de su ubicación. El sitio es un peñasco. Lo que sucede es que cuando uno la ve de lado, la obra parece muy grande y larga, pero si la mira de frente, la segunda puerta parece estar mucho más cercana. De modo que la noción de escala es diferente de un lado y otro de la obra, y recuerda la relación que percibí entre las distancias de las ciudades y la que separa las casas entre ellas. Y no solo eso, la dimensión que se experimenta con el cuerpo es distinta a la que puede experimentarse con la mirada. Es una escultura con diversos puntos de vista; es casi un dispositivo de perspectiva proyectado en el paisaje. De un lado el vértigo, por el otro el abismo.

*Espelho rápido* [*Espejo rápido*], de 2005, es una obra pública de ese tipo. Está en Porto Alegre, a las márgenes de un río. Es el río Guaíba, que en esa región pasa muy lentamente, y la obra puede así dialogar con el movimiento del agua. Para eso pensé un espejo transversal imaginario, capaz de reflejar en todos los sentidos: a la horizontal, a la vertical y en profundidad [Fig. 39].

AJ ¿Podríamos considerarlo como un espejo de tercer tipo?

WC Sí, pero hay que tener una cierta complacencia con mis espejos, porque no funcionan de manera mecánica. Si yo hablo de espejos tipo B, no es porque haya necesariamente los de tipo A. En realidad no existen espejos A. Lo único

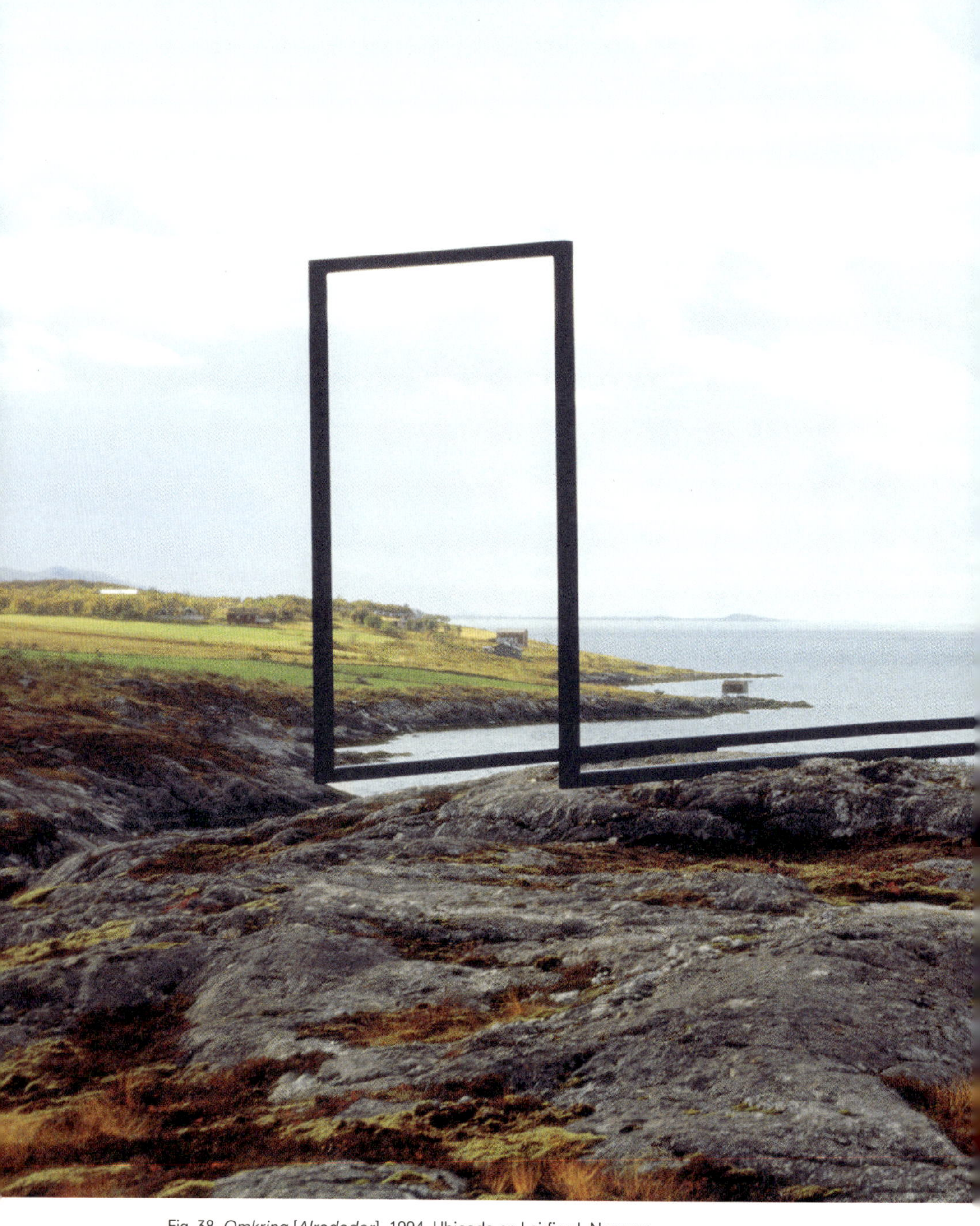

Fig. 38. *Omkring* [*Alrededor*], 1994. Ubicada en Leirfjord, Noruega.

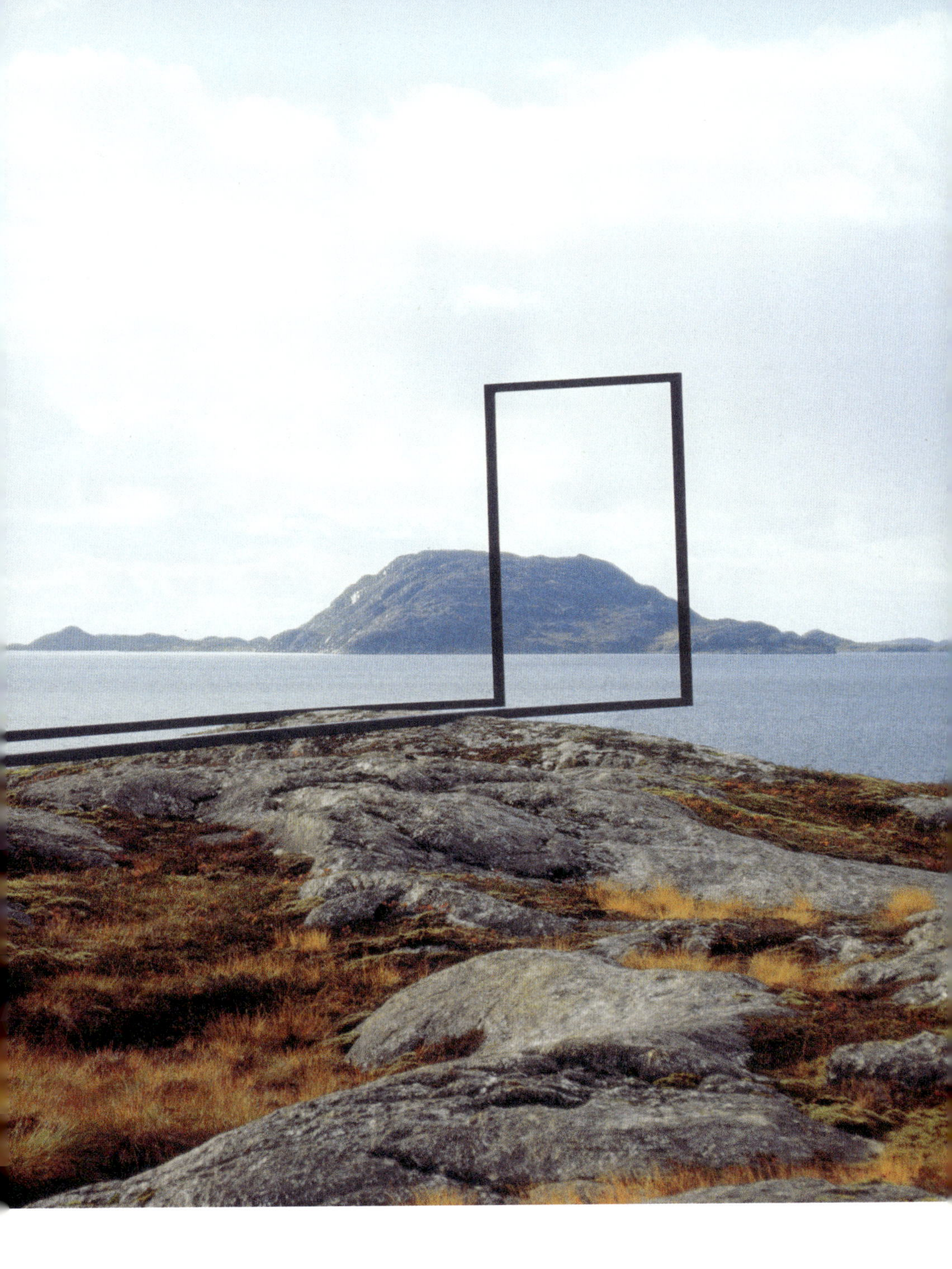

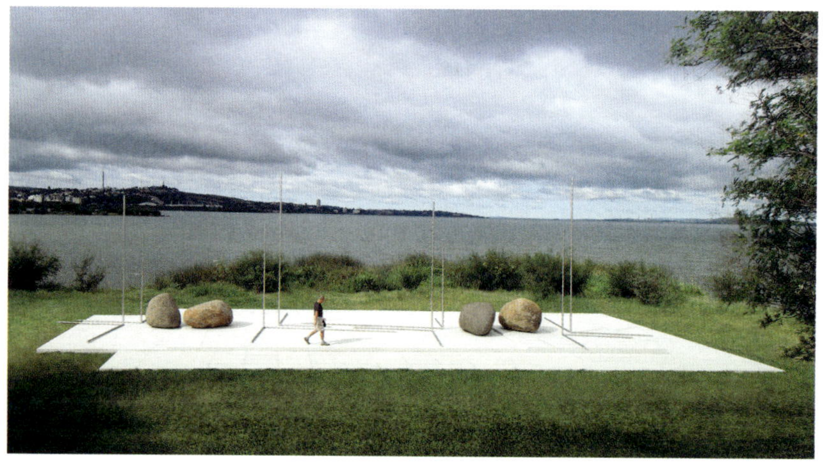

Fig. 39. *Espelho rápido* [*Espejo rápido*], 2005. Ubicado en Parque Mauricio Sirotsky Sobrinho, Porto Alegre, Brasil.

que quiero señalar con ello es que puede haber espejos de otros tipos, o que tienen una forma diferente de operar. Es como si dijéramos que el espejo no es solamente un objeto, sino varios tipos de objeto. El espejo negro, como el de los aztecas por ejemplo, tiene una manera atípica de reflejar, porque lo que sucede allí es muy distinto de lo que podemos observar en los espejos transparentes. Su respuesta es de otro orden. Pero hay otros, como los que describió Borges, que funcionan de manera especial cuando nadie los ve. El escritor sugiere que a altas horas de la noche, cuando nadie está en la habitación, en el interior de los espejos puede escucharse un ruido de armas. Lo que me gusta en estas descripciones es la posibilidad de imaginar un funcionamiento distinto para los espejos. Siempre me hago la pregunta, ¿es posible construir un espejo si solo tuviéramos nociones incompletas sobre ellos?

AJ ¿O solo verbales?

WC Sí, e incluso aquellos que, al concluir su vida útil, comenzarían a funcionar de otra manera; como esos espejos viejos que ya no reflejan nada, pero que se ponen en las casas como elementos de decoración.

AJ Siguen llamándose espejos, y conservan su apariencia exterior, pero ya no sirven como tal, ya no funcionan. . .

WC Eso me hace pensar que los espejos son metáforas del objeto de arte, un espejo que le niega al espectador su propio reflejo, dándole con su imagen una respuesta sorprendente. Otro de los espejos que hice fue uno que estaba volteado contra la pared. Era una plancha negra, de cartón, con un hueco en el centro, revelando la pared [ver Fig. 19]. Ese espejo trae la pared al primer plano de dos formas distintas: realizándola en su imagen y, luego, colgándolo en ella. Y la sola presencia de un soporte indica que debe ser colgado para cumplir su función reflectante. Como si pudiéramos activarlo y desactivarlo. Y cuando lo hacemos, es cuando podemos vernos de maneras distintas. . .

<sup>AJ</sup> Abordemos ahora *O formato cego* [*El formato ciego*], de 1978–82, que es el primer trabajo que haces a escala urbana. Es importante discutirlo porque de lo que hemos visto hasta ahora, este me parece estar más cerca de lo que podríamos llamar una escultura, un objeto en el espacio, y no la creación de un lugar [Fig. 40].

<sup>WC</sup> Lo que sucede en este caso es que está en un sitio donde sopla mucho el viento. Por eso quise construir una escultura que le ofreciera muy poca resistencia. Una masa llena tan solo con el borde del espacio. Lo que busqué con el título fue sugerir que no era el objeto en sí lo que me interesaba, sino su formato, su función.

<sup>AJ</sup> Y sin embargo, cuando uno lee ciego en el título, tiene tendencia a ver esta estructura como un ojo, o como un lente.

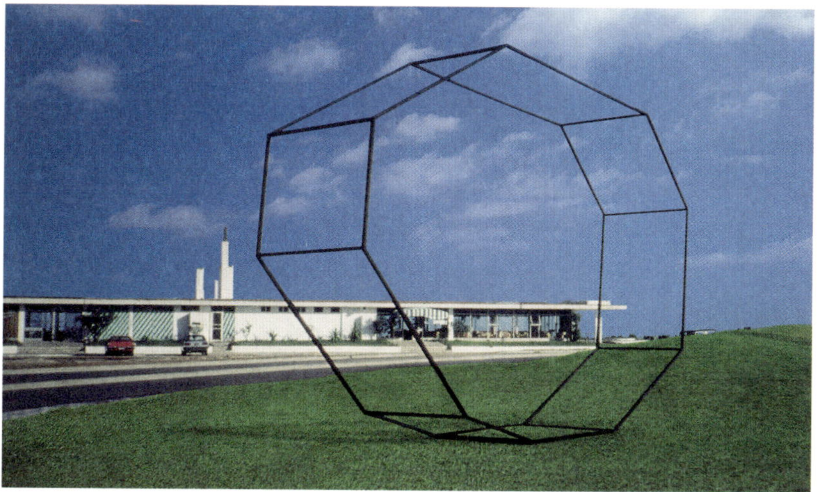

Fig. 40. *O formato cego* [*El formato ciego*], 1978–82. Ubicado en Paseo de Las Américas, Punta del Este, Uruguay.

<sup>WC</sup> Quizás, pero lo que a mí me motivaba era la disolución formal del objeto, su desaparición o su reducción a un simple dispositivo funcional. Siempre me ha intrigado el problema de la ceguera, el hecho de que los ciegos no puedan ver el negro. Borges decía que tenía nostalgia del negro, porque el invidente vive sumergido en una bruma gris. En su carta sobre los ciegos, también, Diderot cuenta la historia de un ciego de nacimiento que, cuando adulto, logra ver por primera vez. Lo que me sorprendió de ese testimonio, es que el ciego quedó muy sorprendido al descubrir que su cuarto era mucho menor que el mundo. ¿Tendrá la ceguera un espacio y una escala propios?

<sup>AJ</sup> Por esa vía llegaríamos al lenguaje, porque para quien ha aprendido a ver, a leer y hablar al mismo tiempo, le parece que la forma del cubo y la palabra cubo coinciden; pero para quien aprende la palabra independientemente de su aspecto visual, no sucede necesariamente así. Y esa era una de las interrogantes que se planteaba Diderot: determinar si ante un cubo el ciego podría reconocer la palabra adecuada para nombrarlo. Es decir, se preguntaba si al tocar un cubo le sería posible saber cuál era la palabra empleada para describirlo.

<sup>WC</sup> Mientras te escuchaba, me vino a la memoria un texto de Francis Ponge, donde decía que la palabra escultura debía ser abolida de los diccionarios. Esa idea de que es más fácil hablar de lo que es una escultura confiando en un espacio vacío, resulta muy interesante, y más verdadera, quizás.

# ASOMBROS INICIALES
## Respondiendo a los estímulos del mundo

AJ Hemos hablado de tu producción —siguiendo una metáfora astronómica— como de un conjunto de objetos que se reunirían en núcleos, como si una afinidad secreta los atrajera para formar pequeños sistemas planetarios, con la particularidad de que esos planetas o núcleos de sentido no girarían en torno a un eje central, sino que irían configurando una estructura constelar variable, y sobre todo siempre abierta a la posibilidad de que nuevos núcleos surjan y se agreguen, modificando la configuración general del conjunto. El sistema funciona, al menos en tu caso, para explicar las relaciones que se establecen entre tus obras, más allá de las analogías formales o de estilo que te acechan, por encima incluso de su aparición cronológica. Y sin embargo, en ocasiones me ha parecido constatar que muchos de esos problemas tienen un origen común. Por eso, me gustaría indagar ahora en tus primeros años de formación, porque intuyo que es allí donde se alojan las experiencias que definen ese funcionamiento, las obsesiones que de alguna manera te imponen determinados temas, y que definitivamente se enlazan con las primeras vivencias de un individuo ante el mundo.

WC El recuerdo más remoto de lo que podríamos llamar una epifanía, tiene que ver con el descubrimiento de la reproducción, en tamaño real, del primer avión creado por un brasileño: Santos-Dumont. Esa réplica, instalada hacia 1954–55 en el zaguán del aeropuerto que lleva su nombre, provocó en mí un impacto muy grande. Tal vez en la época no tenía clara la razón por la cual aquel objeto me había causado tanta emoción, y quizás hoy lo sepa. No era solamente un objeto con ángulos, cuerdas, ruedas, hecho de tela, con un motor; era también la creación de una función. En realidad aquel objeto inventaba el volar, o la posibilidad del vuelo [ver Fig. 6].

AJ Pero esa es, claro, una mirada retrospectiva. En ese momento no podías comprenderlo y menos aún formularlo en estos términos.

WC No, no podía entenderlo por supuesto, pero de algún modo ese encuentro causó en mí un impacto tal que recuerdo haber construido varias maquetas del avión en mi casa. Las elaboré en papel, en madera de balsa y cartón. Podría decir que pasé un buen periodo de mi infancia construyendo y reconstruyendo esa maqueta. Pero su impacto fue aún mayor, porque me mostró la posibilidad de hacer mis propias maquetas. Recuerdo por ejemplo que una vez hice una cámara de televisión, que era un aparato que me impresionaba mucho, porque eran máquinas enormes, con ruedas, y la persona que las manipulaba tenía un enorme aparataje delante de él. De esta cámara en cartón pasé a la miniatura de un estudio de televisión, con sus escenarios y su mobiliario. Quizás, eso pienso hoy, las maquetas que hacía en respuesta a esos acontecimientos me ayudaban a reproducir la sensación que experimentaba cuando las veía, y acaso por eso descubrí una posibilidad de responder a los estímulos provenientes del mundo. Si yo estaba buscando entender el mundo, esa fue, tal vez, la primera noción que tuve de que me era dado entenderlo a través de modelos y representaciones. Hacer algo era como una nueva libertad creativa y personal. Y por eso te digo que cuando pude trabajar en el espacio urbano, en verdad me sentí muy cómodo, porque era como volver a un asombro inicial.

AJ  Y seguramente, mientras lo hacías, tratabas de comprender el impacto que ese objeto había producido en ti.

WC  El niño reacciona a las cosas de una forma muy pura, muy objetiva, sin ningún tipo de especulación. Está siempre, como dice Rilke, dándole la cara a lo abierto. Pero hoy tengo la certeza de que algo, en esa invención del vuelo creada por un objeto que puede ser fabricado con nuestras propias manos, cambió mi vida.

AJ  Me pregunto, incluso, si el descubrimiento de un aparato capaz de despegar y liberarnos de la tierra donde estamos, no se convirtió para ti en una especie de metáfora de liberación más general, de orden histórico, como la de liberarnos también de ese anacronismo que ha pesado tanto en nuestro imaginario histórico.

WC  No sé si los latinoamericanos podemos compartir una misma desesperanza por el anacronismo. Yo creo más bien que nuestras desesperanzas son diferentes. Cada país tiene una manera particular de responder a esos problemas, e incluso un tiempo distinto. Hace algunos días estaba escuchando una entrevista de Ferreira Gullar sobre los tiempos de la dictadura, y él señalaba algo que me parece importante. Él decía que al contrario de la dictadura chilena o la argentina, que comenzaron como tiranías agresivas desde el primer momento, a la brasileña le tomó cuatro años alcanzar el mismo nivel de agresividad, con la represión y las torturas. Es como si nosotros tuviéramos diferencias significativas, en la forma y la manera de reaccionar a las dificultades. Además, no estaría muy seguro de poder interpretar lo que sentía en ese momento.

De cualquier modo, lo que me parece más acertado es que yo estaba incorporando la idea de crear una expresividad artística propia. Como adolescente, yo quería expresarme, tenía necesidad de hacerlo, y encontré en el arte una nueva posibilidad, y una facilidad de expresión. Ser artista era difícil en Brasil, existían pocas oportunidades e incluso contábamos con muy pocos modelos a los que pudiéramos referirnos. Por eso, como ya lo discutimos, cada uno de nosotros tuvo que inventar su propio artista. Y quizás el encuentro con el avión de Santos Dumont, su configuración esdrújula con trozos de tela, de madera y de formas cúbicas ordenadas, me intrigó hasta el punto de preguntarme cómo era posible que aquel objeto pudiera volar. Es decir, fue la extrañeza de su configuración lo que me atrajo. Sin embargo, es evidente que esa preocupación por escapar del anacronismo estaba presente, era y sigue siendo fundamental; se podía percibir en artistas como Hélio Oiticica, Lygia Clark e Ivan Serpa.

Hay luego otro factor que recuerdo como algo muy determinante para mi formación estética –y todo eso sucedía simultáneamente–, y es que Brasilia estaba en construcción, y mi padre, que era ingeniero, hablaba constantemente en casa de la construcción de esa ciudad nueva. También, por supuesto, recuerdo las visitas a su estudio, donde pude ver maquetas de obras modernas en construcción. Había igualmente muchos diseños de casas modernas en el escritorio, y casi podría afirmar que lo vi pasar su vida entera inclinado sobre su mesa de dibujo, calculando aquellas estructuras que apoyaban lo que él llamaba "las audacias modernas". Era como si mi padre pensara que la función de los ingenieros consistía en darle una estructura a esos delirios. No es una casualidad si uno de los arquitectos de [Oscar] Niemeyer fue el gran poeta Joaquim Cardoso.

También en el hecho de que la casa donde vivíamos, que fue edificada por mi padre, respondiera o incluyera algunos de los principios que él consideraba modernos: la casa estaba desplazada en el espacio disponible, no ocupaba el centro del terreno, y se llegaba a ella por medio de una rampa, o sea que respondía a determinadas características que hoy identifico como formando parte de una arquitectura moderna.

La construcción de Brasilia fue importante para toda una generación y yo, a los ocho años de edad, vivía ese "espíritu" moderno. La famosa frase de Mário Pedrosa que dice: "Los brasileños están condenados a ser modernos", era una realidad. Se escuchaban los primeros acordes de la *bossa nova*, una música completamente diferente de la samba a la que estábamos acostumbrados, porque es una música que tenía una espacialidad nueva, fresca, como si una de sus cualidades fuera la de ser una música para el aire libre. Es decir que cualquier composición de Antônio Carlos Jobim, produce siempre la sensación agradable de haber sido hecha para alguien que la escucha afuera, contemplando el paisaje, el horizonte.

AJ ¿Una transparencia?

WC Una transparencia, sí, con la presencia de sombras y agua fresca, de cierta manera. A veces, cuando estoy en un restaurante de Nueva York y tocan una samba de *bossa nova*, siento (quizás por haberlo experimentado anteriormente) que ese espacio cerrado se abre. O sea que siempre vivimos con esa sensación de amplitud de fronteras y de horizontes amplios. Le Corbusier decía que Brasil era el único país que tenía un horizonte íntimo. Por otro lado, vivimos también con la sensación de que Brasil está constantemente en construcción. Es decir, que nosotros no recibimos un país ya listo, sino uno que tenemos que rehacer continuamente.

AJ Es muy interesante, porque si hay una característica clave en el arte moderno y contemporáneo, es precisamente esa apertura a lo posible. . .

WC Sí, solo que nuestro posible ha sido siempre más sorprendente, más desconocido. Pero hay todavía otro aspecto curioso que quizás haya influenciado algunos de mis primeros trabajos durante los años sesenta. Fueron las visitas que yo hacía casi semanalmente a un faquir. Él vivía dentro de una enorme caja de vidrio, sobre una cama de clavos, con algunas serpientes dentro. Se llamaba Silk y, si lo pensamos bien, su nombre era muy gracioso, porque él vivía con muy poco confort. Yo le pedí a mi papá que me llevara una vez por semana a ver aquel faquir. Él estaba en el primer piso de un cine donde pasaban películas en tres dimensiones, y uno necesitaba unos lentes especiales para verlas. Aquel faquir casi ni se movía, sus gestos eran muy lentos, y aquello me impresionaba mucho [Fig. 41].

Quizás algún día pueda saber por qué me impactaba tanto, pero el hecho es que yo me preguntaba cómo era posible que ese señor pudiera vivir así, aislado –o casi–, porque al final él no estaba protegido del público por una capa espesa y opaca, sino por un vidrio transparente. En verdad, él compartía con el público su intimidad, su destino. Y ellos observaban en silencio su figura quieta, que no comía en cien días. Yo veía a ese faquir como la metáfora de un hombre que consigue sobrevivir a cualquier circunstancia. Era increíble que un hombre sobreviviera en condiciones tan extremas. El avión de Santos Dumont, una

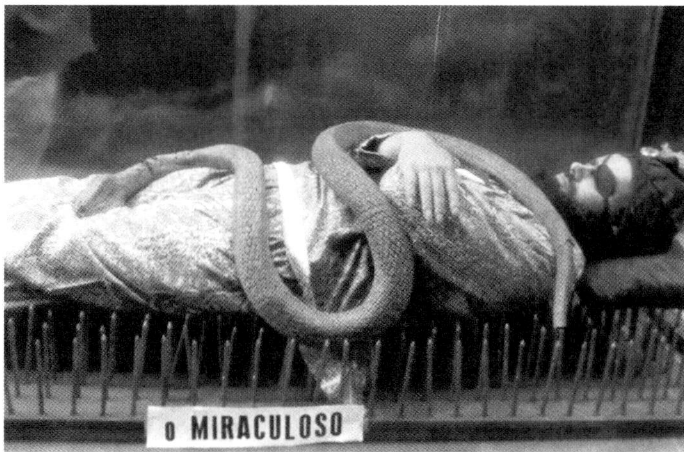


Fig. 41. Silk, faquir del centro de São Paulo, s/f.

ciudad construida para el futuro moderno, el cine en tres dimensiones y aquel faquir, son fragmentos dispersos en mi imaginario. Me olvidé de tantas otras cosas, que no entiendo por qué permanecen estas y no otras. . .

AJ ¿Y no sientes que allí hay una metáfora de tu condición histórica en el Brasil de ese momento? Yo, por mi parte, no puedo evitar ver en ese *faquir* una imagen de encierro dentro de una realidad hostil, y en el avión de Santos Dumont y la construcción de Brasilia, imágenes liberadoras.

WC Sin duda, sin duda. Visto ahora, todo me parece muy coherente, pero en la época. . . , yo era un chico. . . , y encuentro que el arte no es exactamente una prerrogativa para los niños. El arte surge como una necesidad de lenguaje para los adultos, cuando uno tiene que inventarse un destino y responder al mundo, cambiándolo. Quizás haya aprendido entonces que siempre veremos lo que aún no vemos, y que ese proceso no tendrá nunca un fin.

# ABOUT THE AUTHORS /
# SOBRE LOS AUTORES

**Guy Brett** is a London-based art critic, curator, and lecturer. He has written extensively for the art press since the 1960s and has organized a number of influential exhibitions, including *Hélio Oiticica* (1969), *Transcontinental: Nine Latin American Artists, An Investigation of Reality* (1989), *Force Fields: Phases of the Kinetic* (2000), *The Enclosed Openness: Box and Book in Brazilian Art* (2012), *Georges Vantongerloo: A Longing for Infinity* (2009), and *Wols: Cosmos and Street* (2014). He is Visiting Professor at the University of the Arts, London. In 2005 he was Peggy Rockefeller Visiting Fellow at Harvard University, and in 2008 he was Clark Collection Critic/Curator-in-Residence at Victoria University of Wellington, New Zealand. He has contributed essays to many artists' monographs, and was co-editor of the publications *Oiticica in London* (2007) and *Cildo Meireles* (2008). His books include *Kinetic Art: The Language of Movement* (1968), *Through Our Own Eyes: Popular Art and Modern History* (1986), *Transcontinental: Nine Latin American Artists* (1990), *Exploding Galaxies: The Art of David Medalla* (1995), *Mona Hatoum* (1997), *Carnival of Perception* (2004), *Brasil Experimental: Arte/Vida Proposições e Paradoxos* (2005), *Rose Finn-Kelcey* (2010), *Susan Hiller* (2011), and *Abstract Vaudeville: The Work of Rose English* (2015).

**Ariel Jiménez** is a historian and independent curator of modern and contemporary art. He studied art history and archeology at the Sorbonne in Paris, and has curated numerous exhibitions and lectured in both public and private institutions throughout the Americas. He was Chief Curator of the Colección Patricia Phelps de Cisneros (CPPC) for fifteen years (1997–2011), Director and Chief Curator of the Museo de Arte Moderno Jesús Soto in Ciudad Bolívar (2004–2006), Director of the Sala Mendoza in Caracas (1989–1997), Assistant Researcher for the Art Department of the Instituto Internacional de Estudios Avanzados (IDEA) in Caracas (1986–1989) and Director of the Department of Education and Audiovisual Media at the Museo de Arte Contemporáneo in Caracas (1984–1986). He has published extensively about Venezuelan and Latin American art, including *La primacía del color* (Caracas: Monte Ávila Editores, 1992); *He vivido por los ojos. Correspondencia Alejandro Otero / Alfredo Boulton 1946–1974* (Caracas: Fundación Alberto Vollmer and Fundación Museo Alejandro Otero, 2001); *Conversaciones con Jesús Soto* (Caracas: Fundación Cisneros, 2001); *Soto* (Caracas: Fundación Jesús Soto and Fundación Banco de Venezuela, 2007); *Alfredo Boulton and his Contemporaries: Critical Dialogues in Venezuelan Art 1912–1974* (New York: The Museum of Modern Art, 2008); *Carlos Cruz-Diez in conversation with / en conversación con Ariel Jiménez* (New York: Fundación Cisneros, 2010); *Jesús Soto in conversation with / en conversación con Ariel Jiménez* (New York: Fundación Cisneros, 2011); *Ferreira Gullar in conversation with / en conversación con Ariel Jiménez* (New York: Fundación Cisneros, 2012), *Roberto Obregón en tres tiempos* (Caracas: Colección C&FE, 2013) y *Dolor cifrado / Roberto Obregón o una estética de los inconmensurables* (Caracas: Fundación Seguros Venezuela, 2016).

**Guy Brett** es crítico de arte, curador y académico, vive y trabaja en Londres. Ha escrito innumerables artículos de arte desde los años sesenta y organizado muchas muestras importantes como *Hélio Oiticica* (1969), *Transcontinental: Nine Latin American Artists, An Investigation of Reality* (1989), *Force Fields: Phases of the Kinetic* (2000), *The Enclosed Openness: Box and Book in Brazilian Art* (2012), *Georges Vantongerloo: A Longing for Infinity* (2009) y *Wols: Cosmos and Street* (2014). Actualmente es catedrático visitante en la University of the Arts, Londres. En el 2005 fue profesor visitante Peggy Rockefeller en Harvard University, Cambridge, Estados Unidos, y en 2008 fue designado crítico/curador para la residencia de la Clark Collection en Victoria University de Wellington, Nueva Zelanda. Ha contribuido con ensayos a diversas monografías de artistas y como co-editor de las publicaciones *Oiticica in London* (2007) y *Cildo Meireles* (2008). Entre sus libros podemos mencionar: *Kinetic Art: The Language of Movement* (1968), *Through Our Own Eyes: Popular Art and Modern History* (1986), *Transcontinental: Nine Latin American Artists* (1990), *Exploding Galaxies: The Art of David Medalla* (1995), *Mona Hatoum* (1997), *Carnival of Perception* (2004), *Brasil Experimental: Arte/Vida Proposições e Paradoxos* (2005), *Rose Finn-Kelcey* (2010), *Susan Hiller* (2011) y *Abstract Vaudeville: The Work of Rose English* (2015).

**Ariel Jiménez** es historiador y curador independiente de arte moderno y contemporáneo. Estudió historia del arte y arqueología en la Universidad de la Sorbona (París), y ha sido curador de numerosas exposiciones en instituciones públicas y privadas a lo largo del continente americano. Fue curador de la Colección Patricia Phelps de Cisneros (Caracas) durante quince años (1997–2011), director y curador jefe del Museo de Arte Moderno Jesús Soto de Ciudad Bolívar (2004–2006) y director de la Sala Mendoza en Caracas (1989–1997), Investigador asistente en la Unidad de Arte del Instituto Internacional de Estudios Avanzados (IDEA) en Caracas (1986–1989) y director del Departamento de Educación y Medios Audiovisuales del Museo de Arte Contemporáneo de Caracas (1984–1986). Ha publicado, entre otros títulos: *La primacía del color* (Caracas: Monte Ávila Editores, 1992), *He vivido por los ojos. Correspondencia Alejandro Otero/Alfredo Boulton. 1946–1974* (Caracas: Fundación Alberto Vollmer y Fundación Museo Alejandro Otero, 2001), *Conversaciones con Jesús Soto* (Caracas: Fundación Cisneros, 2001), *Soto* (Caracas: Fundación Jesús Soto y Fundación Banco de Venezuela, 2007), *Alfredo Boulton y sus contemporáneos. Diálogos críticos en el arte venezolano. 1912–1974* (Nueva York: The Museum of Modern Art y Fundación Cisneros, 2010), *Carlos Cruz-Diez in conversation with/en conversación con Ariel Jiménez* (Nueva York: Fundación Cisneros, 2010), *Jesús Soto in conversation with/en conversación con Ariel Jiménez* (Nueva York: Fundación Cisneros, 2011), *Ferreira Gullar in conversation with / en conversación con Ariel Jiménez* (Nueva York: Fundación Cisneros, 2012), *Roberto Obregón en tres tiempos* (Caracas: Colección C&FE, 2013) y *Dolor cifrado/Roberto Obregón o una estética de los inconmensurables* (Caracas: Fundación Seguros Venezuela, 2016).

# IMAGE CAPTIONS / FICHAS TÉCNICAS

Pages [Páginas] 34–35, 70–71, 144–145, 180–181 and between 40–41, 88–89, 152–153, 200–201 were specifically designed by Waltercio Caldas for this publication [fueron específicamente diseñadas por Waltercio Caldas para esta publicación].

Cover [Portada]:
*Escultura para todos os materiais não transparentes* [*Sculpture for All Nontransparent Materials / Escultura para todos los materiales no transparentes*], 1985, detail [detalle]
Pair of polished marble hemispheres [Par de hemisferios de mármol pulido]
Dimensions variable [dimensiones variables]
Private collection

Title Page [Portadilla]:
*Água / Cálice / Espelhos* [*Water / Glass / Mirrors / Agua / Vidrio / Espejos*], 1975
Metal, mirror, glass, and water [Metal, espejo, cristal y agua]
42.8 × 50.5 × 14.8 cm
(16⅞ × 19⅞ × 5¹³⁄₁₆ inches)
Chateaubriand Collection

Contents page [Índice]:
Waltercio Caldas, New York, 2014
Photo by [Foto de] Gabriel Pérez-Barreiro

Pages [Páginas] 114–115:
*É =* [*Is= / Es=*], 1986
Polished stainless steel balls on paper [Bolas de acero inoxidable pulido sobre papel]
20 × 50 × 70 cm
(7⅞ × 19⅝ × 27½ inches)
MJME Collection

Introductory Essay [Ensayo introductorio]:
Fig. 1:
*Prato comum com elasticos* [*Ordinary Plate with Rubber Bands / Plato ordinario con ligas*], 1978

Fig. 2:
*Espelhos ausentes* [*Absent Mirrors / Espejos ausentes*], 2003
Stainless steel and marble [Acero inoxidable y mármol]
Luciana and Luis Antonio Almeida Braga Collection

Fig. 3:
*Quarto azul* [*Blue Room / Cuarto azul*], 2007
Installed at [instalado en] *Horizontes* [*Horizons*], Fundação Calouste Gulbenkian, Lisbon, 2008

Fig. 4:
*Anda uma coisa no ar* [*Something is in the Air / Hay algo en el aire*], 2002.
Installed at [instalado en] *Horizontes* [*Horizons*], Fundação Calouste Gulbenkian, Lisbon, 2008.
Andrea and José Olympio Vega Pereira Collection

Conversation / Conversación:
Fig. 1:
*Always* [*Siempre*], 1967
Variable rubber strings on wall [Hilos elásticos en la pared]
180 × 240 cm (70⅞ × 94½ inches)
Collection of the artist

Fig. 1a:
*Always* [*Siempre*], 1967
Variable rubber strings on wall [Hilos elásticos en la pared]
180 × 240 cm (70⅞ × 94½ inches)
Collection of the artist

Fig. 2:
Pablo Picasso
*The Blue Acrobat* [*El acróbata azul*], 1929
Oil on canvas [Óleo sobre lienzo]
162 × 130 cm (63¾ × 51³⁄₁₆ inches)
©2015 Estate of Pablo Picasso / Artist Rights Society (ARS), NY
Image: ©CNAC / MNAM / Dist.RMN-Grand Palais / Art Resource, NY

Fig. 3:
*Maquette II*, 1967
Cardboard [Papel cartón]
57 × 18 × 9 cm
(22⁷⁄₁₆ × 7¹⁄₁₆ × 3½ inches)
Chateaubriand Collection

Fig. 4:
Étienne-Louis Boullée
*Cénotaphe à Newton* [*Cenotaph for Newton / Cenotafio para Newton*], 1780–93

Fig. 5:
Josef Svoboda
Building maquette for [Construyendo la maqueta para] ballet *Juan*, 1959

Fig. 6:
Airplane No 14-Bis by Brazilian pilot [Avión No 14-Bis del piloto brasileño] Alberto Santos-Dumont. Bagatelle, France, October 23, 1906

Fig. 7:
*Maquette V, A noite* [*The Night / La noche*], 1967
Painted cardboard [Cartón pintado]
70 × 50 × 60 cm
(27⁹⁄₁₆ × 19¹¹⁄₁₆ × 23⅝ inches)
Collection of the artist

Fig. 8:
*Princípio de realidade* [*Principle of Reality/Principio de realidad*], 1981
Painted iron [Hierro pintado]
40 × 30 cm (15¾ × 11³⁄₁₆ inches)
Raquel Arnaud Collection

Fig. 9:
*Notas, (   ) etc* [*Notes, (   ) etc*; 2006]
São Paulo: Gabinete de Arte Raquel Arnaud, 2006

Fig. 10:
*Maquette I*, 1967
Cardboard [Papel cartón]
73 × 22 × 18 cm
(28¾ × 8¹¹⁄₁₆ × 7¹⁄₁₆ inches)
Chateaubriand Collection

Fig.11:
*Condutores de percepção* [*Perception Conductors/Conductores de percepción*], 1969
Glass and silver in velvet-lined box [Vidrio y plata en caja revestida de terciopelo]
6 × 40 × 15 cm
(2⅜ × 15¾ × 5⅞ inches)
Private collection

Fig. 12:
*O louco* [*The Madman/El loco*], 1971
Lead figurine in velvet-lined box [Figurita de plomo en caja revestida de terciopelo]
6 × 81 × 8 cm
(2⅜ × 31⅞ × 3⅛ inches)
Private collection

Fig. 13:
*O colecionador* [*The Collector/El coleccionista*], 1973
Watercolor on paper [Acuarela sobre papel]
120 × 120 cm (47¼ × 47¼ inches)
Museu de Arte Moderna, Rio de Janeiro

Fig. 14:
*Ping-Ping, A construçâo de abismo no piscar dos cegos* [*Ping-Ping, Constructing the Abyss in a Blink of the Blind/Ping-Ping, La construcción de abismo en un parpadeo de los ciegos*], 1980
Mixed media [Medios mixtos]
620 × 700 × 350 cm
(244¹⁄₁₀ × 275½ × 137⅘ inches)
Museu de Arte Moderna, Río de Janeiro/Sponsorship Petrobras

Fig. 15:
*Moto perpétuo* [*Perpetual Motion/Movimiento perpetuo*], 1973
Dice on velvet [Dados sobre terciopelo]
50 × 32 × 32 cm
(19¹¹⁄₁₆ × 12⅝ inches)
Chateaubriand Collection

Fig. 16:
*Leitura silenciosa* [*Silent Reading/Lectura silenciosa*], 1975
Pencil on paper [Lápiz sobre papel]
24 × 30 cm each
(9⁷⁄₁₆ × 11¹³⁄₁₆ inches c/u)
Chateaubriand Collection

Fig. 17:
*O limitógrafo* [*The Limitograph/El limitógrafo*], 1975
Wood, metal, glass, and cork [Madera, metal, vidrio y corcho]
55 × 67 × 13 cm
(21⅝ × 26⅜ × 5⅛ inches)
Private collection

Fig. 18:
*Convite ao raciocínio* [*Invitation to Reasoning/Invitación al razonamiento*], 1978
Painted iron and tortoise shell [Hierro pintado y caparazón de tortuga]
15 × 45 × 20 cm
(5⅞ × 17¾ × 7⅞ inches)
Leticia Monte and Lula Buarque de Hollanda Collection

Fig. 19:
*Espelho* [*Mirror/Espejo*], 1975
Cardboard [Cartón]
50 × 50 cm (19¹¹⁄₁₆ × 19¹¹⁄₁₆ inches)
Private collection

Fig. 20:
*Espelho com luz* [*Mirror with Light/Espejo con luz*], 1975
Frame, mirror, and backlight [Marco, espejo y luz]
180 × 180 cm (70⅞ × 70⅞ inches)
Colección Patricia Phelps de Cisneros

Fig. 21:
*Espelho* [*Mirror/Espejo*], 1976
Painted iron [Hierro pintado]
90 × 120 cm (35⁷⁄₁₆ × 47¼ inches)
Private collection

Fig. 22:
*Circunferência com espelho a 30°* [*Circumference with Mirror at 30°/Circunferencia con espejo a 30°*], 1976
Painted iron and mirror [Hierro pintado y espejo]
120 × 120 × 8 cm
(47¼ × 47¼ × 3⅛ inches)
Ricardo Rego Collection

Fig. 23:
*Miroir b* [*Mirror b/Espejo b*], 2005
Stainless steel [Acero inoxidable]
84 × 62 × 9 cm
(33¹/₁₆ × 24⅜ × 3½ inches)
Private collection

Fig. 24:
*Espelho C* [*Mirror C/Espejo C*], 2005
Polished stainless steel [Acero
inoxidable pulido]
200 × 280 × 270 cm
(78¾ × 110¼ × 106⁵/₁₆ inches)
Fundação Calouste Gulbenkian

Fig. 25:
*A distância entre. . .* [*The Distance
Between. . ./La distancia entre. . .*,
Série Veneza III* [*Venice Series/Serie
Venecia*], 1997
Stainless steel and acrylic [Acero
inoxidable y acrílico]
200 × 150 × 150 cm
(78¾ × 59¹/₁₆ × 59¹/₁₆ inches)
Ricard Akagawa Collection

Fig. 26:
Diego Velázquez
*Christ in the House of Martha and
Mary* [*Cristo en la casa de Marta y
María*], c. 1618.
Oil on canvas [Óleo sobre tela]
60 × 103.5 cm (23⅝ × 40¾ inches)
National Gallery, London, Great
Britain
© National Gallery, London/Art
Resource, NY

Fig. 27:
*Ferro pintado* [*Painted Iron/Hierro
pintado*], 1978
Painted iron [Hierro pintado]
120 × 120 cm (47¼ × 47¼ inches)
Colección Patricia Phelps de
Cisneros

Fig. 28:
*Los* [*The*] *Velázquez*, 1994
Digital image on paper, oil stick,
and translucent glass [Imagen
digital sobre papel, óleo, pastel y
vidrio traslúcido]
129.5 × 111.1 × 6.4 cm
(51 × 43¾ × 2½ inches)
Colección Patricia Phelps de
Cisneros

Fig. 29:
Diego Velázquez
*El bufón Don Diego de Acedo "El
primo"* [*The Jester Don Diego de
Acedo "The Cousin"*], 1644
Oil on canvas [Óleo sobre tela]
107 × 82 cm (42⅛ × 32⁵/₁₆ inches)
Museo del Prado, Madrid, Spain
Photo credit: Gianni Dagli Orti/
The Art Archive at Art Resource,
NY

Fig. 30:
*Velázquez*, 1996
São Paulo: Editora Anónima, 1996
Bound offset lithographs on
paper, edition of 1500 [Litografías
offset encuadernadas sobre papel,
edición de 1500 ejemplares]
30.7 × 26.8 × 1.9 cm
(12¹/₁₆ × 10⁹/₁₆ × ¾ inches)
144 pages [páginas], 67 color illustrations [ilustraciones en color]
Colección Patricia Phelps de
Cisneros

Fig. 31:
*Matisse, talco* [*Matisse, Talcum*],
Spain: Centro Galego de Arte
Contemporánea, 1978
Talcum powder over illustrated
book on Henri Matisse [Talco
sobre un libro ilustrado sobre
Henri Matisse]
33 × 51 × 4 cm
(13 × 20¹/₁₆ × 1⁹/₁₆ inches)

Fig. 32:
Waltercio Caldas & Ronaldo Brito
*Aparelhos* [*Gadgets/Aparatos*] . Rio
de Janeiro: GBM Editora de Arte,
1979

Fig. 33:
*Manual da ciência popular* [*Manual
of Popular Science/Manual de ciencia popular*]. São Paulo: Cosac
Naify, 2007. Text by [texto de]
Paulo Venâncio Filho. First published (publicado por primera vez
en) 1982 by [por] FUNARTE, Rio
de Janeiro

Fig. 34:
*Centro de razão primitiva* [*Center
of Primitive Reasoning/Centro de
razón primitiva*], 1970
Gold needles in velvet lined box
[Agujas de oro en caja revestida
de terciopelo]
30 × 10 × 10 cm
(11¹³/₁₆ × 3¹⁵/₁₆ × 3¹⁵/₁₆ inches)
Collection of the artist

Fig. 35:
*A distância entre. . .* [*The Distance
Between. . . / La distancia entre. . .*],
Série Veneza III* [*Venice Series /
Serie Venecia*], 1997, detail [detalle]
Stainless steel and acrylic [Acero
inoxidable y acrílico]
200 × 150 × 150 cm
(78¾ × 59¹/₁₆ × 59¹/₁₆ inches)
Ricard Akagawa Collection

Fig. 36:
*Escultura para o Río* [*Sculpture
for Rio/Escultura para Río*], 1996
Stone and concrete [Piedra y
concreto]
1000 × 1000 × 600 cm
(393¹¹/₁₆ × 393¹¹/₁₆ × 236¼ inches)
Located in [Ubicada en] Av. Beira
Mar, Rio de Janeiro, Brasil

Fig. 37:
*A passagem* [*The Passage/El pasaje*],
2009
Digital maquette [Maqueta
digital]

Fig. 38:
*Omkring [Around / Alrededor]*, 1994
Painted stainless steel [Acero
inoxidable pintado]
450 × 1800 cm
[117³⁄₁₆ × 708¹¹⁄₁₆ inches)
Located in [Ubicada en] Leirfjord,
Norway [Noruega]

Fig. 39:
*Espelho rápido [Fast Mirror / Espejo
rápido]*, 2005
Stone, concrete, and stainless
steel [Piedra, concreto y acero
inoxidable]
600 × 1000 × 2350 cm
(236¼ × 393¹¹⁄₁₆ × 925³⁄₁₆ inches]
Located in [Ubicada en] Parque
Mauricio Sirotsky Sobrinho,
Porto Alegre, Brasil

Fig. 40:
*O formato cego [Blind Format / El
formato ciego]*, 1978–82
Painted steel (Hierro pintado)
600 × 800 × 150 cm
(236¼ × 314¹⁵⁄₁₆ × 59¹⁄₁₆ inches)
Located in [Ubicada en] Paseo
de Las Américas, Punta del Este,
Uruguay

Fig. 41:
Silk, fakir in the central zone of
São Paulo, n.d. [Silk, faquir del
centro de São Paulo, s/f]

**Photo credits / Créditos
fotográficos:** Jaime Acioli,
Waltercio Caldas, Roberto Cecato,
Paulo Costa, Gianni Dagli Orti,
Ileen Kohn, L. C. Lacerda,
Erich Lessing / Art Resource,
NY, Vicente de Mello, Wilton
Montenegro, Gabriel Pérez-
Barreiro, Fábio del Re, Miguel
Rio Branco, Jaromír Svoboda

**Titles in / Títulos en Conversaciones / Conversations**

Carlos Cruz-Diez
in conversation with / en conversación con
Ariel Jiménez  ISBN 978-0-9823544-2-1
E-BOOK 978-0-9882055-1-2

Tomás Maldonado
in conversation with / en conversación con
María Amalia García  ISBN 978-0-9823544-3-8
E-BOOK 978-0-9882055-2-9

Jac Leirner
in conversation with / en conversación con
Adele Nelson  ISBN 978-0-9823544-4-5
E-BOOK 978-0-9882055-3-6

Jesús Soto
in conversation with / en conversación con
Ariel Jiménez  ISBN 978-0-9823544-6-9
E-BOOK 978-0-9882055-4-3

Ferreira Gullar
in conversation with / en conversación con
Ariel Jiménez  ISBN 978-0-9823544-5-2
E-BOOK 978-0-9882055-5-0

Gyula Kosice
in conversation with / en conversación con
Gabriel Pérez-Barreiro  ISBN 978-0-9823544-8-3
E-BOOK 978-0-9882055-6-7

Liliana Porter
in conversation with / en conversación con
Inés Katzenstein  ISBN 978-0-9823544-7-6
E-BOOK 978-0-9882055-7-4

Luis Camnitzer
in conversation with / en conversación con
Alexander Alberro  ISBN 978-0-9823544-9-0
E-BOOK 978-0-9882055-8-1

Waltercio Caldas
in conversation with / en conversación con
Ariel Jiménez  ISBN 978-0-9840173-5-5
E-BOOK 978-0-9882055-9-8

**Forthcoming titles / Próximos títulos**

Tania Bruguera
in conversation with / en conversación con
Claire Bishop

Jaime Davidovich
in conversation with / en conversación con
Daniel Quiles

Alfredo Jaar
in conversation with / en conversación con
Luis Pérez-Oramas

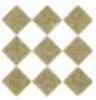

FUNDACIÓN
CISNEROS
COLECCIÓN
PATRICIA
PHELPS DE
CISNEROS